Simply... Woman

Other Books by Crystal Andrus Morissette

Simply ... Woman!:
The 12-Week Body/Mind/Soul Total Transformation Program

Transcendent Beauty:
It Begins with a Single Choice ... to Be!

Simply ... Empowered!:
Discover How to Create and Sustain Success
in Every Area of Your Life

The Emotional Edge:
Discover Your Inner Age, Ignite Your Hidden Strengths,
and Reroute Misdirected Fear to Live Your Fullest

Simply... Woman

STORIES FROM 30 MAGNIFICENT WOMEN WHO HAVE RISEN AGAINST THE ODDS

edited by

CRYSTAL ANDRUS MORISSETTE

SIMPLY WOMAN
PUBLISHING

Published in Canada by Simply...Woman Publishing™, a division of Andrus Morissette Productions, Inc., Uxbridge, Ontario.
www.simplywomanpublishing.com

Simply...Woman™ is a registered trademark.

Library and Archives Canada Cataloguing in Publication data available upon request.

To order books, contact:
1-877-SIMPLY-9 (1-877-746-7599)
info@SimplyWomanPublishing.com

ISBN   978-1-7752602-0-2 (book)
ISBN   978-1-7752602-1-9 (ebook)

Simply Woman frontline editor   **Jackie Brown**
Production/editorial   **Tracy Bordian/At Large Editorial Services**
Interior and cover design   **Kyle Gell**
Proofreading   **Eleanor Gasparik**
Cover photo   **Julia Dantas**

SIMPLY WOMAN
PUBLISHING

Printed in Canada
10 9 8 7 6 5 4 3 2 1

•

For my daughters, Madelaine and Julia,
and all of the brave, strong women in the world

•

Contents

1   **Introduction**   1
by Crystal Andrus Morissette

2   **Dancing Through Fire**   15
by Stacey Chantal Tsourounis

3   **All that Glitters Is Not Gold**   25
by Shelli Lether

4   **Blessed Are the Pure in Heart**   37
by Neyor Karmue

5   **The Secret Keeper**   51
by Sara (Navasi) Hartman

6   **The Living Room Floor**   65
by Dina Strada

7   **What the Soul Cannot Digest**   79
by Dimple Arora

8   **The Princess and the Prisoner**   93
by Katie Kozlowski

9   **The Dark Side of Unconditional Love**   103
by Pam Del Franco

10   **Love to the Fullest**   113
by Raven Thompson

11   **Brook's Story**   125
by Jennifer Mae Kelloway

12   **Life Is Beautiful**   141
by Erin Marie

13   **A Girl from Palestine**   151
by Hamda Wazwaz

14   **Uncertainty in Paradise**   163
by Miriam Engeln

15   **Warrior Goddess**   173
by Naomi Herrera

16 **Three Eleven Elizabeth**   185
    by Katie Seriani Bowell

17 **The View from the Top**   199
    by Karry Ann Nunn

18 **Love Is the Answer**   211
    by Lucy Devi Hall

19 **Dissatisfaction: The Quiet Killer**   225
    by Giovanna Capozza

20 **Sixty Seconds**   235
    by Abigail Nadar Nepaul

21 **Blood and Independence**   245
    by Antonietta Mannarino

22 **I Know Why the Tin Man Smiles**   259
    by Jackie Brown

23 **But He Was My Brother**   271
    by Beth Humphreys

24 **A Mother's Love**   283
    by Elizabeth Walsh

25 **Perseverance**   295
    by Shireen Clark

26 **The Lioness, the Doctors, and the Lawyers**   305
    by Mary Jane Mendes

27 **The Widow's Peak**   317
    by Janice McIntyre

28 **Transcendence**   329
    by Lynsi Anderson

29 **The Remains of Love**   339
    by Toinette LaShawn Benson

30 **Life Always Finds a Way**   353
    by Wendy Gless

    Resources   365

    Acknowledgments   371

A cast of
thousands
begins
with one word
one person
willing
to speak out
touching
upon subjects   *subconscious*
forbidden to   *lest they destroy*
ordinary knowledge   *our own ideas*
a view toward   *of who we really are*
freedom   *God forbid*
of a society   *we find our*
lingering lies   *cruelty*
only have power   *our own discrepancies*
hidden   *all the ways*
kept in our secret   *we harm*
     hurt, maim, mistreat
     and kill
     and who will be
     that one
     to say no
     this is enough
     it's time to stop
     the lies end now.

     — Sara (Navasi) Hartman

Crystal Andrus Morissette has traveled a long road, from living as a homeless teen to coaching A-list celebrities. Now a worldwide leader in the field of self-discovery and personal transformation, Crystal is a media darling: Her work has been featured numerous times on Oprah.com, and her inspirational story and approach to living have appeared in the New York Post and the UK Daily Mail, among others. Crystal is also certified in nutrition, sports medicine, and yoga.

Founder of both the S.W.A.T. Institute, a school that certifies women as Empowerment Coaches (Simply Woman Accredited Trainer) in over thirty countries, and SWAYoga, yoga for women by women, Crystal is also the author of five international bestselling books, including The Emotional Edge, which made the Globe and Mail's bestseller list in 2018. Simply ... Woman: Stories from 30 magnificent women who have risen against the odds is her most ambitious project yet.

Crystal is momma bear to her two daughters, Madelaine and Julia, and beloved wife to Aaron. Crystal and her husband live in a tiny town in Southern Ontario, Canada, with their three dogs, two birds, and bunny.

Introduction

CRYSTAL ANDRUS MORISSETTE

•

*t*he manuscript of my memoir had been sitting on a shelf in my office, collecting dust, for a couple of years. I was too fearful to publish it. What would people think of me? Would telling my story hurt me? Destroy me? Would my family flip out? Would my mother go crazy?

When I first shared it with Izabela Viskapova, professor of coaching at my school, the S.W.A.T Institute, she had a hard time with it. She told me it was too painful. Too raw. Too real. She wasn't sure people would want to read it.

I wasn't sure, I told her. I just knew that I had to write it. In fact, writing it saved my life.

Once Izabela realized I was serious about publishing my story, she got serious, too. Izabela is a brilliant researcher, with a master's degree in both law and psychology.

"Crystal, do you realize you have what psychologists have recently diagnosed as 'Complex PTSD'? You have experienced trauma like no one I've ever met."

Post-Traumatic Stress Disorder (PTSD) is an anxiety disorder that can develop after a person experiences a shocking, scary, or dangerous event (e.g., car accident or natural disaster). The thoughts and memories from the event continue to haunt and affect an individual, and it can make everyday life difficult. When someone experiences prolonged chronic trauma that occurs over months or years, however, this diagnosis often does not fully capture the severe psychological harm that results. Dr. Judith Herman of Harvard University suggests that the diagnosis for these incidences should be differentiated as Complex PTSD. It's also sometimes referred to as Disorders of Extreme Stress Not Otherwise Specified (DESNOS).

Wow. For the first time in my life I understood my brain a little better and why it was responding to stress in a particular way: to protect me. The trouble now was that my own protective coping mechanism was imploding.

Here I was with a lifetime of achievements and accolades — even recently making it on *Oprah.com*, the *New York Post*, and the *UK Daily Mail* as a bestselling author — and yet I was having "dark nights of the soul," as they are known. Although everything on the outside still looked pretty perfect, I was beginning to unravel on the inside. The worst part? I was afraid to reveal this inadequacy to anyone — even to myself.

I was a fearless woman who was afraid.

I'd never admitted to being afraid before. I hadn't shown fear for years. Not since I was a child. I guess I had no one to show it to. No one who would understand or protect me. No one who cared.

Instead, I learned how to channel my fear into jet fuel for success. But don't kid yourself: The fear was still there, raging within.

For the first time in my life, I couldn't stop the anxiety from rumbling ... crumbling ... throughout my body. I started having panic attacks. Fainting. Even seizures. My brain was literally hijacking my body. And I was unable to hide it any longer. My suffering had finally caught up with me. The mess was too huge now.

Don't get me wrong: I could empower other women to get the help they needed, to share their stories, to allow themselves to grow stronger in their vulnerability. I just didn't know how to give that gift to myself.

Sure, I shared some of my "stuff" in my books or with clients during private coaching calls, although I certainly didn't fully disclose myself to anyone. Not even to my husband.

I was very ashamed of parts of my life. Parts of myself. Parts of my family. Parts of my past. I didn't trust that I could tell anyone the truth — the whole truth and nothing but the truth, so help me God. Plus, I certainly didn't want to look like I was someone from a *Jerry Springer* episode. Mortifying. Shameful.

It was then, suddenly, that I wondered what the point of my life was. Why was I even here? Did I even want to be here anymore? Was my whole existence to help others?

But how could I think this way? I was Crystal Andrus Morissette!

Women's Advocate.

Founder of the S.W.A.T. Institute.

Empowerer.

Empowered?

And yet, I didn't want to live sometimes.

I didn't want to live ... *sometimes.*

It was almost as though I felt like I'd done what I came here to do. I had nothing left.

It scared me. I worried that I was collapsing, like a black hole in the universe was swallowing me, stealing my light forever.

I had to change the way I was showing up in the world. I had to change the way I was talking to myself. I needed to acknowledge why I was so angry. Actually, I had first to admit that I was angry.

I was so goddamn angry!

I had so much anger contained just under the surface in a nice little ball of fire. It sat between my shoulder blades and made my neck ache with tension. I had so much pain lodged in my uterus, lower back, hips, groin, and knees. Some mornings I could barely lift my own feet to get dressed. The pain was excruciating. I knew it was buried anger, but I was so embarrassed by it. And worse, so embarrassed to tell anyone about it.

What kind of woman is an angry woman? *Ugh!*

My shame was keeping me isolated. Feeling unsafe. Suffering in silence. And that's when I realized I couldn't just keep passing over my story ... my sorrow, sadness, and suffering. I needed to believe that it mattered. That *I* mattered.

That my pain and heartbreak mattered.

My flashbacks and nightmares mattered.

The sexual abuse, physical abuse, neglect, betrayal, and abandonment mattered.

Pretending I wasn't hurt didn't serve me any longer. I needed to do the same work on me that I did with all my clients. I needed to own my past so it would stop owning me.

I thought I'd forgiven everyone, but I hadn't. I'd turned the other cheek, bit my tongue until it bled, and then continued to accept unhealthy behavior, often from those who claimed to love me the most.

I didn't hold people accountable for their actions. Instead, I'd just disappear. Be silent. Wait for my anger to pass. Wait for the next family gathering where I'd behave as though nothing had ever happened. Lovely. Nice. Politically correct.

Here's what I've learned about anger: Feeling and expressing our anger is where most of us struggle, which is why *how* we deal with our anger is the game-changer. But anger itself is not the problem.

Truth be told, all great change has occurred because someone got angry enough to deal with an injustice. The problem comes when we are so afraid of our anger that we lose sight of our ultimate goal, which is to communicate and advocate for ourselves in a win-win way.

After years of ignoring my own needs, disowning my story, or negating my feelings, I discovered that peace isn't about everyone being the same, thinking the same, or feeling the same. It isn't even about everyone liking you or agreeing with you. Peace is acceptance expanded. It agrees to disagree. But you can't have peace if you're afraid to speak. You can't have peace if you're afraid to listen. You can't find peace if you're afraid to tell the truth. You can't find peace if you're afraid to disagree or, God forbid, have a confrontation or, even worse, put up a healthy boundary and tell someone "no." And yet I'd somehow convinced myself I could just forgive without addressing my anger.

I had some serious and swift healing to do. I couldn't carry the weight of the world on my shoulders another day. I had to stop feeling responsible for other people's feelings — they weren't mine to carry, fix, or heal. I had to transcend my false bravado, pride, and self-righteousness. I had to face my own darkness, sadness, and sorrow. I had to shine light on my deepest shame, guilt, and blame. I had to tell the truth. I had to acknowledge all the pain and suffering buried deep inside me.

My siblings and I were taught that what went on in our house stayed in our house, that no matter what our parents did, we were not to talk back, be disobedient, or tell a soul. Children are meant to be seen and not heard — even adult children. And speaking to a doctor, priest, therapist, pastor, or even yoga teacher was for losers. *The weak needed therapy. The weak needed God. Religion was a crutch,* my father told us.

But I couldn't hold it all in, alone, any longer. All those "bad" feelings that had been bottled up for so long were causing the dam around my heart to crack. All those pent-up emotions started squirting out. My wall was crumbling. My heart was broken. My anger was imploding.

I was imploding.

I had to change. I was done with being the secret keeper. I was done being anyone's punching bag. It wasn't healthy. I had to stop running. I had to see myself — the good, the bad, and the ugly. Becoming whole mattered more than looking good or even being a role model to grown-up women at my own expense.

I realized that I had to be honest with me, first and foremost. I was angry. Although, mostly, I was afraid, especially of my mother. It's hard to believe, but as a grown woman whose had no contact with her mother for ten years (she doesn't speak to any of her children or grandchildren), I was still afraid of her. I was afraid to tell my story, afraid to talk about it for fear of her finding out. Afraid of her retaliation. But by not owning my story, I couldn't own my success. I couldn't sustain peace.

Whatever is repressed will find a way to be expressed.

Patterns continue until they are broken. You have to face yourself and your stuff. You have to dig it up and deal with it: You have to move through it. There is no other way.

This realization was huge! Facing my anger and fear unearthed a massive self-limiting belief that I'd been carrying since I was a child: I was afraid to show my full potential and greatness. I was afraid to be fabulous and successful. I was afraid to really shine. But mostly, yes, I was afraid to outdo my own mother. I was afraid of her jealousy and wrath. I think the rest of my family was afraid of her, too. Which is why no one ever got involved. No one ever protected us kids. *What goes on in your home, stays in your home.*

Looking back, I'm sad that my mother couldn't see my gifts, talents, and leadership qualities as powerful and potentially influential attributes that could help others. Instead, she called me pretentious, fake, and grandiose. And the worst part: She was going to expose me!

Apparently, she'd written a book titled *My Daughter, the Sociopath* and sent the first chapter to people on my Facebook page. Strangers were contacting me in shock over what they were reading. And then she sent some of it to me along with a horrible letter of how I'd stolen her life. *It was she who was supposed to be an author... not me!*

Thank God no one published it. But it still made me very ashamed. And even more afraid. I mean, what kind of mother writes a horrid book of lies about her own successful child who had only ever tried to make her mother proud? All I ever wanted was my mother's love. My parents' love. My family's love. And no amount of success was going to take this pain away. I couldn't bear the shame and abuse any longer. I had reached my tipping point. I couldn't change them. Change their opinions. And I struggled with the notion that maybe my family and I weren't meant to have a close, loving relationship. I just didn't understand how I could be filled with so much love and able to give it to so many people, and yet my family didn't want it. Didn't want me.

I began to consider the possibility that perhaps I'd already gotten the best from them. And that holding on to the secrets — the shameful stories of abuse and neglect and betrayal — was destroying me.

The fact is secrets make us sick, no matter our gender, culture, age, or religion. I don't care who you are: Shame makes you nauseous. Pride keeps you stuck.

I had to write. It was all I knew to do. I did not do this to hurt my family or my mother.

I had to get healthy.

I had to name it, claim it, grieve it, and release it.

This was *my* life!

There were many days when my hands would shake as I was purging emotions ... as I was allowing myself to feel, to remember, to tell my story.

I would sometimes vomit while I was writing. I gagged a lot. With each recovered memory, I'd heave. I couldn't believe what I'd unearthed. I'd cry. Tears would stream down my face, sometimes for days, as I continued letting it all out.

And then finally the shaking stopped. The words slowed down. The suffering began to subside. I could eat some food and hold it down. I'd lost ten pounds in a week as I wrote and wrote and wrote. I'd joke that my next book should be called *The Emotional Release Diet: How to lose ten pounds in a week and keep it off!*

My shoulders were finally settling back down away from my ears, my neck pain was letting up, my locked hip unlocked, and my back stopped hurting. I could start teaching yoga again. My heart wasn't pounding as quickly inside my chest, and I didn't feel like reaching for that glass of wine as often.

I won't lie: It was really scary ... at first. I started worrying that my heart might explode inside of my chest. There was a lot of pressure coming up and out of me. Massive. Emotional. Release. Overwhelming at times. All I could do was sit with it. And so, I sat with it. I allowed it. I stopped resisting and started trusting that I had to release these toxic stories once and for all. I had to tell the truth.

The good news: I never exploded.

Indeed, the chaos was eventually quieted.

I started to feel calmer. Safer. I would never have believed this was possible unless I was experiencing it for myself.

I started to feel the quiet inside growing bigger until it started to feel ... nice. Not nice in a "nicey-nice lovely" kind of way, but nice in a "holy fucking shit, this is good" kind of way. The real way. The only way. The truthful way.

I could be whatever I needed to be. I could feel whatever I needed to feel. I was all things: *I was Simply ... Woman!*

I realized that I didn't need to be perfect, but I also didn't need to be afraid to be my best self. I could be me! Freedom!

It reminds me of a beautiful quote from Marianne Williamson's book *A Return to Love*:

> *Our deepest fear is not that we are inadequate. Our deepest fear is that we are powerful beyond measure. It is our light, not our darkness, that most frightens us. We ask ourselves, Who am I to be brilliant, gorgeous, talented, and fabulous? Actually, who are you not to be? You are a child of God. Your playing small does not serve the world. There is nothing enlightened about shrinking so that other people will not feel insecure around you. We are all meant to shine, as children do. We were born to make manifest the glory of God that is within us. It is not just in some of us; it is in everyone and as we let our own light shine, we unconsciously give others permission to do the same. As we are liberated from our own fear, our presence automatically liberates others.*

Besides, it was amazing what I could remember ... once I was ready.

Freedom. Relief. Courage. Love. Joy. Peace.

Even forgiveness. Real forgiveness.

And then I realized that I wasn't ready to share all the gruesome details of my life with the world — at least not yet. And that was okay. But I still wanted to do something. I decided to cast a spotlight on women who have risen against the odds. Women who were ready to share their stories of triumph, hope, and courage.

At Simply Woman Publishing we put a call out to our readers to share their stories of overcoming personal tragedy and succeeding against the odds. We were overwhelmed by the response. We received hundreds of heart-wrenching yet inspirational personal stories. It was clear we'd hit a nerve, that the time was right for these women to "put pen to paper" and share what they'd been through.

Each woman in this collection was selected by me for her honesty and strength. I was moved beyond words by their willingness to share their stories so they might inspire and help others. Selecting only thirty women was extremely difficult. Although every one of these writers could have filled an entire book with their incredible life stories, we wanted to be sure that this book represented as many of the different lived experiences that women routinely face and overcome as we could. Once we made the final selections, my editor, Jackie Brown, and I were honored to work so closely with each writer during the development of this compilation.

I believe these stories will give you the inspiration, faith, and desire needed to channel your pain and suffering into your greatness. My prayer is that this book helps you feel more empowered to tell your story. Sharing is one of the most cathartic ways of healing.

All of our stories matter.

The world is in a critical time right now, especially for women. Like never before, we are being called to stand up, come together, and rewrite our futures. To remember where we've been, how we got here, and what we want moving forward.

Each of these stories will show you one woman's journey from pain and suffering into wisdom and truth. Let them speak to you. Evoke you. Enlighten and educate you.

And then when the time is right, I hope that you will speak out, too.

When we come together, magic happens.

This is how we heal our legacy.

This is how we heal our future.

This is how we heal the world.

One important woman at a time.

#TogetherWeRise

#TimesUp

A teacher and women's empowerment coach, trained in expressive arts therapy and dance, Stacey Chantal Tsourounis has spent years studying across the globe. Her powerful writing explores the themes of truth and transformation, and has been featured in Simply Woman magazine. She loves performing as a dancer around her hometown of Toronto, Canada, reading Tom Robbins novels, and getting kisses from her dog, Marley. She can be found online at staceychantal.com or on Facebook @StaceyChantalAuthor.

Dancing Through Fire

STACEY CHANTAL TSOUROUNIS

•

*h*er eyes are frightening when I first see them — there's a ferocity, a glowing intensity like nothing I've seen. Her hair is wild and her body's voice so clear and loud that, for a moment, everything else is drowned out. She makes me feel torn: I want to run from her and toward her at the same time. Unable to decide, I release her gaze in the mirror and focus on my feet. I just keep dancing.

•   •   •

I enrolled in this dance class on a whim. I've been in a fog for months now, one that seems to swallow me no matter how hard I try to outrun it, making my life feel blurry and dull. Despite how numb and disconnected I've been feeling, though, something new has been happening over the last few weeks: Tiny pinpricks of light have started to reach me through the heaviness. Usually, this light comes as a tiny kiss of hope or possibility, but sometimes it comes as a whisper that directs me. It was a whisper that told me I needed to move — specifically, dance. Not giving it too much thought, I looked up a few dance studios and found a six-week Afro-Cuban dance class. I called and said I'd enroll and pay in person. I wasn't sure that I'd even go.

I remember how, during my teenage years when I'd first experienced depression and anxiety, dancing was what always brought me home to myself. I'd go into my room alone, blast music, and feel myself cradled by the rhythm, my breath falling in line with the song's pulse. The rhythm was like a strong back I could lean on, and sometimes I'd dance alone for hours. Eventually, I'd reach a place of exhausted release, my body having said all that words could not. Dancing always opened a space of unshakeable strength within me.

The classes have been good for me, and I'm glad I decided to show up. Moving calms me, and getting out to the studio every week is helping me to break out of my solitude. Despite this, I'm not sure dance will bring me to that place of strength this time around; the darkness I'm in now is deeper than anything I'd known when I was younger.

Nearly a year ago, I was sexually assaulted by someone I'd trusted and considered a friend, and I've spent months trying to avoid dealing with it. I've always been known for being strong and perceptive, and I've always believed my instincts made it impossible for anyone to mess with me. I know deep down that my faith in myself has been shattered, but I refuse to admit it.

Instead, I've created an almost-true version of myself: someone who on the outside seems to have it together. This woman is a role I play well, and she's mostly convincing, as long as no one looks too closely. I go to my classes in teacher's college, and do homework and assignments. I see family for holidays. I go out with friends and laugh, smile. Sometimes I feel like I could be this woman forever. Who cares if she's a mask? Who cares if she's just going through the motions? She gets things done, she carries on, and she lets me avoid feeling like a victim.

Here's the thing about truth, though: You can't extinguish it just by putting on a mask or eating your words. It doesn't fizzle and fade. Its embers stay glowing in the belly, softly warm and refusing to be denied, waiting for the breath that will ignite their full flame once again. And I can't help but notice that today the gaze of the woman in the mirror is a spark and something has started to burn.

I lose sight of her as I turn and head to the back of the room again. We're done warming up now, and the instructor, Albena, is explaining the history behind today's movement. We are learning the dance of Oya, the Afro-Cuban deity of storms and change. A powerful warrior and protector of women, she carries a sword that cuts away all falsehood, and her dress of many colors turns like a whirl-wind as she moves. She carries a dark mirror of truth that shows us who we really are, and her movements reflect her essence: deliberate, fierce, and grounded in a powerful grace.

Oya is a force of destruction. It's said that she is the guardian of cemeteries, where she awaits the souls of the dead to guide them as they cross over. When it is time for something to die in our own lives, she helps us to cross over: Conjuring a great tornado, she tears our foundation from its very roots, leaving all that no longer serves to crumble and fall away. Sometimes after her storms pass it can seem like we are left with nothing at all, our lives stripped bare — although this is terrifying, it's never an act of cruelty. Like all manifestations of the Dark Goddess, Oya destroys in the service of transformation, and in the dark spaces of the in-between state, she leads the way to our rebirth.

• • •

A couple of months after the assault, I went overseas. I was headed to West Africa to visit with good friends in Benin and Ghana, and would spend some time traveling alone as well. I'd had the trip planned for a while, but as the date drew closer, I had a growing sense that I shouldn't go. I brushed this aside, of course; I'd gotten good at ignoring what was right in front of me. Looking at the world through the mask I'd created, it was easy for me to explain my insomnia and numbness: I was just busy and caught up with packing and planning. The strong woman would carry on, like always. I traveled anyway.

It didn't take me long to see that this was a mistake. Once I set out on my own for a couple of weeks, the glow of seeing old friends again began to fade. Usually, solitude was a soft cocoon, but now it felt cold and empty, especially at night. I doubted myself constantly and wished I could shut off my thoughts. I tried not to make any of this obvious when I called my family over Christmas, but my grandmother said right away that I didn't sound like myself. I thought about changing my ticket to return earlier, but before I could, I got sick with malaria. If it weren't for the kindness of the strangers who helped me, I might not have made it home at all.

Back in Canada a few weeks later, I struggled to come to terms with the last several months. I could no longer deny that I was avoiding a deep wound, and the close call with my life made me question how well the mask I'd created served me. I knew that I didn't want to carry on in denial, but I also had gotten so comfortable with the role of the strong woman that I wasn't sure how to stop playing it. Feeling torn, I began to slide into a paralysis that was almost hypnotic. I would go to work feeling like a zombie, counting coffees until the end of the day when I could go straight home and crawl into bed. I was exhausted and couldn't seem to get enough sleep.

But after a while, sleep started to become unsettling. Images of my death played out in my dreams at night, coming back to me in flashes throughout the day. I would see myself being dragged into the depths of the ocean by a creature in the dark, or wading through a thick swamp only to stumble over a body that turned out to be my own. I wondered if these haunting images were my mind's way of processing after being seriously ill, but I learned there was more to them. Over time, the messages began to evolve, and in one dream my death was the beginning, not the ending. In this one, after struggling in a raging river, I was pulled underwater and pushed up a hill that seemed to go on forever. At the top, the river turned into a room filled with friends and family wearing suits and dresses, and I wondered if they were there for my funeral. Somehow hearing me even though I hadn't spoken, my late great-grandmother turned to me and smiled. "No," she said. "We're here for your graduation."

• • •

The tempo has picked up. We're turning swiftly, sure-footed, strong arms waving. This is where the drums quicken, the steps become a flurry. I enter a space where thoughts become quiet, and my body takes over entirely — this is the warm, familiar place I remember reaching as a child when I would dance alone, the place where rhythm steadied me and I knew I could trust it to hold the weight of whatever I was carrying.

We move in lines across the floor, and as I get closer to the mirror I catch another glimpse of the woman with fire eyes. This time, though, something has changed, and I don't want to run or look away. The fist of fear can't stay clenched when I'm moving. It has no choice but to fall open in surrender. When at last I'm at the front of the room, my breath catches on the truth in my reflection: The fierce-eyed woman is not another dancer in the room. The face in the mirror is my own. She's me. I feel like weeping. I have denied so deeply what I know and feel that I didn't even recognize myself. I've gotten so familiar with shame that power feels like it couldn't possibly belong to me. This truth pierces me to my core. My chest tightens, and my eyes sting, but I wait until the class has ended and I am home to cry.

• • •

There is no wound so deep and raw as self-betrayal, and it takes me a few weeks to process what the mirror revealed: My mask had become a cage. In my refusal to acknowledge my pain, I could not triumph over it. I'd become numb. In severing myself from the past so I wouldn't be affected by it, I'd uprooted myself from solid ground. I collapsed in on myself, shrinking my world to feel safe and pushing away anyone who came close enough to bear witness to my wounds. All this time, I'd been stumbling under the weight of a responsibility that was not mine. The weight was so familiar I barely noticed it. After all, it's the storyline so many women have heard throughout their lives. And it's a lie.

I began to see what movement had unraveled in me. Stubbornly forcing myself to get on with life, I'd neglected to honor what needs to die. The mask of the strong woman had become a deadweight, suffocating the tender new growth that wanted to be born.

This I know: Our power to create is bound to our power to destroy, and these two forces are both holy and forever seeking balance within us. When we are stuck and stalled and can't birth something new, somewhere within we are resisting death. It is here that we need to claim our right to destruction, as it's the same flame that fuels creation. Without it, we have neither. The pain I'd been carrying haunted me like a heavy ghost, dampening the fire in my belly and leaving me cold. But when I'm dancing, there's no place for this specter to settle: movement makes shame shrivel, and turns guilt and grief into parched kindling. They are a sacrifice, and with them, I make a funeral pyre for falsehood. My anger is the match that sets it ablaze.

•   •   •

One year later, I have found a circle of women with whom I dance every week. Every Sunday morning, I get to the studio, drop into my body, and let myself be carried by breath, connection, and trust. Layer by layer, I've started to uncover untruths in my mind, heart, and body. This is my foundation, my grounding where I sink roots into myself. This is how rebuilding needs to happen: slowly, patiently, from the bones up.

I've begun to learn how to read the body's language, and the tales it tells about our lives. Even if we're not ready for our stories yet, the body holds them for us: perpetually hunched shoulders reveal a heart-seeking shelter; a weak core tells of frail boundaries and dulled instincts. Even though these habits cling like cobwebs, movement in loving spaces sweeps every corner, reminding me that something new is always possible. It is never too late. Where we are stiff and rigid, we can learn to ease into surrender; where we are too soft and pliant, we can learn to sharpen our "no."

The most amazing discovery, however, is that all through this process, the fire-eyed woman was with me. I feel her in the strength of my arms now, the force that lets me fly across the floor. She's also in the power that binds us as we come together not just as dancers, but as women. She's the thread that connects us as we pause silently in a circle at the end of class, honoring where we've come from and where we're going. She is the one who pulls us inward when we're distracted and stalled in the outer world. She is the one who lights the way through our darkness and urges us forward when we'd rather turn back. No matter how many times we've disavowed or abandoned her, we need no permission to return. Her wildness and fury are eternally ours, and her voice lives within everyone. If we choose to listen, she will sing us home to ourselves.

Shelli Lether is a graduate of Coach Training Alliance, a motivational speaker, and an advocate for children, women, and education. Her unique approach blends the wisdom of spirituality, psychology, and neuroscience with strategic coaching. Shelli awakens individuals to their innate intelligence so they can solve their greatest problems and access their inner wisdom. She currently resides in Los Angeles, USA.

•

All That Glitters Is Not Gold

SHELLI LETHER

·

t he three-and-a-half mile drive up Mandeville Canyon in Hollywood, California, dragged on for eternity. The kid's bitching and squabbling about being squashed in the car and the pain of having to stay strapped into their seats was downright crazy-making. I hungered for the relief that my bed linens offered when they were pulled over my head.

As I looked out my car window down into the canyon, I saw mansion after mansion. Ornate iron gates, lavender-lined driveways, and tennis courts surrounded park-like estates. These were the homes of the super-rich and famous, those you'd find on the cover of *People* magazine. The Schwarzeneggers, Tom and Gisele, and Gwyneth Paltrow. Their children played in yards designed by landscape architects and took private swimming lessons in crystal-clean, blue-bottomed pools.

It had been some time since I'd mingled with those kinds of families, now that my marriage to a once-successful Hollywood blockbuster movie producer was dissolving. I looked down at my chewed-off nails and remembered that not long ago opulent diamonds had glittered on my freshly manicured hands.

It wasn't the stuff I no longer had that made me feel inferior to the women of my neighborhood, but rather the lack of fear, shame, and uncertainty with which they navigated their days. Over and over I had watched those mothers call each other on their iPhones and marveled over how they organized charity events and oversaw a new remodeling or decorating project while scheduling playdates, tutors, and Pilates sessions without missing a beat. No matter how hard I tried, I could never seem to be like them. I felt my throat tighten and my face burn with envy.

As my beige minivan rounded another tight canyon turn, I saw housekeepers hoisting residential trash cans to the curbs while others were pushing children on rope swings hanging from trees. I thought of Isabella and Rosemary, Valentina and Camilla, women who used to help me with my children. They left their families in faraway places, walked miles to work, and slept on floors for as little as $80 a day. I was in awe of their resilience and determination to show up and take charge. These women had superpowers I'd never known. Meanwhile, I was drowning in fear that my children and I would no longer be able to fill our trash cans with the wrappings of Whole Foods containers, Neiman Marcus bags, or even a KFC family-size bucket of extra crispy chicken.

Despite the long, noisy drive up the canyon, I dreaded what awaited me when we arrived. The idea of being at home alone with my three kids — nine-year old Leo and six-year-old twins, Ethan and Eli — made me feel like Cinderella pre-ball: stuck in an endless cycle of drudgery. My support system had been shattered. I had never fathomed I would be truly left alone with my kids ... and that *I* would be their supporter, protector, guardian.

I thought there would always be a housekeeper, a nanny, or, as of lately, at least a boyfriend to distract me from my fear that being a stay-at-home mother was a purposeless existence and that becoming a caretaker made me a powerless woman.

I turned down my potholed driveway just as it was getting dark. A rusty and crooked mailbox, half hanging from its post, was our welcome sign. Piles of boxes containing stuff for my soon-to-be ex-husband towered in the dimly lit carport.

I turned off the engine and stared at the steering wheel as if it were a crystal ball. *What's next, Shelli? What comes next?*

I sank deeper in my seat, watching three sets of legs scurry toward the house. *God, why can't I playfully chase after them?*

I wanted to go back to the days when I held them all in my lap. I wanted them to see me smile.

"I'm first!" shouted Ethan.

"No way!" yelled Eli, pushing.

"Come on, Mommy!" Leo called. "I'm hungry."

Entering the kitchen, my stomach knotted. I gritted my teeth. *Fucking dirty dishes in the sink. Is that this morning's breakfast on the floor?*

It didn't matter that there was an art project the boys wanted me to work on with them. The mess made my skin crawl, and it was all I could do not to storm out of the house. I grabbed a bottle of bleach and started scrubbing handprints and food stains off the walls as my father taught me to do when I was little.

• • •

Leo had just turned three, and I was a young, twenty-five-year-old actress. My husband had just produced America's number-two movie at the box office. My life was filled with red-carpet premieres and fancy-pants dinners at the best restaurants in Hollywood. I should have been so happy. So grateful.

Robert called me into our bedroom and slammed the door behind me. I sat on the edge of an embroidered comforter we'd found during a wintertime stroll in the snowy town of Telluride, Colorado. The light from the Tiffany lamp near our bed illuminated the purple birth control packet.

"You've been taking this behind my back! You're a liar! All this time I thought we were trying to have another baby."

I froze and stared at the wooden floor. "Please," I whimpered. "I just started working again. I love my time with Leo, but I can't keep building my career if we have more children."

I reminded my husband of our prenuptial agreement that spelled out everything he was expecting: a child in the first year, raised Jewish, and I would not share equally in the money he'd made should we ever split.

"How would I take care of two children on my own if you decided to leave me?" I said for the hundredth time since signing that lengthy premarital contract.

"Dammit, Shelli, I've already told you, and so did our therapist: Mothers are protected by child support, and the agreement gives you plenty of money. If you want to work on your career first, I understand, but that's not the kind of woman I want to be with."

Robert straightened his jacket and looked me in the eyes, without a hint of kindness. "If you want to stay in this marriage, we're having another baby."

•   •   •

Bleach spray in hand, I shoved past Leo, who was standing at the fridge. I went to the TV room right off the kitchen where Ethan was piecing train tracks together in a circle around a mountain made out of what used to be the folded laundry.

"Ethan! God . . . not the folded clothes!" I spun around to face Leo and pointed to his room. "Homework!"

Singing a song about chickens, Eli ran by, now somehow entirely naked, determined to demolish Ethan's train village. I stepped on a videocassette left out of its box. It was the Flash Gordon movie my dad had bought them on his last visit.

Clenching my jaw, I dug my nails into the palms of my hands. Dark thoughts cycled through my brain as Robert's various criticisms flooded my mind. *Worthless, good-for-nothing cow. You're an insult to working mothers, Shelli. You could have gone to college while the twins were babies. I can't support you forever! Get a job!*

Ethan screamed again, and every nerve in my body felt as if it were on fire. In a split second, all reason left me. Rage took over. Running into the kitchen, I lunged for a pan off the stove and slammed it on the counter with full force.

"Fuck this!" I threw the pan across the room, and it hit the wall with a clang. "Your father does whatever he likes to do while I'm stuck in this place with you!"

The kids ran in when they heard the clang. Ethan's face turned white as paper. Eli froze like a deer in the middle of the street.

"Your father did this to me!" I could feel the veins in my neck bulge as I screamed in their faces. I couldn't stop myself. "I begged him not to make me have you. I told him I wouldn't be able to handle it."

Leo motioned for Ethan and Eli to come toward him.

"I warned him, and his arrogant therapist, and his fucking lawyer. I warned them all."

I turned and found my back up against the wall. I slid down, bleach bottle in hand, sobbing and crumpling to the floor. The bottle tipped over and spilled on Leo's art.

By the time I regained control of myself, it was past dinner, bath, and bedtime. The boys had managed to feed themselves an entire box of Lucky Charms with chocolate milk, and had gone to bed. Standing in the dark, I gingerly rolled one of the pink sleeping pills I had stolen from Robert between my fingers while staring into several inches of vodka poured into a crystal glass. I popped the pill and downed the vodka. As I stepped on the wooden floor, crackles and creaks echoed in the silence.

I found myself standing in the twins' room watching them sleep under the glow of dim light, just bright enough to see their sleeping faces. The now-faded green-and-blue train blankets I had made for their old room draped each bunk bed. Ethan slept on the lower bunk. We called him "our Frenchie" because we'd cut his messy tawny hair in a style that framed his soft face and blue eyes just like a little Parisian boy from a postcard. He was the more timid of the twins and the one most visibly traumatized by me when I'd scream, freak out, or go stone-cold. I had recently told him he'd end up homeless if he didn't do his homework. He broke down in tears telling me he felt like the "dumbest" kid in his class. Overwhelmed by the shape of his sandwich, the collapse of a block tower, or mistakes he made on a drawing, Ethan would fall to his hands and knees and wail as if the world was crashing around him. I wondered where he'd learned that from.

I climbed up the ladder to Eli's top bunk and sat on the edge of his bed. He was named after the prophet in the Old Testament who was known for doing good deeds. However, my Eli was wild, disruptive, and exhausting. He was scolded when he blurted out absurd words, berated when he made strange animal noises, slapped when he stood on the table, thrown out of the car when he tormented and teased his siblings, and manhandled when he acted like he had wax stuck in his ears and couldn't hear. He bit everyone and everything. I'd bite him back and swear that I hated having him.

Asleep, he looked like a real-life angel. I drew the back of my hand along his velvety soft cheek.

"You'd be better off without me," I quietly whispered to him.

"Make them go away!" The voice came from down the hallway. "No. Please, help me. They're coming!"

I quickly climbed down the ladder, and I ran toward Leo's room. He was sitting up in his bed.

"Leo," I grabbed the sides of his arms with my hands, "Leo! Wake up, it's Mommy." It was another night terror. Since his father and I separated, they came like the mailman.

"Leo, wake up."

"They're coming to get me!" He seemed so little wearing his dragon pajamas, alone in the middle of his big bed. His shoulders were shaking. He pointed to something that didn't exist. This was far from our nights of reading stories and having a glass of chocolate milk in our old beautiful estate, down in the valley.

"Wake up, baby ..." I pleaded. He looked straight into my eyes. His face had matured a bit, and I could see in his nine-year-old face the man he would become. I tried to hold him, but he pulled away as if I were a ghost.

"No!" he screamed and jumped out of bed, then grabbed a bamboo stick he'd been saving for an art project and started slamming it down on his bed.

"I hate everything. I want to hurt myself! I'm going to starve myself to death!" His eyes were wide open. "I hate myself so bad."

I'd never seen my little guy this out of control.

"Leo, stop! It's okay!"

He whacked at the floor, the walls, and then he went after his favorite toy dragon collection on his desk, smashing it all.

His arms stopped whaling but his body shook, and his tears began to pour. "Are you going to hurt us, Mommy?" he blurted out. "Or are you going to be like the lady on that TV show who yelled at her family then went to the garage and shot herself in the head?"

His words hit me in the face like a bucket of freezing water. "Leo." I moved toward him.

He dropped the stick. I pulled him close.

"Mommy?" Leo collapsed in my arms, sobbing uncontrollably. "You'd be happier if I were dead."

I held him until he stopped sobbing, then we lay down on his bed. I was still too shaken to let myself think about what he'd just said. I propped him up so he could sip some water, continuing to hold him tight. I ran my fingers through the top of his hair. I didn't release my hold on him until I was sure he was in a deep sleep, then I slowly slipped out from under his covers and tiptoed toward the hall. There I stopped, turned, steadied myself against the door frame, and looked back into his room. A shiver shot through me my head to my toes. I blinked my eyes and suddenly felt foggy; the sleeping pill was doing its job.

In the dimness of the room, I no longer saw Leo. Instead, I saw myself. I was three or four with my thumb in my mouth, trying to rock myself to sleep in a dark corner of my crazy, dysfunctional, abusive, alcoholic childhood home.

"Shelli," I said out loud, "you're sleepwalking through minefields while you're ruining your children's lives. All you've become is a hollowed-out Barbie whose only talents are to dress well and have sex with powerful men."

Again, I looked back. This time, I was wearing a cream-colored babydoll dress and had a yellow daisy tucked behind my right ear. I was clapping my hands with joy, delighting in the sound of my own laughter.

"What happened to that little girl?" I said aloud.

Stepping in the direction of my bedroom I called out, "Dear God, or whoever is listening, if you can teach me how not to destroy my children, let alone myself, I vow to become the woman we need me to become."

Kneeling at the foot of my bed, I knew it was time.

Neyor Karmue is a nurse, humanitarian, and devout Christian. When plans to build an empire of pharmacies across Liberia were interrupted by the Liberian Civil War of the 1990s, Neyor vowed to help Liberia's orphans, many of whom were traumatized by their experiences as child soldiers. With her husband, Alfred, she has adopted over forty children and is raising them with the same amount of love, care, and attention she gives to her five biological children. Her incredible strength and vision is chronicled in Witness: A Child's Account of the Liberian War, written by her son and set for release in 2019. She divides her time between Liberia, West Africa, and California, USA. Neyor's charity can be found at SaveMoreKids.org.

Blessed Are the Pure in Heart

NEYOR KARMUE

·

i come from Liberia, West Africa, a country that has a lot in common with my new country, the United States.

Like the USA, Liberia was founded by Americans who came and settled as freed American slaves, people who had been stolen from Africa generations before. The first ship, *Mayflower of Liberia*, departed New York on February 6, 1820, for West Africa carrying just eighty-six settlers.

We, the Indigenous people who were here before, called these newcomers "Congo people," which means people who came from somewhere else. When they came, they brought what they'd learned as slaves in America — a class system that decides some people are better than others based on their education and their English-sounding last names.

Essentially, what they brought was a system designed to keep people "beneath them." They also brought their holidays, culture, and Christianity.

The Congo people were on a mission to educate most of the Indigenous people with the aim of making them "civilized." They started to influence specific Indigenous groups and individuals who became recruiters among other Indigenous people. They would venture throughout Liberia, going to the villages to recruit men to be soldiers in their army. Most of the people would run and hide in the bush. My father was an orphan, raised by his uncle since he was seven. When the Congo people came, he was a teenager.

His uncle said, "You should stay and talk to them the next time they come here. There may be things there for you in the city — opportunities — which we do not know."

So, when the Congo people came again, my father left my mother behind in our village and went with his uncle to Monrovia, the country's capital. There they met an army captain, a Liberian man named Dr. William, who offered to take him in and train him to be a good soldier. In return, my father washed and cooked for Dr. William and his family. For two years he attended the training bay in Barclay Training Center (BTC). They treated him well, and my father grew to love the man. In gratitude, my father promised that when he had children, he would bring one back to serve them; in return, the Williams would provide education.

My father graduated from the army training and encouraged my mother to move to where he was stationed. Because my father was in the army, we would move around the country every six months. It was disruptive, and it was not possible to go to school in many of the places. I was nine when my father told my mother it was time for him to do as he promised. I was the oldest and was told I had to go and stay with the William family in Monrovia and that my schooling would continue more smoothly there. I did not want to go, and I was very unhappy about it.

My father sat me down and said, "You are going to live with strangers, but I know the man. I know he is a nice person, a medical doctor. His first wife passed away, and I do not know his new wife. I hear she is a Congo person. You are going to go to school. We want you to be humble and listen. Do not speak back to them."

He talked to me so much about what I would learn that I became excited to go. I said goodbye to my mother knowing I would not see her for a long time. My father took me directly to Dr. William's office, many hours' journey from home. Dr. William greeted us, taking off his white doctor's coat to reveal the army uniform he always wore. Tall and light-skinned, I soon learned that he was a quiet, busy man who was rarely at home.

"This is your new father," my dad said, gently pushing me forward. "He took care of me when I was a young boy. I lived with him and washed his clothes. He was nice to me, and I promised I would give my child to him."

The man introduced me to his wife, Ma Lucy, saying, "This is your new mother."

The household had been expecting me, and they were excited to receive a new person as part of the family, they said. There were other children who worked for them, including a girl my age who was also from the Kpelle tribe. Her name was Naomi. She was there with her brothers, Joseph, Aaron, and Samuel.

Dr. William and Ma Lucy had three children: two boys and a girl, Beatrice, who was also nine. Ma Lucy's three nieces and a nephew also lived there; they worked for her, too. They showed me the room I was to share with Naomi, and took me around the house as well as outside in the large yard. I was relieved that there were so many other children.

Ma Lucy was nice that day, trying to impress my father that I was in good hands. She was a chubby, dark-skinned woman and wore her hair in tight, neat braids. She smiled a lot, and hugged me, saying, "This is your new home, feel free!"

It was the next day that I learned the rules. She told us that we would have devotional services each morning and night. And she gave us all a verse that we were to memorize, a verse she said was "ours." Mine was Matthew, chapter 5, verse 8: "Blessed are the pure in heart, for they shall see God."

"Have you ever prayed, Neyor?" she asked. I said no, and Ma Lucy taught me how to pray to Jesus.

Then I learned the rest of the rules. We were put in work pairs: a younger girl with an older girl. I was paired with her eighteen-year-old niece, Mary, a very lazy girl who left all the work to me. We were to mop and shine the wooden floors. Ma Lucy would say we needed to shine them enough to "see your face in them like it's a mirror." If she found a spot that she felt did not shine enough, she would beat us with a stick.

There was not much she wouldn't beat you for.

Although the master bedroom had its own toilet no more than five feet away from the bed, Dr. William and Ma Lucy would use a white chamber pot at night, and this had to be emptied. They insisted that it could not be emptied in the nearby toilet; it had to be carefully carried down the stairs and outside of the house to the septic tank. Ma Lucy would watch you carefully on the journey. If you made a face, she would beat you. If you dared spill even a drop, she would beat you even worse.

Naomi and I hand washed the family's clothes and sheets using a washboard in the backyard. Ma Lucy and her kids would be on the top floor on a balcony that overlooked the yard, watching us rub and rub their clothes and linens on the washboard. She would demand to see our progress from time to time, often yelling down "It is not clean enough!" We would have to keep scrubbing despite the pain in our fingers. When we made food, we were not allowed to eat the food made for them — they would give us different food to cook for ourselves.

Most difficult was the bread making. "You will not go to sleep until midnight, and you must be up at 4 a.m. to bake the bread," Ma Lucy told us. "You will make enough bread to fill up those two large containers, and then you two girls can go to school in the morning after the devotional. The boys will sell the bread in the morning and go to school in the afternoon. You girls will leave school in the afternoon to sell the rest of the bread." If we came back with even one stick of bread, we would be beaten.

Often we would have to beg people to buy the bread, but we could not sell it for less as she would count the money. It was unusual for young girls to walk around town on their own, so I was often very scared, especially in the beginning as I did not know my way around, and Naomi and I had to sell our bread in separate areas.

Ma Lucy's children went to private school, and the rest of us went to the local school. The teacher would ask us, "Is she your real, biological mother?" especially when she would call us out of school to help the boys sell the bread in the mornings, which meant we would miss a full day of school on those days. They knew we couldn't be her real children because of the way she treated us. However, we knew better than to say anything. When questioned we would answer, "Yes, she is our mother."

Naomi would get so angry when we were made to leave school to sell bread. "As soon as my grandfather comes to visit, I am leaving here," she would say.

"No, we have to stay as there are no schools in the villages back home," I would remind her. Although Ma Lucy beat us so frequently I had no more tears, I still felt that I had to stay and be good to honor my father.

One time after Ma Lucy was beating me with great force, she stopped and started to cry herself. "Oh, what have I done!" she would say when she realized how hard she was beating me. She cried, but still she continued to beat us for the smallest things.

One day we were doing the wash, and she and Beatrice were watching us from above. It started to rain, and we thought Ma Lucy had left the balcony, but in fact, she was still watching us. In this rare moment of freedom, Naomi and I danced in the rain. Beatrice came down and wanted to join us, but I said, "No, Beatrice, you better not because I don't know what Mother will say." Beatrice insisted on coming out and got wet in the rain.

When we went to go in, Ma Lucy blocked our way. "You allowed my daughter to come out and bathe in the rain? She could get sick and catch pneumonia! You cannot come in the house! Joseph, do not allow them to come in this house. They are to sleep outside."

As soon as it got dark, we saw neighborhood men enter the yard. We realized they came to use the water pump, to steal water. If they came in the day and asked, Ma Lucy would always say yes and give them some, but it was clear they preferred to come at night so they could take extra. We found a hiding place to sleep that was near the house, but we were terrified.

What would these half-dressed men do if they found two little girls outside without protection? We dared not move or make a noise, but we soon discovered our hiding spot was near a nest of red ants, the ones that bite and sting. We prayed for daybreak, and at 4 a.m. Joseph, Naomi's brother, opened the door so we could go inside to do our work.

Our skin was covered with blisters from the ant bites. Joseph took us to Ma Lucy to show her what had happened. Her reply was, "That is their punishment for letting Beatrice out in the rain."

When we went to school, our teacher burst into tears when we explained why we were covered in blisters. "Thank goodness it was ants and not a snake! We knew they could not be your parents. We knew she could not be your mother!" And we both admitted that, indeed, she was a Congo person and that our parents were in Bong County.

Naomi did leave with some of her brothers when their grandfather came to visit. Whenever my father came, Ma Lucy would never allow me to be alone with him. My father would bring money and food to support my stay in their home. I never got a chance to say a word to him privately. Besides, I figured I had to stay so I could go to school as my parents wanted. Ma Lucy would brag about how well I was doing at school and what a lovely girl I was. She would make sure I was wearing decent clothes for the day.

Although I was given one school uniform, Ma Lucy would not purchase another when it started to fall apart. But one of the new workers who came to the house after Naomi left was a seamstress. I liked her, and I would try to do some of her work. In return, she bought some cloth for me and made me a new uniform, as well as a new dress for the season. But when she left, I did not know how to patch my uniform when it wore out. I had no thread, but I discovered that you could shred palm leaves and create a kind of thread. I'd use this whenever I developed holes in my uniform, but this also meant I couldn't raise my arm in school to answer a question because I did not want the other kids to see the patches and especially what I'd used for thread.

One day when Ma Lucy was sick, she said to me, "Do you know, when we are sick, our kids don't even come to speak to us, but you come in to see us. You take care of us. I will bless you that you will become a nurse and take care of your patients."

Those words were one of the greatest things Ma Lucy gave to me.

At the time, I did not have any idea what a nurse was, but I later became one, and this allowed me and my family to do well financially. My skills also kept us alive when many were dying around us much later during the Ebola virus outbreak, and when I had five kids of my own and struggled to keep them safe from drug-crazed child soldiers during the bloody Liberian Civil War of the 1990s.

But that's another story ... One that my grown son is now sharing in a book of his own.

Ma Lucy's niece, Lazy Mary, married a government official, and Ma Lucy gave me to them to work and cook because Mary still hadn't really learned how to do any of these things. One thing I noticed was that her husband was a gambler. On Saturdays and Sundays, he would invite people to play cards for money and, usually, he'd gamble away his paycheck. Eventually, I was pulled from school because my tuition was late. He would become angry after his gambling losses and take his frustrations out on whoever was around.

One Sunday, I came back from church feeling so happy as I had just been baptized. Instead of saying "congratulations," he slapped me in the face with these words: "So you went to church when you knew I had visitors? And you got baptized? Well, we'll let Jesus pay your school fees. I am not going to pay my money for you." He continued to mock Jesus and insulted my parents.

I was livid. I said, "I have never talked back to any of you, despite my treatment here or with your aunt. My parents and my Jesus are very precious to me. Do not try it."

"You talk back to us?" he said, furiously. "You will not go back to school!"

"Oh, really?" I said. "You said I should ask Jesus for my tuition so that is what I will do. I will go back to school!"

It just so happened that an older girl from school, who'd sort of adopted me as her play-daughter, came to see me as in my absence I had missed an important exam. When I told Eunice what was happening, she insisted I come live with her and her family. I did not want to go as my father expected me to be with Dr. William's family and I was concerned he'd be upset if he did not know where I was. Eunice insisted. She physically picked me up and put in me the taxi when I refused to go. I was fourteen years old. She told her parents I was now their daughter and that I had been living with some Congo people who had mistreated me. She also took me to the school and convinced them to at least let me take the past exam so I could catch up. I studied as best I could, and when I passed with high marks, she asked them to let me come to school, promising I'd have my tuition to them next month.

I introduced Eunice's family to devotional prayers, and I also fasted for three days every other week. Eunice would fast with me. I told her that my prayers would be answered and that Jesus would pay my tuition. She was curious and continued to pray and fast with me until the school started threatening to ban me if I did not come up with the fees.

After school that day she said, "Come with me. I know a man who can help." She took me to an older man's house, and she told him, "You can have her as your girlfriend, but you must pay her tuition."

She was shocked when I said no. "I tried to help you, and you refuse?" she said angrily. "My parents are letting you live here, they are feeding you, and you say 'no'? Do you think God is going to come from heaven and give you physical money? It has to pass through people. You are ridiculous. Just be his girlfriend, and you will have the money."

"No," I said. "Not this way."

We fasted for three days, and on the last day, we were passing a big house, one we passed every day, as did all the students. The security guard came out and stopped us.

"M'am called you. You must come."

We looked past him through the gate and saw a long lane leading to the house.

"Let's go," said Eunice excitedly, and the security guard led us into the house to a room with a long dining table with many chairs. Wokie Tubman, the daughter of the former Liberian president, Tolbert, sat at the table along with her husband and her children.

"I knew it was you because of how you were described," said Miss Wokie. "Don't be afraid. Has anything been bothering you?"

I told her about the first family and the second. I told her about the outstanding tuition. I explained that I was too young to find the money elsewhere and the only person I was seeking the money from was God.

Miss Wokie explained that she had been troubled by disturbing nightmares for the last three nights. God had told her that someone needed something and that she was to give it to them.

"I did not know it would only be 50 US dollars!" laughed Miss Wokie when I told her how much the tuition was. "I am your mother now, child, and that is your seat," she said, pointing to one of the many chairs around the long table.

"Every day you are to come for dinner, and we will not eat until you get here. When you take this money to the school, you make sure that you tell them it was God who paid your tuition."

Eunice and I would enjoy many dinners at Miss Wokie's grand house. I have never forgotten her and how God found a way to help me that time and many more times since. Now I even look back with fondness to Ma Lucy for introducing me to God. How can I remember her with bitterness when that is the greatest gift of all? From Lazy Mary and her husband, I learned the power of prayer. I also learned from them that no one is better than anyone else and, importantly, how not to treat other people's children.

Over my lifetime living in Liberia, I have faced many life-and-death challenges — none worse than the Liberian Civil War. It was my experiences with these families that gave me the resilience and patience to do whatever I needed to do.

When it came time for me to step up and help the orphans of Liberia, many of whom had held automatic weapons against their neighbors during this terrible war, I was ready. I now have over forty orphaned children I call my own.

Despite the ill-treatment I suffered as a child, I am grateful for these lessons, as it made me a woman capable of working hard, staring death in the eyes, and standing unwavering in my faith.

Sara (Navasi) Hartman was a disciple of A.C. Bhaktivedanta Swami Prabhupada from the time she was fifteen, while also exploring the diverse paths of spirituality and mysticism, including becoming a master empowerment coach. A lover of artwork, nature, and writing poetry, she's a proud mother and grandmother to her two grown children and one grandchild. She lives in Georgia, USA, with her husband and their four kitties. You can follow her journey on Facebook @sara.hartman.507 or Instagram @navasihartman.

The Secret Keeper

SARA (NAVASI) HARTMAN

●

We are driving in the car, my father and I, through the mostly empty landscape of central Florida. We are going up to the area his family lives in. I am fourteen years old, and it is May. The school year has ended. He is taking me to stay with his family for a while. They are my aunts, uncles, and cousins on his side of the family, a family I do not know very well.

We drive in silence. I'm watching the landscape of scrub palms and fields go by. We pass the occasional house, set back from the road on a large piece of land. There is nothing but silence in the car. No radio. Only the sound of the car's engine and the tires as they move on the asphalt of the road. The windows are down, letting in the slightly cooler air outside. My father has never talked to me. I'm sure he doesn't know what to say, and neither do I. It doesn't even occur to me that we might talk about anything.

Then, for the first time in his life, he apologizes to me. He takes my hand. I glance at him, then back out the window. He says he is sorry he has not been able to have intercourse with me lately. He tells me he is worried that I might become pregnant. I examine the few remaining balls of white cotton still clinging to the old dried stalks in the fields we are passing.

• • •

I took my sense of self-worth from how well I could stroke my father's penis. I was trained, from the age of five, to do this for him. If I did it the wrong way, with my tiny child hand, he would tell me. Instructions are given. He'd put his large hand over mine and show me. Over and over again.

Yes, it hurts to say this. Why do I want to say these horrible things? I need freedom; I am still holding on to these things. I need to be released from my prison. How many times did he rub his coarse rough hand over my delicate child parts? Digging his sharp fingernails into my flesh as though I would somehow feel pleasure in this. So very painful, always so much unbearable pain. So many times, I cannot begin to count them. Over and over, year after year after year. He slept with a gun under his pillow and told me if I told anyone, especially my mother, she would kill us all if she knew, or he would kill us all, or he'd go to jail. He had guns under the front seat of the car and in the closet, too. Sometimes he cleaned them while I watched. He said, "If your mother were any kind of normal woman, you wouldn't have to be doing this."

I do not remember going to school. I could not tell you the name of the teacher I had in first grade, second grade, third grade, or fourth grade. I do not remember the names of any school friends. Or of anything we studied. These places do not exist for me. I did not exist during those years. I only existed as a sexual tool for my father. Hear me now, my spirit guides. I long to be set free at last. Allow me to hear you, I call out. I get lost in my suffering, as I recall these things.

I cannot remember when, but my father began oral sex at some point. I can only remember the horror and the disgusting things he did and the sounds he made. It fills me with disgust and shame to even recall this, but I must, so I continue. I cannot stand to be near a foam rubber pillow. Because of the horrible stench of his foam pillow as I lay in his bed at night. When he was through with me, he'd pull the covers up over my head as if I didn't even exist. Did I remove them so I could breathe? No. I did not deserve that freedom. I simply endured, and tried to find enough oxygen anyway. I lay there in stillness until I heard his loud snoring. Only then would I move the covers slightly just to breathe more freely, a little air for me. I dared not move or wake him.

• • •

It is Easter. I am ten years old. We are gathered at my grandmother's house for the holiday. I can hear my cousins laughing and playing. Usually, I'd be playing with them. Not today. One of my cousins is wearing a beautiful pink, frilly dress. I love the dress, but my mother has dressed me in a plain blue dress. No ruffles, no frills. It's not the dress; it's the filth I feel I am inside. This blue dress is somehow exposing that. She laughs at me because I'm upset over my dress.

I sit by myself on the black antique wooden bench that I still have today, inherited when my grandmother died. The laughter makes me feel even worse. I am alone. I am not good enough to be with my cousins. I am secrets. I am silence.

I make certain no one knows how my father has been taking me into our travel trailer in the driveway. I lie there on the edge of the trailer's small bed. My legs bent at the knees. Feet on the bed. Spread and laid bare. I stare at the jar of Vaseline on the ledge of the window. This is what he uses to lubricate me with. I endure the unbearable pain, always so much pain. I have noticed lately that my panties have some awful discharge in them all the time. I am ashamed, and I wonder what is wrong with me. I am the silence. I am the secrets. On and on it goes.

The first Christmas after we moved to Florida my father was there. He wasn't living with us again, yet. There was no room for him in the tiny two-bedroom duplex. On Christmas day, I was almost eleven. My brothers and I played with our gifts that were left under the tree. I had wanted a "Thing Maker" for Christmas that year. It was a toy that you made little plastic lizards with by squeezing gelled plastic into a mold that was then cooked and cooled to become the lizard. I loved it and wanted it so badly. I got one, and I was thrilled with it. Of course, it needed to be plugged into an electrical outlet, so I took it into my mother's bedroom. I plugged it in and started to squeeze the plastic into the molds. So exciting. In came my father. He looked at my "Thing Maker" for a moment then he shoved his hand down into my pants and started the infernal rubbing. My toy became dust and mold and soot and tears. Thing Maker.

When I was twelve or thirteen, my brother, his best friend, and I somehow started talking about what sperm looks like. I had a crush on the friend and wanted to show him and my brother that I "knew things," too. I went into the kitchen and mixed up a few choice ingredients and spread it on the back of the toilet in the bathroom. I told them to look — that's what sperm looks like. The friend looked at me shocked. I was pinned. "How do you know?" he asked. *How-do-you-know*. The secrets are harder to keep inside. I never made a mistake like that again.

• • •

As an adult, I have a recurring nightmare, which I wake from in terror and panic. It is a dream where I did become pregnant by him, and my parents took me to a doctor for an abortion. The doctor gave me something that would make me forget the whole thing. But that is just a dream I've had. I remember coming back from somewhere with them when I was about twelve, and I had a horrible migraine. Then we were watching the moon landing on TV. It was a big deal then. It meant nothing to me; I didn't even believe it was real. But you had to act excited.

While I am staying with my father's family, my cousin and I ride horses through the orange groves of Florida. I love horses. We had horses and ponies in New Jersey when I was growing up. These horses are a little larger but I love them, and nothing compares to the feeling of their strong bodies racing beneath you, the wind in your hair, the long stretches of the orange grove on either side, the sandy soil beneath their hooves.

One of my aunts asks me a question. "Does your mother drink?" she asks. I say yes. This somehow gets back to my mother. She is on the phone screaming at me. Furious. I can't say a word. She goes on and on. "How could you possibly do this? How could you tell someone that I drink!" I broke the silence. Never break the silence.

She decides she doesn't want me with my father's family anymore. She tells me I have to come to Tallahassee and live in the temple with the devotees. She and my brother are living in the dormitory because she's working on her master's degree in psychology.

There is incense. Strong scents of sandalwood and patchouli. Hardwood floors polished to a sheen. It is cool and calm here. Like an oasis from the outside world.

Devotees are chanting *japa*, gazing at posters on the wall of Krishna, Radha. Hare Krishna, Hare Rama. It is quiet; it is calm; it is peaceful. *Silent night, holy night, all is calm, all is bright. Om.* Transcendence. No one is fighting here. No one is drunk. There is no screaming.

At night I sleep on a sleeping bag in one corner of the dining room. My little piece of paradise. I have never encountered such kind, gentle people in my life. God. Love. Spirituality. Peace. Just Krishna and more Krishna.

The temple president and his wife are like angels to me. I adore them. I am in love with them. I crave their time and attention. I crave being with them. We go together out into the world to try to get people to take copies of the Krishna book. And hopefully, give us a donation for them.

In the mornings, when it is time for Mongol Arotike, at 4 a.m., the temple president sits near me and chants *japa* for a few moments, telling me gently it's time to get up. "Jiv Jago. Wake up, sleeping soul."

I wish he had been my father.

He gave me the devotional service of cleaning and decorating the altar. I had trouble finding flowers, though, and he took me with him in the dark early mornings down to the graveyard. There were flowers there that we could pick. Sometimes I'd use the ones growing on the oleander bushes around the house. His wife had a vegetable garden growing in the backyard. We'd work on the rows, sometimes picking beans for the dhal. I didn't want to wear a sari, and they didn't make me.

At 4:30 a.m. we would gather in the small temple room for Mongol Arotike. Dancing and singing the prayers together. I had no idea what we were singing or even exactly why, but it felt nice to be there, with them.

One day everyone at the temple goes to Gainesville to see Prabhupada. It is August by now. As I enter the narrow hallway, I see before me a tiny man seated on a dais. He is Indian and dressed in flowing saffron robes. He is tiny, but the power he radiates fills the space and beyond. Above me, on the stairs, his followers are lined up, a row of eager faces, so attentive they appear not to notice their surroundings. To the left of me, crowding me and the entire hallway, more followers. The room he is seated in is the tiny living room of an average house now turned temple. It is also packed with his followers. I am watching, awestruck, as I listen to his Bengali dialect. I cannot understand a word. I am fourteen years old, in my bellbottoms with long blonde hair. A child of the hippie generation. As I watch tears begin to stream down my face. I am so overwhelmed by this man. My rebellious teenage brain says, "He's just a man, just an ordinary man. Why are you crying?" But the tears continue, a flood of emotion I have never before experienced.

He continues speaking, looking around the room. He gazes past me, then stops, turns his head quickly back to me, and looks into my soul. In that instant, I knew my entire being, all that I was or ever would be, my soul, had been witnessed in a way I had never been nor ever would be. The tears continue.

After meeting him, I change my mind about wearing a sari. One of the women told me, "Prabhupada doesn't like women to wear pants." That was all I needed to know. The next day we all went out to the college campus because Prabhupada was going to speak there. I was wrapped in the heavy cotton saffron sari that was exactly like the one all the other women, except the married ones, were wearing. The married women wore yellow.

Before he spoke, Prabhupada led a kirtan. We were all dancing there in front of the little stage he was seated on. He kept looking at me, just like he had in the temple room the other day. I thought maybe I was wearing my sari wrong, and I kept looking at the other women to compare. I watched the way they danced, too, and tried to do it the same way. Still, he kept looking at me. I was worried I was doing something wrong.

On the way back to the Tallahassee temple, in the van, I kept thinking about him. The only thing I didn't understand was that I never saw him smile. That worried me. That night I had a dream. In the dream, he appeared, and he was smiling the biggest smile I'd ever seen. It was just his face, up close. I loved him from the moment I first saw him. Now he was also smiling.

I stayed on living at the temple in Tallahassee, even after my mother and brother left the dormitory and went back to Fort Myers Beach. By the end of September, school had been in session for some time, and I wasn't there. One day police officers came to the temple and took me to the home of a Christian woman. It was there or a detention center I heard them saying. This woman and her family were kind and took me in for a night. I slept in a bed that was so clean and had sheets on it, the room so pretty. I felt like I didn't belong there, I was not meant for such nice things. I was too dirty for this.

In the morning, they wanted me to come downstairs and eat breakfast at the table with them. Her children looked up at me, trying very hard not to stare, but I could tell where I didn't fit in. I couldn't sit at the table with these people. I wasn't good enough. I didn't belong.

I was made to go back home to Fort Myers Beach, for about four months because my father was demanding that I be in school. Everything of mine was gone. No trace of me in sight. I slept on the couch or a sleeping bag on the living room floor. I had been getting severe migraine headaches for a few years that would make me so sick I'd vomit and feel like I was going to die. I had no medicine for them. Once I stayed home from school because of one and was lying on the floor trying to cope. He came over, and I told him I couldn't do anything with him because of a migraine. He told me sex never made a headache worse, only better.

•   •   •

We had a second one of the very few talks we ever had. Again, it was in the car, this time as it was parked in the driveway. He asked, "Don't you miss sex up there in the temple?" He then said those people at the temple were just hippies and all they wanted were drugs and sex and didn't I know that. I thought of Prabhupada and the temple president and his wife. I knew it wasn't true. There was no point saying that, though. I could see my reflection in the glass of the window, and I wondered who I was.

Finally, my fifteenth birthday was coming in early February. My mother asked me what I wanted for my birthday, and I told her I wanted to go to the Tallahassee temple. Just for a visit. When I got there, we found out the temple was closing, and everyone was going to Dallas, Texas, where they were opening the first temple school in the movement. I wanted to go along, and since it was a school, I was able to convince my father to let me go. My mother explained to him that it was a real school and I'd be taking classes. When I got there, I was treated as an adult and didn't take any classes. I just helped open the temple there and take care of the children.

I lived there for about six months, then was sent to Detroit, Michigan. It was so cold there, and I didn't have proper clothing, only a windbreaker and a pair of rubber garden boots someone had donated. I remember standing outside in that freezing weather trying to get people to take magazines. Most people hated us in those days.

I was very lonely there. I was fifteen, and people constantly mistook my age for twelve. The other men and women were all adults and experienced ex-hippies, too. None of the people I had known from Tallahassee were there. The mood was very different. I tried to keep up with the impossibly hard schedule, but I had trouble.

After a few months, the temple president told me I had to come to his office because of something I'd done wrong. These lectures continued night after night, always some new infraction I had to be chastised for. He was twenty-five years old and had demonstrated quite a bit of physical violence. I was afraid of him. He was soon touching me. I asked him to stop. I told him I didn't want that. It meant nothing. Finally, one night as I was trying to leave he grabbed me and held me back from the door while he bolted the deadbolt. Then I was on the floor of his closet with him on top of me, in the pitch-dark. This went on for two months, during which time he told me if I didn't show up every night and do what he wanted or if I told anyone he'd throw me out on the street. I had no money at all, not even a dime, and nowhere to go in the middle of winter. The other threat was that he would just kill me. I turned sixteen during this time. My birthday present that year was him and his sexual needs. Finally, after two months of every sexual act that two bodies can engage in, I didn't care if he killed me anymore, so I told someone. He was removed from his position and sent away. I was told to get married, so I did.

The abuse in my life continued. By this time, I did not even see it as abuse anymore. I only saw it as somehow my failing. I was also told it was my failing. If I had been better, "more pure," more careful, more devoted, more intelligent, not so lustful. It was somehow my fault. But the result was the same, one abuser after another. I started to appreciate the suffering and willingly endured it. I needed to punish myself because I knew who I was inside deserved to be punished, hurt, abused, and betrayed.

My mother had always said "suffer a little, it's good for your character," so I felt I was developing tremendous character. Soon enough it didn't even count as suffering; it was just my ordinary life. If you had asked me then if my life was ordinary, I would have said it was.

I kept my secrets carefully. Keeping secrets was my specialty. I was proud of my secret-keeping abilities. I was proud of the fact that no one could get a secret out of me if I didn't want them to. These secrets nearly destroyed me, and they destroy the lives of other little girls, and women, even now.

Abuse doesn't end when one abuser is caught. Abuse lives on inside the victim, and they find new abusers and the pattern repeats. This is how grooming works and why grown women stay in terribly brutal situations and relationships.

On the other hand, many women either don't live long enough to write a story about it in a book like this ... or they don't believe sharing it will ever help. But sharing it is the only way we can change it ... heal it ... stop it.

There are women right now, just like me, who are out there and who need our help. By removing the shame, we remove the need to keep the secrets.

Secrets kill. Secrets corrupt. Secrets protect the perpetrators and destroy the innocent.

I am not a secret keeper.

Dina Strada is a Los Angeles-based writer who's had a long love affair with Hollywood and a twenty-five-year career in the entertainment industry. A certified life coach and intuitive, known for her willingness to be vulnerable, raw, and brutally honest in her writing, Dina's work has been featured in numerous online publications, *including* Huffington Post, Elephant Journal, Thought Catalogue, Elite Daily, The Good Men Project, Chopra, Simply Woman, Rebelle Society, *and* Tiny Buddha. *You can read more about her work at dinastrada.com.*

The Living Room Floor

DINA STRADA

•

*t*he rug was soft. I loved lying on the rug in this room. I had spent countless nights on it over the past two years, from using it as a yoga mat to laughing and playing on it with my son, both of us in pajamas. Often, I would lie on it as I stared up at the ceiling snuggled up in the crook of my husband's arm, laughing about some funny thing that happened during our day. It didn't feel quite the same at this moment. Now it was rough and scratchy, wet with my tears. It smelled like chemicals mixed with the shit of wet diapers ... a perfect metaphor for what my life had just become.

I was breathing heavily into the thick fibers. Using it as a way to muffle my sobs. Well, if I'm honest I don't think

I was actually breathing. Hyperventilating is more like it. Yes, I remember now. I was hyperventilating ... gulping in small, shallow breaths. I was having a panic attack.

This is not happening. It can't be happening. It can't be happening. What did I do wrong? Why would you do this to me?

A deep, animal-like wail erupted from my chest. "No! No! No!" I screamed over and over until I was hoarse and choking on my sobs. Blood-hot rage filled my lungs, my head, my entire body. I rocked back and forth in a fetal position, still sobbing. My head was pounding so hard I couldn't lift it off the floor.

Flashes of her ... long blonde hair, leaning in close to my husband. I had seen it in visions that I'd brushed away as "silly wife paranoia" that comes with the territory of having a good-looking husband who spends a lot of time around other women at the office. At that point in my life, I didn't accept or want to own the gifts of intuition I'd had most of my life. Yes, I saw and felt things before they happened — things that people would confirm later actually happened — but I was too practical to take all that woo-woo crap seriously. Those visions, these feelings you're having in your body ... they aren't real, I told myself when the faceless blonde appeared.

Now I knew who the hair belonged to. I knew the face. And I hated her. I hated her with every fiber of my 4'11" being. I wanted to destroy her for taking a fucking wrecking ball to what should have been the most blissful, exciting time of my life: being pregnant with my second child ... a little girl I had dreamed of having my whole life.

Instead, I was lying in a fetal position on my living room floor seven months pregnant, hardly cognizant that my three-year-old son was crying and calling out to me from his bedroom one floor above me. I cradled my swollen belly, the belly I had grown so proud of, trying to protect my unborn child from this nightmare that was now happening in our home.

I will never recover from this. I will never be the same. My life is over. I'm over. I'm nothing now. I will never get off this living room floor. Not ever.

Except I did. Because this is not where my story ends. It was just the beginning.

Eight years earlier ...

We met at work. Technically, he worked for me where I spent most of my time in meetings and barked the occasional request at him as I ran in and out of my office. He used to joke years later that I didn't even notice him while he was pining away for me. I think he's exaggerating, but he may have been right. Love with the young boy working in my office was the last thing on my mind at that time in my life.

But one night on an invite from him to join his birthday party, the two of us found ourselves on the dance floor together. I had never socialized with him outside the office and never noticed how cute he was. He had dark, sexy eyes, a charming smile, and abs that went on for miles! It was lust at first dance.

That lust quickly turned to love. It happened so fast, my head was spinning. I was still grieving the loss of the relationship I had recently left and was not ready to start another one. If I'm honest, I was just looking for a little harmless fun to fill the void. But the connection between the two of us was intense and hypnotic. We fell for each other fast. He told me he loved me just a month later, and I felt the same for him.

Although my family and close friends were wary at first that I had jumped into something so quickly after my last relationship, they couldn't help but love him. Nobody had seen me so happy. We were *that* couple, the one that couldn't keep their hands off each other. We stared into each other's eyes, we kissed in the most inappropriate places, and we were often told to "get a room" because, as my sister said looking so pleased for me as she expressed it, "when these two are in a room together they get lost in each other."

And it was true, we did.

On paper, it never should have worked. We were ten years apart and at different stages of our careers and in life. But it just did. It was the most natural, most effortless relationship I'd ever been in. He made me blissfully happy. Three years later he proposed on a beach in Maui, and we were married a year later.

We had the perfect wedding, saying our vows on a cliff overlooking the Pacific Ocean. But what made it even more special was that we had just found out seven weeks earlier that I was pregnant with our first child. A blessing and miracle, as I was in my late thirties and was told I would have a difficult time getting pregnant. We nailed it on the first try! Who gave a shit about having a glass of champagne to toast our nuptials when I had a perfect little life inside of me? Just seven months later I gave birth to a beautiful baby boy. I felt like I was living a dream.

That dream, however, slowly began to unravel into a sleep-deprived nightmare. Parenthood was tough, and the demands of balancing our careers, a colicky newborn, bills, and the usual stuff every couple navigates started to take its toll on us. My husband was a rock through it all. Where I was falling apart, he kept us together. He was a fantastic father, often taking my son when I collapsed into tears from frustration and exhaustion. I fell even more in love with him.

What I didn't notice as time went on was that he was throwing himself more into his work, and spending more time at the office. He was a hard worker and very ambitious, something I admired about him. Although my intuition told me something wasn't quite right, I ignored it. I was living my fairy tale, and I didn't want anything to ruin it.

When we talked about having a second child, he was understandably hesitant. We were still struggling with our first and scared that we might not be able to handle another one. After see sawing back and forth for months, we both agreed we wanted our son to have a sibling. I think we both felt the difficulties we were going through at the time were normal. When I discovered I was pregnant again at the age of forty-two, I was ecstatic. I thought he was, too — although when I broke the news to him, I could sense something was off. He didn't react with the same excitement and enthusiasm that he had the first time I got pregnant, and my spidey sense kicked in again. *Something isn't right.*

Nevertheless, I pushed aside my feelings of unease and plowed forward.

Remember, I wanted the fairy tale.

•   •   •

Back to my living room floor. The one with the soft rug, wet with my tears of rage and shock and humiliation and pain that was cutting so deep into my heart, I knew my baby girl could feel it through the umbilical cord.

I believed at that time that the heartache I was feeling in that moment after discovering that my husband was having an affair was the worst it was going to get. That once I could pull myself together and pick myself up off the living room floor, it was going to get better. I had confronted him about the affair, although I still couldn't believe it was actually true. He would never do this to me ... to us.

But he had. When he finally admitted that it was true, he apologized over and over again. He told me how sorry he was for making me feel like I was crazy all those times I had suspected something was going on and he denied it.

For all the times he lied to me and insisted that they were just friends and I was being ridiculous by accusing him of anything else. He seemed genuinely devastated for hurting me and causing me so much pain. He swore that it was over and promised me that he would never see her again. And I believed him. I believed he loved me and didn't want to lose me or our family. So I thought, *I got this*. I can fix this. I fixed everything.

But I was wrong.

Three months after our daughter was born, I lay peacefully on my bed nursing her. She was so beautiful. I used to call her my little angel. Just having her soothed my broken heart. My husband was working late again, so I grabbed the laptop to check my email. And there it was . . .

An account he had forgotten to log out of. I felt my heart start to race and the blood leave my head before I even clicked on the messages tab. The pounding of my heart in my ears was deafening as I scrolled through message after message after message.

The full truth of what had been going on not just months but over a year was splayed out in front of me. Not just the evidence of his affair, which was still going on, but the admittance that he was in love with her.

Which meant I couldn't fix this.

He moved out of our house the next day. I was in such shock that I completely shut down. My friends organized a forty-eight-hour vigil to get me through that first week-end alone. Each friend took a shift and stayed with me for several hours at a time, helping me with the kids, feeding me, making sure I slept so I could still nurse my daughter, and holding me through another round of hysterical crying.

As the days turned into weeks, life went on and I had to pull my shit together. I had two kids to take care of and was back at work from maternity leave, so I had to soldier on and get through the days without falling apart. Most days I wasn't successful. Every other day it seemed like another bomb was dropped on me as more information came to light that I was in the dark about. Each bomb felt like another annihilation.

He didn't just move out. He moved directly in with HER.

I didn't just lose being with my children every day and being able to bond with my baby.

They were now spending half the week with HER.

I didn't just feel humiliated and rejected like every other woman who finds out her husband had an affair. I had HER shoved in my face every week, standing on my front porch glued to my husband's side every time they dropped off the kids, her eyes silently screaming, "He's mine now ... in case you had any delusions that he may come back to you."

Yeah, I got it, girlfriend. You win.

And so it went. The emails back and forth between us with HER copied on each one. Every text message my husband sent to communicate about the kids had HER copied on it as if we were being policed by the Gestapo. When I asked to speak to him privately about something, he refused, telling me that she would be a part of every single conversation we had and I better get used to it since she was going to be part of my life and our children's life FOR THE REST OF THEIR LIVES.

I died a slow death that year.

• • •

So, what's a woman to do when confronted with this hot mess of a situation?

Stop fighting it. Accept what is. Step it up. Pull my big girl panties up because my situation wasn't changing. We can only cry, complain, and stay the victim of somebody else's behavior or a given situation for so long before we get sick and tired of being a victim.

And I was sick and tired of being a victim.

I made a conscious choice to do the deep inner work to heal my wounds and let go of the self-defeating patterns and stories I had held onto my entire life. The "I'm not enough" story was destroying me and getting old. I had to deep dive into where that came from and reviewed every choice I had made in my life where I played into that story ... feeding it like a hungry wolf that was never satiated. I went through every past relationship I'd ever been in and saw where I had denied my intuitive gifts and feelings, often pushing them to the sidelines so that I could have what I wanted.

I started to see how many times I had betrayed myself. When we don't trust ourselves and our intuition, that's the single biggest act of betrayal to the self.

Some people choose to go the traditional therapy route to work through their stuff. I chose to take a chainsaw to my inner being and go a hell of a lot deeper. I felt broken and shattered into a million tiny pieces. I was being forced to co-parent with the woman who in my eyes at the time "took my husband" from me and ripped apart my family. I had to learn to take my power back and rebuild my self-worth and self-esteem. Traditional therapy wasn't gonna cut it.

I did energy work, worked with renowned healers, and even took part in sacred ceremonies in Peru, Hawaii, and Costa Rica. The most massive transformation and break-throughs I had during my journey to healing took place during these ceremonies, giving me a new perspective and deeper awareness of myself and others that was integral to letting go of the pain and trauma I was carrying around.

I was a writer from the time I was a child, but I put writing to the side as my career in the entertainment industry took off. As I dealt with the daily pain, depression, and setbacks over the months that came, I began to write again.

I wrote not just to process my pain but to also give a voice to other people who were struggling in the world. I unabashedly shared stories about my healing. I wrote about my dating disasters, single parenthood, depression, self-love, owning your own shit, empowering yourself, letting go, sex, intimacy ... you name it. I used my own experiences as a way to reach people and let them know they weren't alone in whatever they were going through.

Something magical happens when you become willing to sit with your loneliness and solitude as opposed to looking for someone else to make you happy. You learn to be your own best friend. You learn how to take care of yourself. You discover things about yourself you never knew existed, and usually what you discover is how damn capable you are. You start to enjoy your own company. You stop looking for validation from another person that you're funny, beautiful, sexy, smart, worthy, or good enough. Because you know what happens when you finally choose yourself? You learn that you are enough. You don't personalize anything anymore. If someone doesn't want to be with me, I don't personalize it anymore. "Oh, you don't want to be with me? That's cool. Must not be a fit." Not "Oh my god, what's wrong with me that he doesn't want me?" That makes it personal. Self-love eliminates that.

And for those single moms out there struggling, thinking you aren't a real family without that man? Let me tell you: nothing can be further from the truth. If there is an area in my life where I can proudly say I "stepped it up," it was with my children.

I used to lie in my bed sobbing, thinking I wasn't ever going to be a good mother because I couldn't give my kids a two-parent home like the one I grew up in. I believed that I could never do it alone.

Well, I'm doing it.

Am I a perfect mother? Of course not. Nobody is the perfect parent. But I let go of the story that "this wasn't supposed to happen to me" and that I and my two children can't be a real family with just the three of us. We are a real family. We're a beautiful, whole, complete, and happy family of three. And when they're with their dad, they have the same.

I'd like to say I wish this hadn't happened to me, but I don't think I would have become the woman I am today if it hadn't.

Just know I would have told you I was strong and resilient before this happened. I was always a pretty tough cookie. What I wouldn't have been able to say is that I'm no longer defined by a relationship or another person. I couldn't have said that what I know for sure is that we define ourselves by how we choose to take everything handed to us in this lifetime. Both good and bad. We can always find the nugget of gold in there and turn it into something positive and powerful that will elevate us if we're willing to believe in ourselves.

And the best part about all of this? My story doesn't end here.

It's just beginning.

You've seen my descent. Now watch my rising.

— Rumi

Dimple Arora is the founder of Mindful Evolution — a mindfulness movement that aims to guide women and children towards self-love, positive
connection, and inspired action.. Dimple is certified in life coaching and
alternative healing modalities. She holds degrees in mathematics, business, and education. As a licensed Heal Your Life teacher and a registered holistic nutritionist, Dimple is a "foodie" who advocates for healthy,
authentic living. Dimple currently lives in Toronto, Canada, with her supportive husband and beautiful daughter. Please visit dimplearora.com.

What the Soul Cannot Digest

DIMPLE ARORA

•

The old healer to the soul:
It's not your back that hurts, but the burden.
It's not your eyes that hurt, but injustice.
It's not your head that hurts, it's your thoughts.
Not the throat, but what you don't express or say with
*   anger.*
Not the stomach hurts, but what the soul does not digest.
It's not the liver that hurts, it's the anger.
It's not your heart that hurts, but love.
And it is love itself that contains the most powerful
*   medicine.*

—Unknown

i love food, but for most of my life, my body hated it.

On my first date with my husband, we meditated on the beach and ate shawarmas and falafels afterward. It was perfect. We married a couple of years later and planned a big, fat, magical wedding. My life seemed like a fairy tale. I was a young, vibrant professional, a former beauty pageant contestant, married to the man of my dreams and surrounded by loving family and friends. I'd even attracted the wonderful mother-in-law that I had diligently prayed for my entire life. My heart was wide open, as it had always been.

Our honeymoon was in Hawaii. I stepped off the plane into the warm breeze of the open airport knowing my lifelong dream of a happy partnership was about to begin. At that moment, I noticed that I was unusually stiff.

The week progressed, and things got worse until every inch of my body began to hurt, even to the touch. The vibrant colors of my surroundings were too bright for my eyes. Every excursion was a difficult task. Still, it did not stop me from indulging in romance and being intoxicated with love. I would not let anything ruin my honeymoon, not even my body that had so often betrayed me.

When we returned home, the pain did not subside. Even in the afterglow of vacationing at one of the best places on the earth, I found myself crying for hours on certain days of the month. My moods became erratic and unpredictable. One day I threw a glass across the room. On another day, I threatened to kill our wedding photographer. I couldn't understand why I was so angry.

Most days, it took a lot of energy to complete simple tasks, such as bathing. But on this particular evening, I finally mustered up the energy and stood under the showerhead. I was in so much physical pain that I could not lift my arms to wash my hair. Each stream of water against my sensitive skin felt like a bunch of darts. My eyes welled up with tears. I cried, out loud, as though someone close to me had just died. Sinking to the shower floor, sobbing, I remember thinking, *How did I become this broken, dysfunctional version of myself?*

I had a sudden insight: I could not recall a single day when I had not been on one medication or another. My body had created a horror story and was screaming for me to listen. That night I tuned in, finally. I knew something — everything — had to change.

• • •

My parents' story is nothing short of a Bollywood romance. They met in Canada and fell in love overlooking Niagara Falls. My father was raised as a Hindu in India, following Radha Soami principles. My mother, whose ancestors are originally from India, was raised in Guyana as a Muslim. The union of a Hindu and a Muslim was considered taboo, and their parents refused to permit them to marry. In a culture where "fair skin" is valued, my mother's deeper complexion was not accepted. My dad, heroic in nature, and my mom, strong-willed and determined, fought for the right to their love and eventually married anyway.

However, life didn't continue "happily ever after" as it does in Bollywood movies. My parents struggled with the pressures of in-laws and extra responsibilities for their families. They were focused on creating a successful life for their children. I didn't make it easy for them, particularly at mealtimes.

As early as I can remember, I expelled absolutely everything I ate. My mom says it started when I was a toddler. As strange as it sounds, I also had to leave the table to defecate each time I attempted to have a meal. Eating was a constant struggle. I avoided it. My tummy hurt, always. I tried to explain that I had a lump in my throat that made swallowing difficult. I held spoonfuls of food in my mouth for hours, unable to eat, and too fearful to reap the consequences of spitting them out. My parents lived in a state of frustration. Emotions ran high in our home. Sadly, rather than console me, my mother often hit me, cursed me, and tried to force me to eat.

One morning, she thought maybe freshly squeezed orange juice would be the solution to my eating problems. She carefully prepared it, crying, and praying as she watched me drink it. She sent me to school, which was just across the street from our home. On the way there, I vomited continually, over and over again, until I reached the school gate.

My parents shifted me from doctor to doctor. No one could explain why this was happening. The doctors concluded, "She is a lazy eater." Reluctantly, my parents accepted this diagnosis. They also accepted all the conventional medical treatments for eczema, asthma, allergies, bronchitis, and ear infections.

Still, I thrived in every other aspect of my life. Even though I was labeled as too dark, too sick, and cursed, I was also labeled as gifted, a social butterfly, and a brilliant child who was wise beyond my years. I believe that's when the perfectionism started.

• • •

When I was ten years old, we moved into a new home, and the vomiting miraculously stopped, just like that. It was also no longer only my brother and me; my younger sister was a welcome addition to our family, bringing much joy into our lives. With the focus shifted to my sister, the next few years of my life dramatically improved.

Unfortunately, by the time I got to university, I was addicted to a white, refined substance that my brain couldn't live without: Sugar was my drug of choice. I didn't know it at the time, but the sugar was destroying my immune system. I was always battling one health issue after another. I had the worst case of hives and endured constant colds and infections. It didn't matter, in one sense, that I steered away from alcohol and recreational drugs. I popped medication like it was candy, daily, to appease the ailments I was plagued with. Essentially, I was a drug addict. When I graduated from university, I carried on, ignorant that there was a better way to live.

Five years later, I met my husband, and started teaching high school. I was a second-year teacher, staying up late at night working on lesson plans, while caught in the whirlwind of planning my wedding. I didn't realize how depleted my body was until I stepped off the plane in Hawaii.

The next few years after the wedding were a blur. My brain was foggy. I had constant muscle spasms. My bones hurt. My energy levels were low. It took time for me to get out of bed each morning. My stomach blew up like a balloon after each meal. Three times a week, I saw a bodywork specialist just to get by. Although I looked radiant on the outside (friends often suggested that I'd held onto that "newlywed glow," giggling about it), on the inside, I felt nothing close to radiant.

Socializing with friends was the only activity that energized me and allowed me to forget about the pain. My husband and I partied like rock stars on Saturday nights and slept until noon the next day. Little did I know that I was further damaging my body, my vitality, and eventually my career.

My spouse was the only person who emotionally supported me at the time. No one understood the extent of my physical pain and no one had answers. Multiple doctors tried to prescribe antidepressants, but my higher self knew that I wasn't depressed. My body was just extraordinarily imbalanced and broken. I tried counseling but was told that I seemed well adjusted to life, confident, and happy. My inner perfectionist was a master at insisting that I wear a smile and come across as exuberant, regardless of how I felt.

I was beginning to lose faith in doctors — the one profession that I had trusted my entire life. By the fifth rheumatologist, I finally agreed with the diagnosis of fibromyalgia. I was referred to a doctor who was researching fibromyalgia. He understood me. For the first time, I felt heard. When I received the news of his death, I cried like a baby.

I dreaded each weekday morning, waking up for work and struggling to get out of bed, stiff and unable to straighten my torso. I was like a crippled, old woman in a young body. Tasks that should have been second nature to me, like putting on socks, seemed like immense undertakings. There were days when I didn't even attempt to be on time for work. I was defeated before I even tried.

The twenty-minute drive to work was what I feared the most. My mind raced as I contemplated how I would make it through another day. Then the moment finally came when I became so physically weak and exhausted that I collapsed in the staff room. Within five years, my teaching career was over.

At the same time, my husband was climbing the corporate ladder, always occupied. A few doctors had suggested that I needed physical human touch, but I couldn't handle going for massages and I spent my days and evenings alone.

Lonely and bone-tired, feeling like my body had failed me, trapped under an avalanche of pain, there I was that night in the shower, knowing something — everything — had to change.

That evening, crying in the shower, I stopped the journey of my soul in its tracks. I switched from having suicidal thoughts to having an epiphany. I realized that despite being married, despite having family and friends, it was just me, myself, and I. No one was going to save me. It was my responsibility to save myself. I thought about my future and what I wanted in life.

A fire ignited in me, and I gained an internal strength that I had never felt before. Turning a blank page, I made a conscious decision to rewrite the story that my body was intensely trying to share. It was then that my Higher Self guided me away from all pain medication. I had a sudden desire to know my body, to feel my body, and feel everything that embodied my existence. That night, I made it my mission to heal and feel better than ever. My motivation was to become a mother.

A few days later, one bright afternoon, I pulled out the book *You Can Heal Your Life* by Louise Hay. Louise's motto was "change your thoughts, change your life," or maybe more accurately "heal your thoughts, heal your body." That day, unable to affirm that I was healthy, I started with the affirmation "I am healing."

I am healing.

Louise suggested metaphysical causes for specific ailments and positive affirmations to shift the issues. This concept made sense to me. It felt like truth. I suddenly became fascinated with the idea of self-healing.

The universe was in favor of my profound determination. Opportunities and ideas started showing up in my life to lead me on a remarkable pilgrimage of healing, unlearning, and self-discovery.

I started a healing protocol. My body was toxic, both physically and emotionally. I eliminated sugar, gluten, dairy, and grains from my diet and took a few supplements to start. The healing crisis was almost unbearable. I got worse before I got better. Despite suffering from diarrhea, shivering, mental impairment, extreme irritability, and limited energy, I stayed committed for months. Four months to be exact!

Four months of a dramatic lifestyle change created massive healing in my body.

I started to feel like a new person. The stomach aches stopped. Digestive issues were on the mend. The brain fog was gone. My energy levels improved. My spine seemed more aligned. I became passionate about healing through food and mindset. Wanting everyone to feel this good, I enrolled in a two-year program to become a registered holistic nutritionist. I dug deep into what my mind, body, and soul could not digest. I grew convinced that we could positively affect the turnover of each cell in our bodies, and I was determined to do just that. I had a desire to relearn my entire way of showing up on this earth. After all, the programs that my body had been running were no longer serving me.

Over the next year, I underwent successful surgeries on each hip. Interestingly, my hip issues began precisely two weeks after I stopped teaching.

In Louise Hay's book, she believes that our hips are what carry the body in perfect balance; they are the primary thrust in moving forward. Problems with the hips are associated with fear of making significant decisions or that there is nothing to move forward to.

I started to see my body as a messenger.

However, the journey to health came with its challenges, too. My propensity for visiting doctors was replaced with seeing alternative practitioners. Prescription drugs were replaced with natural supplements. Scared to move my body for fear of pain and having to recreate muscle memory, I still had not learned to fully trust myself.

I became aware of the emotional connection to pain and how to heal the little girl inside of me — my inner child. One by one, I removed the emotional charge of any incident from my past that I could recall hurting me. Realizing that forgiveness is a one-person job, I forgave everyone, for everything. I chose to no longer poison myself with resentment and anger. The process took years and, actually, it's never-ending.

I learned about the "mother wound" and the generational patterns that we can carry forward. I gained an incredible sense of understanding and compassion for my parents. Finally understanding my mother and her deep love for me, I forgave her a million times over for all her past actions. I cut the old cord with her and reattached a new one. Feelings of gratitude, love, and peace overcame me. Today, she is my biggest supporter, and I love and admire her more than ever.

Over the course of three years, I examined my beliefs in every area of life and reprogrammed the ones that were no longer helping me to thrive as a person. I practiced extreme self-love and self-care. Eventually, the pain in my body completely disappeared. I started to live in a state of Zen. I felt relaxed, centered, and grounded. Mood swings became a thing of the past. The frequent infections were gone. I no longer felt bloated, ever. I developed a beautiful relationship with food and started building a career helping others heal.

I was finally healed.

I healed myself.

Healthy Self = Heal Thyself.

It was then that I knew I would have a daughter — a healthy, beautiful baby girl. My intuition had become so honed, two years later my precious daughter was born. I set a clear intention that when I became a mother, I would do it with the utmost love, patience, respect, and wisdom.

The conception, pregnancy, and birthing process were easy. I think it's because someone had once advised me "be with the pain." Having my daughter was like offering paradise to the earth. This time in my life was the healthiest I had ever felt. I was calm and in my power, ready to embrace motherhood.

As they say, life doesn't always give us what we want, but it does give us what we need. At times, my body throws me a curveball, as all bodies do, and my mind forgets what's been reprogrammed. When health challenges arise, I have learned to listen to myself and trust my inner compass in bringing my body back into balance.

Presently, I live a life of harmony and peace of mind with my body. I can eat. I can breathe freely. I can think clearly. I can love openly. I can trust my body. I can move and dance, and I often do! I feel calm — most days — and I am no longer addicted to practitioners or supplements.

Freedom!

When I was in teacher's college, I wrote a mission statement: "To empower myself physically, emotionally, mentally, spiritually, and socially and to help others do the same." This mission statement still resonates with me today.

Yes, we can change the stories that our bodies have created. We are not our stories or our circumstances. My most significant lesson is that the soul can digest everything we experience in life, and it is love itself that is the most powerful medicine of all.

Katie Kozlowski is a professional voice-over artist and singer from Connecticut, USA. She holds certifications in multiple modalities and is a dynamic speaker, healer, and artist who combines emotional expression, creativity, imagination, storytelling, and spirituality to deliver truth and freedom to all those ready to find their awakening and joy. Katie loves using her creative gifts to reach others and inspire them to express their true selves inside and out. Visit Katie at katiekozlowski.com or on Facebook @iamkatiekozlowski or Instagram @iamkatiekozlowski.

The Princess and the Prisoner

KATIE KOZLOWSKI

•

i used to be two people, but you'd never know that if you met me.

On the outside, I was a bubbly, bright, whimsical girl with blonde hair, a curvy figure, and a toothy smile. On the inside, I was an ooey, gooey, deep, emotionally rich being.

This duality made me feel like an unsolvable puzzle. I could never seem to make the pieces fit in a way that made sense. So I decided one of those two people would get to stay and the other one would have to be imprisoned forever.

It wasn't a hard decision. I was smart. By observing others, I learned that if I acted a certain way, I could make other people happy. Unless I was being adored, I was worthless, and there's nothing less adorable than someone who's a mess of emotion. So I chose the "put on a happy face and make them laugh" girl. (Of course, the other girl lived tucked away deep inside me. She was like an imaginary friend I could hang out with only when no one was looking.)

•   •   •

At my very first dance recital, when I was six, my best friend pulled down my tutu while we tiptoed in a circle to *Somewhere Over the Rainbow*. Instead of running offstage crying, which is what I wanted to do, I turned around and slugged her. The audience went wild, and I liked it. I took my place center stage, in the spotlight. I reveled in the applause. It felt good to know they were watching me and laughing.

When my grandmother passed away when I was ten years old, I told myself it was my job to keep it together. I sang a solo for her at church. Even as my lips quivered and I swallowed my tears through the words of *You Are My Strength*, I never cracked. I knew our friends and family were counting on me to make them smile while they all came apart. When I was done, I was so proud of myself. I'd pulled it off.

As I got older, I got really good at keeping my secrets tucked safe inside. When things went wrong or someone hurt me, as long as I smiled and said "It's okay," I'd stay safe and feel accepted. It's how I got through my adolescence. In front of others I played the gregarious actress, but when no one was looking I struggled with my thoughts. There were times I even fought the urge to cut myself. I wanted to let the feelings out. Instead, I performed happily because I didn't want anyone to know what was hiding inside me.

The longer I behaved this way, and the more positive response I received, the harder it was for me to feel anything. I wanted to express myself, but all I could do was grin and say thank you.

When I got to New York City at the age of twenty-one, I was certain I was destined for stardom. But it didn't come as sweetly as I had envisioned. I began to lose myself. I struggled to find my persona: I was constantly trapped between the person my agents wanted me to be and the woman I knew I was inside. For the first time, I couldn't figure out what they wanted. Comments about my smile being too big, my shoes too clunky, my hair too flat, and my clothing too tight were constant. It seemed no matter how hard I tried I couldn't please them.

I'd be offered auditions, but mostly for roles playing dumb blondes and prostitutes. As a voluptuous woman, I struggled with my body image and my weight, yet I found myself standing in my bikini an awful lot. This wouldn't have been so bad except every time, at every audition where it was a requirement, I was reminded that being a size six and 5'3" was neither thin enough nor tall enough to be on TV because "the camera adds ten pounds."

I can still remember standing in the room alone in my skivvies auditioning to play Eve, the first woman in the Bible, who was described in the casting breakdown as a "real woman" (code for "she has curves"). I waited as the casting director took a break. She returned, saying, "I'll save you the embarrassment of doing the audition. You're just too big." I was often reminded that "while you are beautiful, you are not a supermodel."

Being told "no" over and over again can take a toll on you. After three years supporting myself as a cocktail waitress and five years as a spokesmodel, I was beginning to slip into dangerous waters. I felt myself drowning all my feelings and rejection in anything I could find, including food, unavailable men, and lots of booze.

My agents suggested that because I was so unique and hard to cast, I should write my own show. So as everything started to turn sour at once, and I seemed to think it was funny, I decided to get creative and take all the messy embarrassments and turn them into comedy. I became so proficient at telling stories about the humiliating occurrences in my life and turning them into jokes, I accidentally gave birth to my alter ego, who I lovingly named *Sick Bitch*.

Sick Bitch and I were bubbly and likeable with girlish charm, just like my favorite heroines Carrie Bradshaw and Bridget Jones. I was always stepping in you-know-what, and I mastered the art of making suffering, misery, and mishaps cute. Me and Sick Bitch shared the curse of being "dick magnets": blonde hair, big boobs, and Sagittarian. When I was date raped by my boss, I quipped, "At least he bought me a pizza."

I even had a serious relationship for a few years with my own Mr. Big: a charming and handsome older man who I met at a charity event. He became my hero and savior. He took me away from my fears and financial woes and covered them up with five-star hotels, Dom P, and shopping sprees at Anthropologie. It felt like love. But when I began to realize that I couldn't stay a kept-woman forever — or I'd never be free — I broke it off and went back to fending for myself. I was left with full rent for a two-bedroom apartment in Manhattan, a car payment, and many other bills I'd become unaccustomed to covering, so I took a high-paying job as a Scotch ambassador, selling whiskey in bars, and began drinking my fair share of it on a daily basis.

I started to care about my well-being less and less while putting myself in danger more and more. I knew I was from a family of alcoholics with a legacy of suicide, and my behavior was starting to feel all too familiar as I drank on a daily basis, sometimes upward of six Scotches at a time, and wandered home through New York at all hours of the night. I was involved with men who were unsavory in their behaviors, at least one of them married. While I wasn't necessarily happy with my life, it felt normal, like an endless merry-go-round I couldn't get off, so I just kept on going.

I went on like that for almost two years until one chilly fall night it all changed. And for the first time in my life, I realized it wasn't funny. It hurt.

I was sitting in one of my favorite accounts doing my final whiskey event of the night when my current boyfriend, who I'd known from high school, failed to show up when he said he would. This was not the first time he'd gone dark when he'd promised he'd be there and then didn't respond.

I was so despondent that I couldn't even drink. I turned down a whiskey, which was very unlike me, and opted instead for one of their famous 1100-plus-calorie bacon cheeseburgers. I looked at my phone, waiting for a message, but nothing came. Where was he?

When it came time to leave it was only ten, but I was feeling beaten. I moped out of the bar like a child who'd just had their puppy taken away. I couldn't imagine where he was, and all I could think about was him and how much it hurt. How could he do this to me?

I felt a gnawing sense of disappointment and rejection, and when I came to the corner to cross the street, I paused and sighed. I looked at my phone, and it was dead. And then the thought returned, the thing I would think to myself every so often when I was certain no one loved me: *I wonder if anyone would care if I wasn't here anymore.* But this time I meant it.

I stepped off the curb and a cab struck my left side. I gasped as the wind was knocked out of me and I was propelled over the hood of the moving car. I hit the ground, and the cab continued, speeding away while I was doing a barrel roll — *Just like Wonder Woman*, I thought as I landed, back on my feet, standing in the middle of the street. It was over in a matter of seconds.

I checked my face. I checked my knees. I checked my elbows. No blood. No broken bones. Not even a scratch or a speck of dirt. Perhaps it was the knee-high black boots and long black trench coat or my stage combat training in college that saved the day. Regardless, I was physically unharmed and started to walk away.

I was already on the opposite corner when I heard the crowd coming. People were screaming, a young girl and her father came to me, others called the police. Some people were chasing the cab. It stopped, and the two women who had been riding inside promptly got out and ran away.

The crowd gathered around me in a circle, confused by what had just happened and what they had seen. Some urged me to go to the hospital because I'd been hit by a taxi going full speed. People asked me how I had managed to survive; they had expected me to be a bloody, mangled mess.

I was slow to reply, but all I could say was, "You don't understand — I'm not like everyone else." I didn't know what that meant, but it was all I could say, and it felt quite natural to me.

The police arrived and pushed their way through the crowd to get to me. I let them do their checks, but I was determined to go straight home. I refused the ambulance and said I'd walk, to which one police officer joked, "Maybe the cab that hit you might like to give you a ride."

For the first time in my life, I didn't laugh. The bright, bubbly girl was still standing there, but I felt something new stirring inside me. I turned away and began my walk home through the West Village to 25th Street in Chelsea, where I lived.

As I walked, I asked myself, what does it mean to not be like everyone else? Why did I have the opportunity to be hit so hard yet walk away without a scratch? I knew that something had changed and I would never be the same. I had gotten the message: It was time to start living life as if I mattered. But why?

Sometime later — maybe a week, maybe longer — it occurred to me that the impact had broken something inside me, but it wasn't a bone or an organ. It was a wall of that prison. Those pieces that never quite fit were fused back together. I stopped feeling like a broken puzzle, and things started to make sense. All the feelings in my body came back, and I could express myself again. That girl I had locked away was free. But this time she wasn't separate from the outer me, now I was one. And I finally felt safe to be fully and wholly me.

Pam Del Franco is a spiritual medium, counsellor, author, and workshop facilitator. She has spent over twenty years helping women trust their intuition and feel more empowered. Pam graduated as a social service worker in 1994, and is a certified hypnotherapist. She's been studying dreams since 1986 and has developed a dream interpretation app called Dulcis Somnium. Her memoir, Walking Out of the Fire, published in 2006, describes her experiences with physical, mental, and emotional abuse and how she survived against all odds. She currently lives with her fur-baby, Molly, and enjoys spending her free time with family and friends. Visit innernetwisdom.com or find Pam on Facebook @pam.delfranco or Instagram @inner.wisdom.

The Dark Side of Unconditional Love

PAM DEL FRANCO

·

People who know me see me for who I am: a strong, independent elder trusted and affectionately called "Nanna" by younger women. More than twenty years ago, a man I'll call Domenic broke my heart, and it's never fully mended. I'm in my late 60s now, and when a song or a scene in a film triggers the dormant pain of that heartache, the sudden jolt reminds me of how much I've grown. My experience with Domenic inadvertently molded my intuition and empathy because of the energy I used trying to force him to love me. I used to think Domenic was the biggest love of my life. In retrospect, he was the biggest lesson of my life: My time with Domenic was time well wasted.

• • •

I better get straight home, I thought, *just in case Domenic calls*. It
had been weeks since I heard from him and, as it was not
the weekend, I figured it was likely he would call. I had the
buyers sign the last few pages of the contract, said good
night, and locked up the sales office. Sometimes I stayed
after eight, but I felt anxious. I had to get home. On the
drive home, I imagined his voice on the other end of the
phone, and I felt just as excited about the possibility of
seeing him as I was when we first met fourteen years ago.

As soon as I opened the door to my small apartment, I
looked over to the answering machine praying that it was
flashing, but there was no red light in the darkness. I kicked
my shoes off, put my things away, and stood in front of the
fridge with the door open just staring into the empty space.
I couldn't be bothered to eat and certainly didn't want to
cook, but I managed to grab some cheese and munched on
a few crackers. I don't even remember what TV show was
my distraction that night, but it was enough to make me
sleepy, so I headed for bed at 9:30.

I lay there trying to figure out why Domenic didn't call.
What is he doing? I wondered. When will he call? What else can
I do to make myself irresistible? All that was spinning around
in my mind when the phone suddenly rang. I flew across the
room, stubbing my toe on the edge of the bed as I grabbed
the phone before the fourth ring would prompt the answering
machine to kick in. I didn't feel any pain. "Yeah" was all he

said in his deep sultry voice. That's all he ever had to say, and I was done for and already planning what I was going to wear.

Domenic never ever actually invited me down to his place; he would just wind me up to a point where I would ask if I could come down to see him. Then he would casually say okay. So, after trying on two or three outfits, I was in the car for the forty-minute drive. *He's standing at the top of the stairs to his small apartment above the store when I arrive. He pulls me into his arms.* "I was a fool to make you wait so long," he says. Suddenly a car horn honks and the driver gives me the finger, snapping me out of my reverie.

I thought I had sensed something a little different from him on the phone earlier, and when I arrived at his place, I swallowed the lump in my throat. I walked up the stairs and saw him sitting on the couch in his underwear, smoking. When I sat next to him I managed to contain my excitement about seeing him because Domenic's not the demonstrative type — real men just aren't that way. I glance down at the rainbow effect on the hot knives. He calmly places them down, takes the last gulp of his drink, and says, "Let's go."

I am somehow even more enamored by his decisiveness, and just watching him pull on his pants and zip makes me silently swoon. Domenic is walking toward my car with the poise and stealth of a leopard stalking its prey. On the way to our favorite Greek restaurant, I sensed something bad was about to happen, like an antelope sensing it's the prey.

Truth be known, it had become more and more difficult for me to ignore the signs. A few weeks between visits was normal in our relationship, but in this last year or so those weeks had stretched into months at a time. I pumped up the volume on the radio as Whitney Houston belted out *I Have Nothing! Nothing! Nothing!*

Domenic's momentary silence gave me a spark of hope that things were okay, but the antelope was already on high alert. He turned the volume down and, not for the first time, uttered the words "I don't think this is working out anymore."

The restaurant was small with cheesy decor, but I loved looking at the curves of the white plaster walls with the hand-painted scene of Greek houses stacked against the edge of the Aegean Sea. Each table had a carefully placed candleholder on a white tablecloth and wine glasses ready for filling. The smells of freshly baked bread, herbs, and grilled fish wafted through, making my mouth water as the hostess approached. Domenic let me lead as the hostess asked where we'd like to sit. He knows it's important for me to be away from the kitchen, the washroom, or any family with small children. These meals with him were my chance to exercise some control over getting his undivided attention. As we sat down I thought about how he might be kidding about the breakup. He teased me sometimes, just to get me worked up, and then he would say "I'm just kidding, dummy! You're so gullible."

We had been to that restaurant enough times that the owners stopped by the table to welcome him. Domenic was cool and calm, and chatted with them casually but with an air of status. It made me feel proud that he was my man. The waiter took Domenic's drink order. They already knew I would have water, no ice. For dinner, I desperately wanted to start with the saganaki, then order moussaka or chicken with a side of roasted herbed potatoes, but I needed to make sure my meal could be eaten and portioned in the most ladylike way. I settled for the wonderful production made over the flaming cheese, feigning lack of hunger, while Domenic ordered his second drink.

The waiter took Domenic's plate away and paused with his hand close to my not-quite-empty plate.

"Have you finished, ma'am?" he asked.

"Yes," was my automatic response, even though I could've finished the little bit that I left plus a second helping.

"Can I show you the dessert menu?"

Domenic leaned back in his chair waiting for his chance to order his Courvoisier. I politely declined dessert, and the waiter took the empty bottle of wine and Domenic's wine glass away to bring the proper glass for cognac. He left my clean wine glass on the table. His focus shifted to follow the money. Domenic didn't just order his Courvoisier: They also had a brief conversation about Napoleon giving his artillery companies a ration of this expensive cognac during the war. I sat quietly admiring my man's worldly knowledge.

I desperately wanted to talk about what he said in the car, and while he chatted with the waiter and sipped his cognac, I was thinking, *What if we make another investment together?* I'd find another perfect property like the ones I bought a few years ago, and make the same arrangement. I put up the money for the deposit, then I show him all of the properties I think are best so he could approve one, then I'd renovate it, sell it, and we'd split the profit 50/50. That could take upward of nine months to a year to make happen. If this time he meant it, and we were going to break up, it would be a way we could stay close. Before I had a chance to say anything, he pushed his chair back and stood up.

"Let's go," he said.

I paid the bill and left, trailing behind him.

He walked to the passenger side of the car and got in. As I slid behind the wheel, my mind was spinning with how I could invite myself up to his place and change his mind about leaving me if he did mean it. On nights like this, we didn't have a set routine: Sometimes he would invite me up and sometimes he wouldn't.

Tonight, he had not invited me up, but I figured it was still okay because that wasn't different. Different is dangerous. Different is a sign that things are changing. *Good*, I thought, *he must not have meant it.*

And besides, there was still time. Maybe when we got outside his apartment he'd invite me up to share a joint. He smoked them almost as much as he did cigarettes, and on occasion, he would draw me close to him, breathe in slowly, and then blow the smoke into my mouth. I loved when he did that because it was a definite sign he wanted to be with me forever. He used to tell me you can't have both people in a relationship drinking or high, so those times when he'd share a puff or two with me made me feel like he was trying to see if I would fit into his lifestyle. My response had to be perfectly executed: One or two inhales, and I'm cool. More than that, and I'm not wife material.

We pulled up outside his apartment, and I waited to be told to turn the car off and come upstairs. He leaned over to me. The antelope quivered. He kissed me on the cheek — the leopard was going in for the kill.

"Goodbye. Have a good life," he said, as he exited the car. I watched him calmly walk to his apartment door.

My eyes blurred, and I felt the hollow caving in of my stomach. I automatically covered my belly with my hand in an attempt to comfort myself while I fought back tears. At that moment, the leopard could have dragged this bleeding antelope into his cave and I'd have been okay with it. Instead, my frontal lobe won over my primal instinct, and I drove away.

In the darkness of the night, the loneliness of window wipers squeaking in rhythm with the rain began to lull me back to my soul. *He's breaking up with me, but if that's what he needs I can do what's best for him*, I thought. *Love is unconditional.* Patsy Cline's "Stand by Your Man" resonated with me. I let the tears roll down my cheeks as I forced out her words, my voice breaking.

We're together in this one, sister, but don't worry, I know how to fix it. I know how to love properly, deeply, I told myself. Mine wasn't romantic love; it was deeper than that. It was more important: It was spiritual.

My Stockholm syndrome was raging. Back then I wasn't sure what Stockholm syndrome was, but I've since learned how people can overlook abuse and in some cases even develop feelings of trust or affection toward the person who is victimizing them.

"The love of my life is breaking our fourteen-year relationship, without even a conversation, but if that's what he needs, I can do what's best for him. I can dig deeper into my soul and support that decision for his sake — at any cost to me."

That was the last time I ever saw him.

• • •

For too many years, I clung to the idea of unconditional love, regardless of the profound cost to my soul. Do you know that overused expression "the path I took made me who I am today"? Well, isn't that a way of dismissing the responsibility that is asked of us, as empowered women, to look at how we behave in our love relationships? It's okay to love deeply and passionately, but in the meantime, your heart is begging the same from you.

Listen to it.

Now when I see women taking a back seat in their relationships, it makes me want to look them in the eyes, shake them by the shoulders, and shout, "Look at me! Look at the years I wasted trying to be somebody else, somebody I guessed might be loveable on his terms. Stop putting yourself last! Your soul needs you to be you, and the world needs you now more than ever."

That's what I learned from Domenic, and why I am a beloved Nanna to so many.

Raven Thompson graduated from the University of Toronto with an undergraduate Honors degree majoring in equity studies and Caribbean studies, with a minor in African studies. She has a Master of Education degree in curriculum studies and a teacher development degree. A certified yoga teacher, Raven has always had a passion for promoting healthy minds, bodies, and spirits. She's a strong advocate for the criminal justice system and mental health. Raven is a single parent of two amazing, caring young men. You can reach Raven at raven.rachel@hotmail.com or on Instagram @RavensBreathYoga.

Love to the Fullest

RAVEN THOMPSON

•

My first kiss was with a boy from my neighborhood named Kayon. At that moment, he held my heart. The way he made me feel gave me life. I wanted to be happy, in love, and to have a purpose rather than just struggle like those I saw around me. I wanted a life where I would love to the fullest.

I grew up in the 80s as poor as everyone else in the rough part of town, Scarborough, located on the outskirts of Canada's biggest city. Such a community provided ample opportunity for aggression, frustration, and street hustle. Although tension and violence existed on the streets, there was also a sense of loyalty. Solid bonds and commitments were forever formed.

We were fourteen when we took the bus to the group home with his mother and little brother. I didn't really know anything about such places. When I walked into the home, an older man gave us a brief tour. I held Kayon's hand tightly as the man led us to a room with several bunk beds. A boy with sandy-brown hair and a white tee-shirt who looked younger than us sat on one of the top bunks holding his pillow. He looked terrified and just stared at us. It seemed as though he had been there a while; he was settled in. I knew right then that Kayon was spending the night.

I only saw him sporadically after that. I'd just randomly bump into him, and we'd spend a few great hours together. I'd expect to see him again, but then he would disappear. Much time had passed, but my feelings for him had not. I was confused by his lack of interest in me. I continually asked myself what I did wrong. *Maybe he thought I wasn't pretty enough? Maybe it was because I didn't have sex with him? Maybe it was because I wasn't worth the effort?*

•   •   •

I was in my second year of college when I met a new man, who was the opposite of Kayon. Sean was quiet, shy, extremely funny, drove a car, worked a good job, and lived in an upscale neighborhood. He had a two-parent family, was 6'4" with sandy-brown hair and ocean-blue eyes — and he was white! This is not what either of our families expected. Our dramatic differences caused a lot of tension, and I even lost some friends. People used to stare or point at us, or they'd talk behind our backs. I honestly never thought of color when I was with Sean. It was other people who reminded me of our differences.

Sean not only liked my looks, but he also wanted to get to know me. We had beautiful conversations about travel, adventure, and rap music. He didn't ask for anything in return. I was skeptical at first. What did he see in me? What was his game plan? I soon found out that he had none. He was a genuinely kind, compassionate soul. I stepped out of my comfort zone, and I allowed myself to fully try at this relationship. I began to love.

God has a way of testing us!

About a month into my relationship with Sean, I was standing in the train station on my way home from work when I suddenly saw Kayon. Even after so many years, my heart started pounding in my chest, and I got those familiar butterflies. I was nervous but tried my best to stay cool. He smiled at me, but I did not smile back: I held a straight face. I was angry at him because of all the times he promised to come back to me and didn't.

I thought I was over him. I knew part of me still loved him, but I was tired of his empty promises. I told him that I had moved on. In my heart, I needed him to say something to me to change my mind or to give me a reason for his unexplained absences from my life. He said nothing. That night we walked away from each other with our issues unresolved.

• • •

I soon found out I was pregnant with Sean's baby. We were happy, but shocked! We never talked about having kids or what the future held for us. We were young. That night Sean packed his bags and moved in with me.

A few days later as I was watching the news, Kayon's face flashed across the TV screen. My heart sank, and I began to panic. I had no one to talk to because I had lost contact with everyone who knew "us." I was in a state of shock and began to cry uncontrollably. I looked around guiltily even though I knew Sean was not home. I was confused by what I was seeing and hearing. It could not be true: the station repeated that a warrant was out for Kayon's arrest, and that he was "armed and dangerous."

My head hurt, and tears burned my eyes. I fell to my knees and prayed, chanting, "God, I will see him in twenty years. God, I will see him in twenty years. Please keep him safe."

I guessed that, should he be caught, he'd be looking to serve over twenty years in jail. Not for one moment did I believe that he was capable of such a crime, but I could no longer pine for a man who did not want me, especially as I was now carrying another man's baby.

• • •

My life with my new family was wonderful. Eventually, Sean and I got married, despite my relationship with his mother.

From day one she was not fond of me at all. I have always believed that she wanted Sean to marry someone of his own race and was disappointed in her son's decision. Sean loved me, and although I had some issues with his parents, he stood by me.

Sean and I weathered many storms, as all relationships do. We went to marriage counselling to help strengthen and seal the gaps in our marriage. He was a wonderful husband and a great father to our beautiful son, Quinntin. Our family was everything to Sean. In 2000, the company he worked for offered him a full-time position, which meant we needed to move to a city I'd never heard of before. Like any good wife, I went with my husband. I left my job, my friends, and my familiar surroundings to make a life in the unknown.

Life in this new town was strange for me at first. It was a complete culture shock. I didn't see another black person for months. I was the only one. I was "different." I stood out. As I began to meet folks, I started to build real, solid friendships. I had a full life: I was a wife, mother, and a friend. I had a beautiful home, cars, and a great job. My relationship with my husband was wonderful, and we had a second beautiful son named Ethan. For five years, this was my home. Until the day my husband was diagnosed with stage 4 non-Hodgkin's lymphoma.

For months I'd been telling Sean that he needed to get the large tumor on his neck checked out.

Why didn't he listen to me? Why did he wait so long? Why didn't I force him to get checked out earlier?

Sean went through chemo, radiation, injections, and ample amounts of medications. He had constant seizures and several surgeries. Against his wishes, Sean spent most of his time in hospital undergoing tests or hooked up to an IV machine. He was such a brave fighter and tried his best to be strong for his boys and me. He loved us so much and just wanted to be with us every moment he could get. It was the hardest ten months of our lives. I don't remember much. I was on autopilot until the very end.

I do remember the day the doctor came and told me that Sean was dying. I asked when. It was just a matter of time, he said.

That day, I left the hospital and planned Sean's funeral, from the flowers to the casket, and even the food. Over the next couple of weeks, I just listened to him talk about all the things he still wanted: to eat pizza and sour candies, and drink Coca-Cola. He wanted to see the water again, so the boys and I took him on a ferry boat ride across the harbor. He also wanted a Tommy Hilfiger watch with a red face, so I bought one for him. He loved it. He wanted to be at home, to sit in our backyard and watch the boys play. That was his true happiness.

But tension mounted with Sean's parents. Their wishes for their son were different than what I wanted for my husband, but I humbly stepped back. I allowed them to make decisions for their only son — and that is my biggest regret. One night, as Sean lay in ICU, a priest asked if I was okay. I looked at him and said, "There are three things that I must do before you can ask me that: Sean must take his last breath, I must tell my boys that daddy isn't coming home, and then I must bury him. Then you can ask me if I am okay."

That night our eight-year-old son Quinntin went to the ICU to see his father. Before he went in, I told him that if your father squeezes your hand, he loves you. I still don't know what made me say that. We went in, and I said, "Sean, Quinntin is here," and then I placed Quinntin's tiny hand in his father's hand. At that moment, Sean squeezed his hand. That was the last time he ever moved. We lost Sean shortly after.

The funeral was beautiful. I had tremendous support and love from friends and family. My wedding vows echoed in my head: "in sickness and in health ... till death do us part."

When it was all over, and everything had settled, and everyone had gone back to their lives, I stood in my kitchen and looked up to the heavens. I realized that the best part of me had died. The only love I could find was the love of my beautiful sons, who were soundly sleeping. Their love saved me that night and many years after. Without them, I had no purpose. I was in a cycle of hurt, pain, and misery. I had hit bottom.

It was the love of my sons that allowed me to see my divine light.

Years later, as I began to step into my greatness, I asked God to send me a man who would love me and always put me first. He needed to be smart, funny, loyal, sexy, brave, passionate, spiritual, humble, and have a story that was worse than mine. I was tired of people feeling sorry for me. (Poor widow.) God soon granted me my wish.

I had decided to go back to school to earn my teaching degree and happened to bump into a childhood friend that had known of me and Kayon. She and I started talking, and I asked about him. She said that she would inquire around for me. I gave her my phone number to pass along, just in case.

I had no expectations. I didn't even know for sure if he remembered me. All I wanted to say was sorry for how we left things unresolved. I think I was seeking closure. Two nights later he left a message on my answering machine: "I've missed you and always loved you ... I thought you knew."

I listened to the message over and over again. It was the first time he said he loved me — and no, I had not known!

It was my fortieth birthday, and the first words that came out of my mouth were "God, I get to see him." I did not realize it but twenty years had indeed passed.

The man I want and wish to spend the rest of my life with has been incarcerated for the past twenty-three years. He is still in prison. And I have been committed to him since that first night we reconnected on the phone. It's been five years now.

In many ways I could be labeled a prison wife. I am doing my time on the outside because of who I love. Every day when he calls, I wonder, *Could this be the last time I hear his voice?*

My heart breaks when I hear the dial tone. I have learned to cherish the times we spend together, the love letters we write, and the words we say. This love in my heart started years ago with that first kiss. We started on the same road but chose different paths that still led us back to each other. I have committed to him just as I did my husband, and I will not leave him or bail. I am standing behind the man I love, despite naysayers who question my choice. I am rewriting our story and expect a happy ending. His is a source of true love.

I was not there the night his world turned upside down. I am not the judge nor the jury. I cannot imagine the pain and anguish his family has endured all of these years, nor that of others involved. I believe that he has served more than his fair share of time, and that as a human being he deserves the love I am offering him.

I have been given a second chance at true love, and I am accepting it all with an open heart. I have reconnected with a man who respects me, loves me, supports me, and puts me first. For a while, I kept my love for him a secret as I didn't feel the need to explain it to people and I just didn't want the judgment. He is getting out soon, and we are preparing for that. We no longer deny what we have. I see life and breath now as a gift and blessing from God.

We only have the moments that we create, so we must cherish them and not take the things and the ones we love for granted. Why would I throw away such a great love when I know his heart is true? We must be our authentic selves and stand in our truth. All of us. My truth is I love a man who is currently incarcerated.

It is not trauma or pain that defines us — it is how we choose to fight, rise, and overcome it that defines our character. It is through kindness and love of ourselves that we can demonstrate kindness and love to others, and slowly begin to heal our hearts.

I have stepped into the light and choose to love to the fullest with no regrets or hesitation.

I love him.

From the age of seven, Jennifer Mae Kelloway knew that she wanted to be a teacher and a mother, but it wasn't until she was faced with her own mortality that she realized just what type of teacher she was meant to be. Jennifer is a human potential life and business coach with a background in psychology, an accreditation as a CFP, neuro-linguistic practitioner, and certified DiSC trainer. For the past six years, she has been arming her clients with life tools to allow them to overcome adversity and reach their optimal potential. Jennifer currently resides near Toronto, Canada, with her loving husband, two healthy children, two dogs, and two cats. You can connect with her on Facebook @facebook.com/CoachKelloway.

Brook's Story

JENNIFER MAE KELLOWAY

•

*l*ooking back, I know that I was experiencing post-partum depression when I had my daughter. I felt as though I had done something unforgivable to my first-born child — my son. I couldn't comprehend how I could have enough love for two children. Shane had been my world, my everything.

Caught up in my emotions, I was ignoring several comments concerning how jaundiced Brook was. I thought all babies were jaundiced. I was, however, about to find out just how abnormal it was.

As the weeks went by my postpartum improved, and I started asking the midwives if I should be concerned about Brook's color. They reassured me over and over again that she was okay. One said, "Your husband has quite an olive complexion, and Brook is going to be the same. It's that simple." Those words still haunt me today.

It was after the six weeks of midwifery care ended when I was paid a visit from one of my oldest friends, Tracy. I was in the middle of taking pictures of Brook when she knocked on the door and all but demanded, "Get Brook dressed now. I am taking you to my doctor for a second opinion." Tracy is far from the aggressive type, but I knew she meant it and could see the concern in her eyes.

In a whirlwind that took less than an hour, we were sent from her doctor to the hospital to speak to a pediatrician — the third opinion. As my husband and I sat across the table from the doctor with our six-week-old daughter, my palms started to sweat. "I can't tell you what it is, all I can tell you is that it's not good," the doctor said.

His words seemed to echo off the cold cement hospital walls. He repeated himself several times before my husband said, "If you say that one more time, I cannot be responsible for what my wife might do."

What I wanted to do was jump across the table and attack this man who was giving us this horrible news with the worst bedside manner ever.

He continued, "We are referring you to SickKids. Go home, and they will be in touch."

I don't think my husband and I said a word on the drive home. It was like time had slowed down, and it seemed to take forever to get to the safety of our house.

I sat on the couch with my baby's car seat in front of me on the floor and sobbed. I didn't know what was happening, and the loss of control over the situation was too much to handle. I remember wondering how we would cope.

The ring of the phone broke my trance. It was SickKids. Boy, they move fast. I don't know how she did it, but the woman on the other end of the phone was able to immediately console us. She assured us they would get to the bottom of the problem and that there was no better place for our daughter to be than at the best hospital in the world for sick children. We were to be there by 10 a.m. the next morning.

I had a sick child.

Upon our arrival, an entire team of doctors and nurses got to work. The first goal was to figure out what was going on with Brook. That meant blood work, lots and lots of blood work. The first time the nurse drew blood from my baby's little six-week-old arm, I felt completely and utterly helpless. Little did I know what was to come would be a hundred times worse. If I had, I might have handled it better.

That evening my husband went home with our son, Shane. As I stared at them from a window on the sixth floor, watching them leave, I felt like I had just been sent to prison. I felt claustrophobic and started to hyperventilate. I just wanted to go home ... go outside ... anything but be there.

After a week of testing, our team delivered the news. Brook had a rare disease that destroys the bile ducts of the liver, preventing it from filtering out toxins: biliary atresia.

It's a name I wish I had never heard. One in 15,000 people have it, and there is no known cause.

The first thing we were going to do was a procedure called a kasai, a surgery, the doctor told us.

After the filth of the word "surgery" had washed off of me, I threw myself into research mode. I started reading every piece of material they had given me on the disease, including the next procedure.

"It has a 33 percent chance of working," I said to my husband, Glenn.

"She will be in the 33 percent. It's going to be fine," Glenn responded.

Oh, how I wanted to believe that, but my gut was telling me differently.

A few days later we were escorted to the surgical waiting room. I was overwhelmed by how many parents and children were there. To think that the despair we were feeling was shared by so many brought tears to my eyes. We settled in for the long wait and, as usual, began people watching. We overheard a few people discussing what their child was there for: a broken bone, a brain tumor, and one parent had backed the car over their daughter.

My husband and I started to notice that some doctors came out to the waiting room to deliver an update on the children while other parents were brought into a private room.

"That's probably where you go if it's not good news," said Glenn.

I felt as though I had swallowed a rock.

We looked at each other in silence. *Please don't come and take us to that room.*

Not long after, our doctor appeared.

Thank goodness, I thought. *It went better than planned.*

That's when he asked us to come with him into one of the rooms. I thought my legs would give out and my heart would explode. It was the most fear I had ever felt.

"Her liver is too far gone. She's going to need a transplant. She has six to nine months to live, and the waiting list is two years so you may want to consider a live donor option."

It is hard to describe the look of complete anguish on Glenn's face. After what seemed like only seconds, I absorbed what had happened, and I was ready to solve the next problem.

"I *knew* it was only a 33 percent chance of working," I blurted out, "and I've read everything on live donors already. I know that I am a blood match so we can get this going right away."

"No, no, dear," Dr. Ing responded. "You need some time to absorb this information."

"No, Doctor. I don't need to absorb this information. With six to nine months, we have no time to waste."

Glenn still appeared dazed. I don't think his thoughts had caught up to the conversation. He managed to say, "It should be me, then."

But I was having none of it. Survival mode had kicked in, and the mother in me was going to fix her daughter.

They agreed to have me worked up as a possible match and sent us home to wait for various appointments. After several weeks of ultrasounds, X-rays, blood work, CT scans, MRIs, and psychological testing, it was official: I would be Brook's live liver donor.

Now we waited for a surgical team to be assembled and an open spot in an operating room at the hospital. Time seemed to stand still while we waited and waited and waited. As the weeks passed, Brook began to get sicker. Septic poisoning from the toxins in her body had distended her tummy, and she was almost green. Nothing could soothe her except being in our arms, and she slept at most for forty-five minutes at a time. We were utterly exhausted in every sense of the word. I was so angry that my baby girl had to suffer while we waited for a team of doctors and a surgical room. We were left to watch her die, cell by cell, as the days passed. Every minute felt like an hour, every hour like a day, and every day like a week. Friends would visit and bring us food and pay our bills. Gift baskets from total strangers were left on the porch, and as grateful as we were, at the time I couldn't have cared less. I just wanted life to be normal again, my baby girl to be healthy, my son not to have to spend every day at a hospital, and to have the unbearable weight of despair lifted off our shoulders. I felt as though I had not taken a breath in months.

Brook become too ill to stay at home so we were finally admitted to the hospital to wait. The nurses had to come hourly to check her temperature. If she spiked a fever, her surgery would have to be postponed. The stress was unfathomable. I remember telling the nurses, "If you come in here and tell me she has a fever, I'll shoot you." I was furious and feeling as though I was becoming unhinged. I had been ruminating on why they couldn't do the surgery "now" for so many months that it was starting to eat away at my sanity.

They sent the hospital psychiatrist to see me. Ha! Emily was her name. And she was amazing. She would sit with me for hours as if there were nowhere else for her to be. Which I knew was not the case as we had met many families while living in the hospital, many of which were just as bad off if not worse.

Emily gently sat me down and in her angelic-like voice said, "Jennifer, you cannot tell people that you are going to shoot them or they will not let you donate."

The reality of her words terrified me, so I immediately stopped threatening to shoot people.

On the evening of June 25, at 11:15 p.m., the hospital phone rang. It was time. They had a golden liver for Brook. It meant that a mother and father somewhere in the world had lost their baby and donated the child's organs. It was the strangest feeling I have ever had. An immense amount of hope for the first time in a very long time as a full baby liver was better than a portion of mine but also pure raw devastation for the family who had just lost their child. We were told the surgery would take place the next morning.

Brook was in the operating room, opened up, ready to go when we got word that the golden liver couldn't be used.

The vessels were too tiny to attach. At 8 p.m. that evening, I was told I would have to go into surgery the next morning or Brook wouldn't survive. She stayed in the ICU with mesh screening over her open belly. We all hoped she'd make it through the night. I was Brook's last chance.

The next morning at 5:45 a.m., I entered the hospital across the street. Remember: SickKids is only for kids, and I wasn't a kid. The nurses prepared me by putting in four art line IVs, which are attached to significant blood supplies in the body in case a blood transfusion is needed. I had one in my hand, one in my neck, and two in my arms. Thankfully, I have no fear of needles, but as I looked over at my sister, I thought she would pass out and fall right off that tiny red hospital chair.

"I'm okay, Margie. You can go to the waiting room until they are done." But she wasn't leaving my side.

Before I knew it, it was time to go. The surgeon came to talk to me accompanied by the nurse who would hand deliver my organ to SickKids. I somehow managed to find my sense of humor and asked the nurse to make sure she crossed at the lights.

"I do not want anything to happen to that liver," I joked.

The last order of business was to prepare my last wishes in case anything went wrong with the operation. The surgeon told me that they had never lost a live donor yet, but that it was like walking around a golf course in a lightning storm, so we had to hope for the best but be prepared for the worst. (As I write this, I am debating reading my last wishes; it's not something I've done since writing them.)

The next thing I remember is waking up in the recovery room with a soft voice asking me if I knew what day it was. Sweet as the sound might have been, my response was somewhat abrupt: "Once you tell me how my daughter is doing, I will tell you what day it is."

The nurse immediately picked up the phone, and the next thing I knew my surgeon was at my bedside ready to provide an update.

"It went as well as it could have," he said.

Now my interpretation of that statement turned out to be entirely different than the reality. Although I felt hesitation in the doctor's voice, it was still magic to my ears. I was so relieved and felt so light for the first time in months. It might have had something to do with the morphine, but I was elated. My baby girl was going to be okay. I wasn't able to see Brook for three long days because of my recuperation.

Finally, my husband put me in a wheelchair and took me through the underground tunnel that joined the two hospitals. The walls of the tunnel were cold and colorless. The sound of our voices flat. It resembled a bomb shelter, or at least what I thought one would look like. As we got close to the neonatal intensive care unit (NICU), we passed a couple we'd met a few days prior whose son had gone into a diabetic coma.

"Hello," I shouted in an almost inappropriately happy voice, "how is your son doing?"

There was a long pause, and I began to realize that the father had tears in his eyes.

"It's not good," he said.

His wife interrupted, "We have one more day with him, and we are thankful for that."

My mind couldn't process, and I just smiled awkwardly and said, "I'm so sorry."

Glenn wheeled me through the doors of the NICU. The room was quiet, lights dim. Their son was in the first bed to my left. Lifeless, with only the sound of the monitors keeping him alive. As I focused on the room, I quickly realized that I wasn't prepared for what I was seeing. Brook's bed was the next bed in the room. She had five IV pumps stacked one on top of the other. She still had an art line in her head and her hand. She was under a plastic cube hidden by her pink bunny blanket to keep the light out of her eyes. This tiny baby was holding on for her life.

Glenn began to fill me in on what the past three days had been like. Brook had flatlined three times and was experiencing many of the possible complications of surgery but somehow was still managing to be adorable and smiling.

I started to talk to her in a quiet, loving voice. She responded with a smile, and my mood changed yet again. I was on an emotional roller coaster. I would go from feeling complete and utter despair to hope and gratitude within seconds of each other. The ride left me feeling nauseous. As challenging as it was, I was allowed to pick her up and breast feed her.

The nurse said, "Well, that's a first. I've never seen a baby in this unit having the comfort of being breast fed."

I knew I would likely lose what little milk I had left as a result of the trauma of my surgery, but I just wanted to give her and me the comfort of being able to do it one more time. I had so enjoyed breast feeding Shane and was heartbroken that I would no longer have milk to breast feed Brook. I felt as though I was letting her down. I knew how important it was for her immune system, so I had pumped everything I could before the surgery so she could at least have a few more days of it. (My milk dried up a few days later and never came back.)

In the grand scheme of what was happening, you would think breast feeding wouldn't be a big deal, but it was very emotional for me. When I breast fed, I felt like a mother, a protector, and a provider. I felt like I was doing a great job in the most important role of my life — being a mother. During the many months we lived in the hospital waiting on Brook's surgery, I would take her from her crib, IV lines and all, drag my cot close to her IV pole, and place her beside me and breast feed her. Many of the nurses did not understand why I did that, but I did, and that's all that mattered.

•   •   •

Although we didn't think it was possible, the next several months presented even more challenges. First, there were bleeding ulcers, then a rejection of the liver, so they increased the steroids. I had seen what some of the other children who were on high doses of steroids looked like and was concerned about the side effects. There were many tests to try to sort this out. X-rays, ultrasounds, and a biopsy. The most significant challenge of these tests was that Brook often could not have anything to eat for up to eight hours prior. We thought it was all some kind of sick joke. After everything Brook had been through, we had to starve her every other day. It was pure torture.

They then discovered that she had a blockage that would require yet another surgery. Back to the second-floor waiting room. This time, however, things were looking better — the doctor came out and sat on the couch beside us to say everything went fine.

After several months of battling even more problems like her electrolytes being out of whack, they told us that they had never seen a baby experience every one of these issues and come out the other end doing so well. Brook was exceptional in every way. Tests or no tests, she was the strongest, cutest, happiest little baby with the personality of a soul much older than she was. She slept like an angel, had an enormous appetite, and smiled and giggled all the time. Shane had become very attached to his sister. He would climb into the hospital crib and hug her and kiss her and talk to her.

After nine long months, it was time to go home. I have no memory of packing up our things or saying goodbye to any of the nurses or doctors, yet I know that we did. When I walked out of that hospital, I never wanted to look back. Ever!

Although everything seemed right in the world again, the trauma of the experience poured over us like hot tar and it was difficult to wash off. Don't misunderstand me: We were elated to be home with a happy, healthy baby girl. We were thrilled to be back in the real world and to see people and go places. I felt as though I had been starved of human contact and was immensely grateful to see and spend time with friends and family, but we just couldn't believe what we had been through. Did it all really happen? The experience was unfathomable.

People didn't understand, I suppose, and mostly kept it to themselves with a few brave souls who would remark "You should be happy, she's doing so well." But I wasn't so happy.

Eventually, it was Brook's first clinic visit with her whole team of doctors. Every street sign, every landscape, turned my stomach as I remembered so freshly the drive back and forth daily. We made this trip for nine months, back and forth, and I never wanted to make it again.

They greeted us with warm smiles and open arms, happy to see how well Brook was doing.

"So, we have named a syndrome after Brook! Any child who experiences every one of the side effects of transplant and is now doing well, we have labeled the Brookie Syndrome!"

I guess that should have made me happy?

As Brook grew, we realized that she would never remember most of this experience. It was a joyous realization.

Except for constant blood work for the rest of her life, most of it is no longer in her conscious memory.

As time passed and we realized how this experience had stayed with us, I decided to begin a journey of stress management. I was damned if life was ever going to throw adversity at me again without being armed with some life tools to help me deal.

So, I sat down in my home office and typed "stress management" into the Google search bar. I started to take notes furiously. There were many techniques, tools, scientific approaches, mindsets, etc. Little did I know, it was the universe preparing me for an encounter with my greatest personal fear: cancer.

But that's another story ...

A soul coach in the women's empowerment industry, Erin Marie has helped many women to heal, grow, and live their best lives. As a visionary and author, Erin dreams of a world filled with peace, harmony, balance, and love. She lives with her partner near the beautiful redwood trees in Northern California, USA, and is currently working on developing her gardening skills. You can learn more about Erin at erinmariesoulhealing .com or find her on Instagram @erinmariesoulhealing or Facebook @erinmariesoulhealing.

Life Is Beautiful

ERIN MARIE

·

i am standing in a crowded marketplace, feeling surprised and curious. My eyes lock with this beautiful, tall, dark-haired, goddess-like woman. She's surrounded by spiritual items and trinkets that are for sale in this mysterious-looking city that I don't recognize. She tells me that she has been waiting for me. I have this feeling that she is here to help me in some way.

She beckons to me to follow her. She begins to run, and suddenly, we've been transported to my secret childhood spot.

How did we get here? I wonder. But there isn't any time to think. I lose my footing and fall. My leg starts bleeding.

When I look up, the woman is standing in front of me, smiling, with love and wisdom in her eyes.

"You can heal yourself, Erin," she says gently.

I feel her message down to my core. I place my hands over the wound and feel an inner power activated. My hands begin to channel energy, the pain starts to subside, the bleeding stops, and the wound closes up.

I wake up and realize I'd been dreaming, and even though it was a dream, it felt so real. I feel a deep sense of awe and wonder. I know in my heart that this dream was sent to me. That it represented something big and important. It was a message ... and I received it.

•   •   •

The truth is when I had this sacred dream I wasn't in a good place. I'd fallen into a deep hole of darkness. I was struggling with suicidal depression, extreme anxiety, substance abuse, and addiction. This had been going on for years, starting around the age of fifteen, when the people who were my family — the people who were supposed to love and protect me — forgot that I existed. And that is when I began to take their neglect out on myself.

I felt so trapped by my family and life, like I had no power over my circumstances. I became hopeless. My distress and anger began to implode, creating a dark hole; my depression felt inescapable. And that's when I became a rebellious teenager — drugs, alcohol, and cigarettes offered an escape. I even started a dangerous relationship with painkillers. And even though I made it through high school and even went off to college (far from home), a new truth emerged: Wherever you go, there you are. I'd always blamed my family for the state of my life, but by the time I got to college, I was already in too deep. The drug use continued — the street drug "molly," cocaine, weed, Adderall, acid ... literally anything I could get my hands on — and I constantly felt like I was drowning. I was in pain.

Deep down, though, I knew I was not meant to be living like this. I knew my life was meant for more and I was disappointed in myself. Ashamed.

That is when I had my sacred dream.

At twenty years old, I knew it was time to heal myself, and that my life depended on it.

• • •

I dove into the healing abyss. Within weeks, I signed up for a winter-term course at a beautiful ranch in New Mexico, alongside six other young women. We had the most amazing wise woman teacher who'd take us daily into a special sacred circle where we'd take turns sharing our deepest secrets, shame, and guilt. We journaled, journaled, and journaled some more in the most quiet, beautiful, and peaceful settings you could ever imagine! I stopped drinking, smoking, and using drugs. I began to make friends with sober people, and I spent many days hiking the red mesas and cliffs in the magnificent desert landscape. I soaked in hot springs, witnessed native rituals, visited sacred sites, and vision-journaled for the first time. I learned about yogic philosophy, and practiced yoga daily. At night, if I felt brave enough, I'd sit outside in the dark and watch as the night sky lit up so brightly with billions of stars. I found out that I was in the same town where Georgia O'Keeffe, a famous American artist, began her career. The land was ancient and preserved, even dinosaur remains were found here. All of this gave me a glimpse of how beautiful life could be, and I wanted more of it.

By the spring, I'd received so much in this magical land and I was ready to move on. Next stop, Nepal!

•   •   •

I took on three summer jobs to save up, and by Thanksgiving, at the age of twenty-one, I took my first solo travel trip abroad.

I volunteered at the Children's Peace Home — one of the most amazing children's homes and schools in the world — and even though at times I was the only native English speaker around, I loved being there. The views were amazing: rolling Nepali countryside and beautiful women wrapped in saris, tending to day-to-day duties and working the land. Tall, handsome Nepali men selling food, clothes, and bus tickets on the side of the road. I felt happy, free, content, and deeply alive. I was in love with life!

Soon other volunteers joined me from the UK and USA, and we became fast friends, traveling the land together.

We visited Bardia National Park in western Nepal, where we searched for wild, one-horned rhinos and Bengal tigers. We camped out overnight by a river, where the local people helped us to make fire, set up camp, and fed us. On our way back to Peace Home, we rode on top of a bus, hanging on for dear life, eating peanuts and small oranges, our bags tied down.

For one week, we hiked in the Himalayan mountains for over five hours a day. We ate the local Nepali cuisine and stayed in homes that were open to trekkers, some no more than a shack in a mountainous forest or on a snowy mountaintop. We took turns having baths in the local stream where a group of wild water buffalo met us to let us know it was their turn.

My days were filled with hiking, eating, and hiking some more. My body had never been pushed so hard ... and yet I had never felt this good before either.

One night we arrived at our next stop just in time to watch the sun set over the mountaintops. Our dinner was cooking, and my friends were laughing, messing around, and taking pictures. I plopped down at the edge of the cliff and began meditating. I quickly fell into an altered state of consciousness — an almost dream-like state. I felt a deep sense of peace, comfort, and love. It was as though my angels and spirit guides were speaking to me. I had never experienced something like this before. It didn't last long.

The most pivotal moment of the trek, though, was while we were at the highest altitude, at the top of a snowy mountain. We were debating about staying for a bit when our guide spoke to us in broken English, telling us that we must go back immediately as there was a bad storm brewing.

We packed up and left, but as we were hiking back down the mountainside, the storm hit. Thunder, lightning, and downpour. The other hikers quickened their pace, but my body was at its breaking point. One step at a time was all I could do. Then something magical happened, and I felt the power of Mother Earth cocooning me, giving me a sudden surge of energy and strength to carry on. I trusted that I was safe. I reveled in this powerful energy.

When we finally made it back, we ate like queens for days. My legs were so strong, I could climb anything, effortlessly. And the adventures didn't stop there. After a night of dancing, we all decided we'd go paragliding the next day.

I was the first in our group to jump off a cliff with a professional Nepali paraglider strapped to my back. We had to run as fast as we could for about 200 feet before jumping. If we didn't run fast enough, we wouldn't get enough momentum. You can bet I ran as fast as my legs would go! I flung myself into the air and trusted that the straps would hold my weight

I was wearing purple overalls with peace signs, rainbows, and elephant patches sewn all over them, an orange tee-shirt, and green Converse sneakers that I'd bought after I'd lost my shoes riding an elephant. Afterward my friends told me, laughing, that I looked very vibrant gliding through the air. They cheered my bravery and my unique way of spreading out my arms and legs like a star as I flew through the air. To me, it symbolized my deep sense of complete surrender, trust, and freedom.

When it came time for my friends to go home, I knew my time to leave was coming soon, too. After five months in Nepal, I was ready to move on.

Next stop, India!

• • •

As I climb back up the hill to my rented room in Bhagsu, India, with my new Polish friend, Marika, all I could think about was food. I was finishing up a month-long yoga intensive and an Ayurvedic whole body detox called Panchakarma.

Marika laughed and reminded me that we had to stick to the food they give us at the Ayurvedic Center in order to receive the full benefits of the healing process. And boy did we detox! But for some reason all of this yoga and cleansing had me craving chocolate. Unbelievably, we were surrounded by many amazing eateries that served cuisine from all over the world.

How is there a German bakery all the way in the northern, mountainous region of India? I wondered.

In those seven months of travel, I learned more about love, being a woman, relationships, and true friendship than I had in the twenty-one years I had been on this planet. I had a newfound sense of purpose. I'd shifted and healed tremendously.

On the final night of our yogic graduation ceremony, we ended our time together by having a sober dance party. We danced all night together and had so much fun!

As our yoga group broke bread together for the last time, we talked about our future plans and where we were off to next. I sat beside our yoga teacher, Manu, and he asked me what my plans were. I told him I'd be departing in the next day or so, and that I was sad to be leaving this amazing place.

"Then don't go!" he exclaimed. "Why don't you just stay?"

He described what they would be up to in the next couple months. They were planning a trip to meet their guru, and he invited me to continue on with them. I knew in my heart that my time in India was up, and I told him so. I knew that it was my purpose to return home and begin to assimilate all that I had learned throughout my travels. To create the life I desired in my heart, on my own terms. To share all that I had learned in order to help others heal as well. I now knew life didn't have to be so hard.

You can heal yourself was my new mantra. As I began my long journey back to the States, my heart exploded with joy and gratitude for this crazy, beautiful thing we call life.

Hamda Wazwaz is a women's master empowerment coach, the founder of Truly Empowered Women's Coaching, and an international business consultant with a degree from the University of Phoenix. Born in Jerusalem and raised in the United States, she now lives in Palestine. Compelled and determined to create change by standing up to injustice, she spends her days helping women lead the lives they were meant to live. A loving mother to five beautiful children and a wife to her beloved husband, Hamda is a true storyteller and empath. Visit trulyempoweredwomen.com or find Hamda on Facebook @hamda.wazwaz or Instagram @hamda.wazwaz.

A Girl from Palestine

HAMDA WAZWAZ

•

*i*t was a typical school night. I had put my five kids to sleep, and the house was finally quiet. I sat alone on the couch watching a movie, waiting for my husband to come home from work. Something made me get up to check my phone, and I saw that I had three missed calls from my mother. I must have left my phone on silent. Knowing my mother rarely calls during late hours, I had a feeling that something was very wrong. I called her back, and my heart dropped when there was no answer.

I called again, and she hung up on me. Now I was sure something was wrong. I called my brother, and he answered. His voice was heavy with emotion. I could tell he was trying to hold himself together.

"Hamda, Candy is missing. We found her car by the river, but she's not there."

I put my hand over my mouth, my eyes open wide. I sat down and tried to reassure my brother, telling him that she might be with a friend.

"No, Hamda, you should come," he said.

I called my mom again. I was shaking as the phone kept ringing. All I could imagine was my mom, 2,000 miles away, falling apart. My sisters were also far away, in Dubai, as were a few of my brothers. I needed to be there with her, so I kept hanging up and then calling back, praying she would answer. And then she did. She was crying hysterically. I will never forget the fear in her voice as she screamed into the phone over and over again, "Hamda, she gone! Candy is gone. She's in the water! My Candy, your sister, she is gone!"

Shaking, I screamed, "Candy?! No, Mom, please tell me this is not real!"

She kept crying. I took a sharp breath in and listened: In the background, I could hear a police officer talking to her. I gripped the phone so tightly my knuckles turned white.

This was real. I couldn't move. I was holding my breath.

I was in the Palestinian-occupied territories, far away from them. My mother, my family in the United States needed me. I called my husband at work, sobbing. He came home and found me curled on the couch, shaking, crying soundlessly. I couldn't say a word. I couldn't move. My husband grabbed my passport.

"You need to go to them," he said.

I knew that, but I was terrified.

By 6 a.m., I was on my way to Jordan with only the clothes on my back and very little else packed in a small bag. Because as Palestinians we are not permitted to use the Israeli airports, my only way out of Palestine was to cross the Allenby Bridge to Jordan. I knew I had a long way to go because we are not allowed to use the same roads as the Israelis. The streets we use have armed checkpoints at which we are often required to exit, where you must remove your shoes, your belt, and the rest of your clothes to be strip-searched. Once at the bridge, we are required to do all this and then switch buses.

I was distraught as I sat on one bus, knowing the hassles and irritations before me. I expected this, but I needed to be with my family and find Candy. Tears streamed down my face, and fellow travelers asked me, "Are you okay?" I couldn't even reply. I could only cry.

I thought of my sister's beauty. Candy, with her long, dark hair and tan-colored skin, looked like an Arabian princess. She had a radiant smile and a fiery personality: She was very wild and fun. She had called me a couple of weeks prior, begging me to visit, as she often did. I had said, "But Candy, I have school, and what will I do with all these children? I can't leave them alone?"

I felt guilty. I knew there wasn't a time when I needed her that she had not been there for me, and here I was on a slow, continually interrupted journey to get back to her.

She was always the strong one. Maybe she had been trying to tell me that something was wrong and she needed me, but I missed it. I only hoped it was not too late.

Finally, I got off a full, un-air-conditioned bus at 4 or 5 in the evening — nearly twelve hours for a commute that should take no more than an hour in another country — and entered the airport in Jordan. I was exhausted from lack of sleep, from the worry, from the stress of checkpoints, from the smells, heat, and humidity of the city of Jericho, and from the effects of being far below sea level. I got checked in and knew that now I faced a nineteen-hour flight to get to my mother and there was nothing I could do to get there any faster. I was so jittery I couldn't sit on a chair and instead collapsed on the carpeted floor, sobbing and praying for the safety of my sister.

My brother met me in Minneapolis, at the airport. He looked pale and as though he'd slept in his clothes. He picked up my small bag, and we headed to his vehicle. We said little as we drove to our mother's house.

Soon after we got there, my mom and two sisters, from Dubai, arrived. They had been at the St. Croix River in Minnesota's Interstate Park the whole day and were now home because the search party had ended. My sister had been missing for two full days. We'd go back in the morning to keep looking.

My mom looked so weak and broken. She was a woman of strong faith, and although she had already lost my father and my brother, when he was nineteen years old, I had never seen her like this. She just sat on the couch, sobbing. None of us knew what to say or do for her.

The next morning at 7 a.m., we went to the river to begin our search again. The drive to the river was an hour and a half long, much of it silent. I looked out the window and thought of how my sister had reacted when I told her I was going to Palestine to live with my new husband.

That was when my life took a dramatic turn ...

I remember Candy shaking my shoulders, screaming at me. She acted like she was losing her daughter, not her younger sister. I was eighteen, and she was twenty-three, but she had raised us all — nine of us — after my father died. I admired her strength and beauty.

"What are you doing? I will break his neck before I let him take you," she said, her eyes blazing. "I blame him," she pointed to a photo of us taken on our wedding day, "for taking you away from me like this. I will never forgive him. How dare you cheat on me with him, you are my wifey," she screamed.

Somehow being called her "wifey" made us both stop and laugh. We laughed and cried as we said goodbye. I insisted I wouldn't be gone forever. I could come home to visit anytime I wanted.

And so my life began in a small town in Palestine, where I had no one but my husband and child. Just like any beginning, it was not an easy move, especially here. I was born in Jerusalem, and although I moved to America as a child, we had a second home near Jerusalem that we spent each summer in with my mother, father, and nine siblings. And yet, now that I lived in Palestine, I was no longer allowed to enter into Jerusalem unless I had a permit from the Israeli government. It was heartbreaking to know that going to the city I was born and raised in was no longer an option. An apartheid wall was built soon after, and entering Jerusalem became something I didn't even consider. I was too afraid and, as a result, felt imprisoned in my own home.

I looked around and saw the hopelessness of my neighbors — their freedom taken from them, a sad look in each child's eyes. I saw the oppression. I felt it. I no longer had the freedom to live my life the way I would have back in America. I couldn't go to certain schools, cities, or other places without being harassed. The opportunities available are little to none for women, let alone for Palestinians. The racism is astounding.

Trying so hard to belong, I quickly began doing everything I could to feel accepted, all the while losing bits and pieces of myself in the process. Knowing that my options and hopes for a future were limited by the occupation, I felt devastated. I could not imagine going on like this, and I slowly began to lose hope. Candy was my lifeline to the world, and I would wait daily for her call. Although she was not there with me physically, she was the only source of inspiration I had. And now, I hadn't heard from her for days ...

I got out of the car with my family, now back in Minnesota. I shivered. I had not brought the right clothing for the weather. September in Minnesota is much cooler than in Palestine. I wrapped my scarf around my head real tight. I had selected a heavy one that made me feel protected, like I was wearing sunglasses. When we got out of the car closer to the St. Croix River, it was even colder.

Despite the temperature, it was calm by the river. It was peaceful and quiet. Families were relaxing on the grass together, and I could smell their barbecues. I felt calm yet terrified. A strange combination. And that is when I walked over to the rock where they had found Candy's shoes, her phone, and her keys, and I immediately started to doubt she was in the water.

Are you kidding me? I thought when I saw the spot. *She couldn't have drowned here.*

The water was so shallow you could wade out for some distance, which is why it was a spot favored by families. I guess I was expecting a cliff or some bridge, but instead, here we were at a peaceful park and it just didn't make any sense. I convinced myself it was going to be okay. I figured she just wanted a break and had gone somewhere. She just wanted some time alone. This was the story I had to tell myself to stay sane. To keep looking. To have faith.

When the searchers found nothing, we went home. I even started getting angry. Feeling mad felt more empowered than feeling sad: Maybe she created this elaborate trick to force me to come back to see her? I was sure she was going to call and say, "Surprise! Of course, I'm okay. I needed you to come back, and now you are here."

The next day by the river was very windy. I felt empty inside and had a sick feeling in my stomach. It was the fourth day since we had heard from Candy. We watched the search crew lower their sonar equipment for any signs of her in the water. Helicopters flew overhead, and members of my family were interviewed by the FBI.

The FBI was searching for my sister. It was like something out of a movie. I couldn't believe this was happening.

I remember the feeling when I saw the Missing poster with her picture on it. My heart was broken. Candy's beautiful face constantly flashing online, on TV, on social media sites. It was a nightmare I couldn't wake up from. Search teams of people would come, looking at us with sympathy as they grabbed a bottle of water and resumed their searches. It was the search dogs that intrigued me the most. They kept going to the spot my sister's shoes were found then jumping in the water. That's why the police were convinced that she was in the water, because of those large German shepherds.

It was then that I saw a familiar face. Rita, a friend of Candy's, had come to the river. She ran to me, tears streaming down her face, and told me she had been praying for Candy. Rita was a Christian who said she did energy healing. She came to the spot where Candy's objects were, and she offered to pray and try to see if she could sense Candy's energy near the river. We stood around her, desperate for answers. "Did you see anything? What are you feeling? Did you feel any signs of Candy?"

"I feel no sign of life," she said, which to me meant that Candy was nowhere near this spot where we were gathering each day to look for her. "There is no way Candy would do this to herself," Rita said.

Although my faith says not to believe in psychic things, Rita's words gave me hope, and I left the search area early, taking my two sisters with me, to go back to our mother's house to make some food. No one had eaten for days. No one had slept. No one was functioning correctly.

As I made soup for everyone, I imagined that Candy would open the door at any moment and say something to make me laugh. I thought about how she'd dropped out of school to take care of us after our father died. How Candy made sure we had the best birthdays, holidays, and vacations. She was always making things fun and showering us with attention. She encouraged me to go back to school, so I enrolled in an online college, the University of Phoenix in Arizona. I was terrified to leave my house in Palestine, so this was amazing. I had three kids at the time, and although I did not believe I could do it, I admired Candy and trusted her. She believed in me even when I didn't. Her soft yet commanding voice still rings in my ears as she would say, "You got this!"

We knew the search ended at 6 p.m., so we were expecting our mother and the others to arrive home before 8 p.m. I kept looking toward the door, but nobody came. It got later and later. I got no answer when I called my mother's cell phone. When the phone finally rang, vibrating in my hand, I jumped. It was my sister-in-law.

"Hamda," she said, "they found her."

Immediately, I started screaming.

I fell to the ground. My sisters and younger brother came running. They didn't need words to understand why I was screaming, and they began screaming, too. Our immediate reaction was to run outside. We didn't have a car, so we ran into the street hoping someone would help us to get to the river. My brother, who had dropped us off earlier, arrived and we drove there, to meet the others, in complete silence.

The police reported there were no signs of foul play. They said a man had called reporting a body floating in the water 11 miles from the search area. We knew it was her when they described her beautiful long, dark hair.

I had experienced the death of my father, two brothers, and a son, but this was beyond any pain I had ever felt. Candy was the light of our family. I no longer had my best friend, the person I could call at any time of the day. I wondered how any of us would get through this.

Seeing the grief in my mother's eyes at the funeral, I felt torn to shreds.

I returned home to my family in Palestine, but the pain was too much to bear. I was thousands of miles away from my family who needed me ... and I needed them. Life seemed to stop. I fell into deep depression and had interest in nothing.

A month passed and my husband could see I was falling apart. He told me I could go back if I wanted to, but I couldn't live torn between these two worlds. I had to choose.

I found myself broken beyond repair. Looking at my kids, I could see the sadness in their eyes. They knew their mom was not okay.

I needed to make a change. I couldn't allow the guilt and grief I was going through to take over my life. I imagined my sister Candy telling me to get my shit together, and that made me smile.

I began to think of ways I could keep her with me, part of my daily life. I didn't want to forget her. I needed to keep her spirit alive. We would always dream about how she would fly me back to the States for my graduation from college. I wanted to make her proud, so I finished up my remaining classes and got my degree. I know she's watching over me still.

•   •   •

I now work as a women's empowerment coach, counselling women both here in Palestine and around the world (what a saving grace our online world has provided to women like me). In my most vulnerable moments, I know Candy held my heart with a rare blend of delicacy and encouragement, and that her legacy in lifting others and helping them heal inspired me in so many ways. As a woman and mother, who at one point lost all strength and confidence in herself, I know the importance of having a mentor and person of inspiration in someone's life. My dream is to be a source of strength and inspiration to my daughters and others, as Candy Belle was to me.

A breast cancer survivor, Miriam Engeln strongly believes that the cure to almost anything is positive thinking. Growing up in the Netherlands, she always dreamed of living in sunny weather. In 2000, Miriam left Amsterdam to spent time in Thailand, Spain, and Belize, and eventually ended up in Aruba, where she's lived and worked as a real estate agent since 2004. You can follow her on Instagram at www.instagram.com/arubaconnections or on her blog at arubaconnections.blogspot.com.

Uncertainty in Paradise

MIRIAM ENGELN

•

*t*he doctor chose his words carefully: "The test results are in, and they are not good. You have breast cancer."

It was 2014, the year I use to remember the major events of my life.

The years before or after cancer.

•   •   •

A few days before Christmas 2013, I called my doctor and explained to the doctor's receptionist that while showering that morning, I'd felt a hard lump on the top of my right breast. Usually, I am very level-headed, and by no means a hypochondriac, but I instantly felt a sense of dread. I tried to hold back my tears as I told her I was worried it was a tumor. She booked me in to see the doctor that same day. Since I was so worried, my husband came with me. The doctor checked my breast and felt the hard lump. He confirmed what I intuitively knew.

"It doesn't feel good. I will send you for tests and schedule you with a specialist."

Within a day, the hospital admitted me, ran a multitude of tests, and told me to wait until they called. Christmas came and went, and for another week, I tried not to think about it. I didn't want to worry anyone, so other than my husband, I certainly never told a soul, not even my mother who lives here in Aruba, too.

In complete honesty, I never dreamed that I would ever have to face cancer — or any sickness for that matter. I had a great childhood in the Netherlands. I was a very healthy girl, never sick. My sister and I were raised well by my mother, a single parent. Growing up, there was lots of singing, cooking, talking, and laughing. I had a carefree youth, and even though Mum and Dad got divorced when I was six, I had a blessed life where I studied and traveled abroad with my sister and Mum. I fell in love with a Dutch boy, who I had been friends with since I was fifteen. I traveled with him to Thailand to do volunteer work with Gibbon apes in Phuket for three months. We would treat their illnesses and, if successful, place them back in the jungle. After Thailand, we began to travel and see the world.

We drove to the south of Spain, with one suitcase each. I started working in real estate sales. After a year or so, we moved to Central America, where my sister and her boyfriend lived. I opened a real estate office in Belize, near the border of Guatemala. My Dutch lover and I got married on top of a Mayan temple surrounded by friends and family. Life was magical.

Once my mother moved to Aruba, it was less than a year before we joined her. Aruba is a tropical, sunny island in the Southern Caribbean, located just north of Venezuela. I have lived in Aruba since 2003, and I work as a realtor. I walk the beautiful white sandy beaches every morning and continuously feel blessed by the paradise I live in.

When my doctor called me to come to his office to review my test results, I knew the news was bad.

My worry was confirmed. "Yes, you have breast cancer ... but you are young! Only forty-five years old. We will do the most aggressive treatment possible, and we will get you better." *Blah, blah, blah.*

The rest is a haze. I really couldn't focus on much after receiving such bad news. I couldn't believe this was happening to me: I felt good, I looked good, I ate healthily. *They must have taken another patient's file and confused it with mine by mistake*, I thought.

But nope. It was real, and it was my file. My husband later told me what the doctor had said since all I could hear was a loud thumping sound inside my head. Apparently, the oncologist suggested that he would operate to remove the breast tumor, then I would undergo chemotherapy, followed by radiation. I had to come to terms with it. That was that.

My mother was the first person I told, and she was in shock. She had lost her three sisters to cancer, and cried so hard when I broke the news. She was so scared she would lose me. She grabbed me in her arms and hugged me tighter than she'd ever hugged me before. I was more worried about her than myself.

Since I was born in Amsterdam in the 1960s, I was used to seeing people smoke weed, although I never did it myself. I started reading articles online to educate myself on cures for my illness. I read that by smoking weed or taking hemp oil, the tumor could shrink. *Maybe I could become a pot smoker and skip all the other treatments and live happily ever after*, I thought.

Unfortunately, my doctor insisted hemp wasn't the answer to dealing with my type of cancer, HER2, the most aggressive form possible. Instead, he insisted, "Our team of specialists have met and discussed your 'file' [I think that meant they'd discussed 'me'], and we believe what we advised for you will work. You will make it."

When a studied specialist tells you that you will make it, you almost forget about your research on oils, hemp, and all the alternatives. My doctor said I would make it! That was that!

After the first chemo treatment, I vomited once and was then fine. My taste buds changed; food started tasting like metal. I craved melted cheese often, and my husband and mother would take turns cooking for me. I ate well — lots of smoothies, yogurt, and fruit. My hair started falling out a little bit, and that was when we realized there were no real-hair wig salons in all of Aruba. Mum had some savings so she bought us each a plane ticket to Miami in the USA, plus three nights in a hotel. Mum had this way of always making life an adventure.

I wanted a wig that looked close to my natural hair so people would not notice I was sick. I still had much of my hair at that time, but I knew what was coming. I didn't want pity. I didn't want anyone to know. I wanted to continue to work. I didn't want anyone to think about or give cancer any power. So we walked around Miami and found a great wig salon that made beautiful wigs from real hair. The owner of the store was going to a wedding in Israel the next day, but she told us there was one last appointment available before she left on her travels.

She placed me in the chair, and seated my mother next to me. As soon as they began fitting me with the very first wig, my strong mother began to cry. She looked so sad and fragile, I didn't know what to do. It was heartbreaking for her to see her child like this.

The business owner asked what was wrong. She told us that most of the women who came to her salon were Jewish and that many Jewish women wear wigs in public because they are not to show their hair outside of their homes. We had no idea!

That's when Mum told her that I was sick with breast cancer, and that I would soon lose my hair. From that moment on, I got the royal treatment. She gave us drinks and all kinds of extra attention that afternoon, and it felt really good. I am a very private person and never want to bother people with my misery, but in sharing my cancer story, I saw that people could offer love and support.

The hairdresser took pictures of my hair so they could copy the highlights on my wig. The owner offered to drive with us to her other salon, where the highlights would be done. And so, we went. Afterwards, she offered to show us around her house, a mansion located just north of Miami. She was so sweet and gave us the full tour. I will never forget how a stranger can become a friend so quickly. After the visit with our new friend, Mum and I took a cab back to the hotel.

The next morning I had my hair cut short, and in the afternoon, we picked up my wig, which turned out nicely and looked a lot like my real hair. I was worried it would feel uncomfortable or itchy, or that I would look ridiculous, but my fears subsided as soon as I slid the wig on. It was an emotional moment I will never forget. I looked cute, and I was very grateful for my mum arranging it all for me. We flew back to Aruba so I could get the rest of the chemotherapy treatments.

• • •

After the second chemo treatment, my hair really started to fall out. Thank God for that wig! Losing my hair was the first time I cried about the whole ordeal. I asked my husband to shave my head since I was losing more and more hair every day. It was time to start wearing a wig. My husband got the shaver, and within minutes I was completely bald. We both were silent and sad.

From that moment on, I wore my wig whenever I left the house, even when I went to the doctor's office or chemo treatments. At home I would wear a little cap. I found it interesting how so many people would compliment my new hairstyle, especially the bangs I had cut to cover my lack of eyebrows. It felt so good, and it was a great relief to realize they didn't suspect I was sick.

Here's the thing: When people notice you are sick, they normally start talking about their illnesses and experiences, and about the medications they think you should try. I didn't want to listen to any of it. I got lots of attention from my mother, my sister, and the rest of the family, as well as a tiny circle of friends who knew.

I slept a lot, lost not just my eyebrows but my eyelashes, too, and by the end of the six treatments my period stopped. Thankfully, I was already childless by choice so going into menopause was kind of nice — although I think my husband found my sudden menopausal personality a bit trying at times! Here he was with a sick wife, low on energy, no sex drive, wearing a wig, and, on top of that, experiencing hot flashes. I felt bad for him, so I tried to smile as much as possible and think happy thoughts. We are not the type of people who speak easily about our feelings, so we did not discuss it much. In fact, I was always taught to keep my secrets to myself. I did not want to discuss cancer at all. (It was a fault that I would later fix, and then all would be fine again.) But I had always believed "what you think about, you bring about," and I wanted to bring about great health and lots of happiness, so I tried to stay positive.

I had to travel to Colombia for six weeks of radiation treatments as we did not have those machines on our island, so I took some private Spanish lessons. While I was in treatment, my need to see the world got stronger, as well as my need to enjoy every single day I was alive for the rest of my life. But I was scared because my marriage was changing.

Once I got back from Colombia, my husband started to distance himself from me. He stopped going out in public with me, and he became reticent. I kept asking him what was wrong. I'd read somewhere that when a spouse gets seriously ill, roughly 75 percent of men will leave their wives compared to just 25 percent of women who leave their husbands. And that's when he told me that he'd fallen out of love with me. After all, we were going through and had been through, he wanted to leave me ... Now. Could my life get any worse?

After thirteen years of marriage, and living together in four countries, owning a home in Aruba and loving our cat, he was leaving me! I asked him if there was somebody else, which he denied. I suggested marriage counseling, but he didn't want to work on our relationship. He'd made up his mind. I was so sad. We decided because he was the one who chose divorce, he would leave the house and find a rental property in Aruba. Within twenty-four hours he was gone.

Twenty-four hours and every sign that he'd lived in our home was gone.

In the weeks that followed, I kept myself busy listening to love songs and watching romantic movies and crying. A lot.

Life, I've learned, doesn't always make sense and sometimes bad things happen to good people, no matter how happy you try to be or how much you pretend bad things aren't happening. The good news is that in 2018, I'm cancer-free. I still have my regular checkups twice a year, and I eat healthily. I became vegetarian, I'm still a positive thinker, and I enjoy time with my family and friends. One of the biggest lessons I've learned is that sometimes we need to talk about things — even hard things. Cancer. Your relationship.

Looking back, maybe I could have saved my marriage had I communicated more. Or maybe not. Who knows? What I do know for certain is that no matter what life throws at us, we can overcome. As I walk the beach looking out at the clear blue waters of Aruba, I know that I am home. I am loved. I am healthy. I am still in paradise. And that is enough.

Naomi Herrera is a peer counselor at Greater Lakes Mental Health-care in Washington, USA. She uses her experience as a trauma survivor and her expertise in holistic healing to inspire hope in those she serves. Naomi is dedicated to connecting people to their personal power and intuition so they can heal themselves and design a life they love. She is the founder of Warrior Goddess Evolution, which supports individuals through one-on-one empowerment coaching, divine feminine workshops, and group retreats. You can connect with Naomi on Facebook and Instagram @WarriorGoddessEvolution or via her website at warriorgoddessevolution.com.

Warrior Goddess

NAOMI HERRERA

•

i was nine years old the first time I thought to myself, *I want to die*. I felt alone and depressed, and was convinced suicide would be my legacy. This suffering continued in the ensuing years. By the time I reached full adulthood, I was at the peak of my "party girl" phase, squeezing out every ounce of life I could. There was no experience that was "too much." I used drugs and alcohol to avoid the whirlwind of emotions that existed just beneath the surface, left stagnant from years of unaddressed trauma.

It was during this time I met my unlikely savior. He was a tall, dark, handsome soldier covered in tattoos. He was the answer to all my dreams … and fears. After four months of dating, we were married and soon moved to Germany.

Within two years, he was deployed to Mosul, Iraq. I was given the space to sit with myself and reflect on the direction in which my life was proceeding. It was time to do something for others, something that consisted of meaning and purpose.

In September 2008, I ventured to Tanzania to summit Mt. Kilimanjaro in support of the American troops and volunteered in a juvenile detention center. Upon my arrival, I met other women who, like me, felt that something more needed to be done. We dove into our work, determined to make a difference. With weekends at our disposal, we planned excursions to explore the beautiful country that we now called home.

Diary Entry, September 12, 2008:

We packed our bags and loaded them into the extended Land Cruiser. By 1:15 in the afternoon, we headed out to begin our safari adventure. Our guide, Jafari, sat in the left passenger seat in front of Elizabeth. I sat behind the driver, Edward.

I watched the driver put on his seat belt, which was a rare sight in Tanzania. This caught my attention. I turned to Elizabeth and asked if she thought it was a sign that we should put ours on. She said it wasn't.

Minutes later, I heard a dreadful sound. It instantly triggered fear. I reached for my seat belt but was unsuccessful in my attempt to fasten it. For a moment, I felt paralyzed. I knew what was coming. I took hold of the seat handles as we swerved erratically across the highway. The vehicle lurched left, preparing for the inevitable roll. Mid-roll, I told myself to let go of the handles and be a rag doll. I remember thinking about drunk drivers and how they often survived accidents that should have killed them. This would be my third rollover accident. I wasn't surprised by my ability to think midcrisis. To prevent any broken bones, I let go. I failed to think about the seat belt I was unable to fasten. The vehicle flipped numerous times before resting on its side. I yelled for everyone to get out, catching movement all around me ... except for one place, right next to me. My eyes fell upon her. She was completely still.

That day, Elizabeth died.

I remember people wrapping my wounds, others trying to get me into a vehicle that had no seat belts. I couldn't do it. I waited in pain, wishing for an ibuprofen and beer, the military "cure all." I was carried to the next vehicle, unsure of my fate, thoughts focused on my family, wanting desperately for them to know how much I loved them. As I limped onto the bus, I looked around and saw I was surrounded by nuns. This sight filled me with hope and a deep sense of calmness. With my head in the lap of one of the other volunteers, I spent the hour-long ride sharing messages with her to relay to my loved ones while listening to the methodical melody of the nuns' prayers. I was completely at peace, welcoming death, the answer to an old dream.

I survived. Sadly, my marriage didn't. My husband was unable to support me emotionally or listen to my stories regarding Elizabeth's death. We divorced the next year.

Baby step by baby step, I began healing, the spark of hope growing ever so slightly with each battle I won. I used this energy to refuel my passion for travel. I enrolled in an internship with a classmate, Chris, and in 2010 was on my way to Lima, Peru. Three months into the internship, I decided to travel to Arequipa. It was the city that captured my mom's heart, and I was determined to find out why.

Upon arriving, Chris and I prepared for our two-day Colca Canyon excursion. So far, our trip was everything I had expected. The larger-than-life condors flying overhead, the inviting hot springs to ease our sore muscles, and the markets where the locals created and sold their crafts. It was a dream come true. We returned to the hostel and headed out for a quick dinner.

Exhausted from our excursion, we left the restaurant at 9 p.m. and continued down the main strip, looking for a cab. Chris and I weren't your typical tourists. We'd previously worked in developing countries and took every precaution to avoid trouble. We knew to avoid the small yellow cabs in Lima, but in Arequipa, there was no other choice. We picked the perfect cab — a sign on top with a legitimate advertisement and an identification number painted onto the side of the vehicle.

We told our cab driver where to go and settled into the back seat, making sure to lock the doors. It was always the first thing we did when getting into a cab. It had become second nature. I viewed the lock as my protection from the dangers of the outside world. It gave me what I would later see as a false sense of security.

Ten minutes into our ride, Chris mentioned he didn't recognize the route we were taking. I began to worry, not enough to question the driver or make a scene but enough to take notice. I said to Chris, "Maybe he's taking a more direct route?" As I said the words, I noticed my body tense up and my senses awaken. I realized I was on high alert. Was there something more to this comment Chris had just made or was he making something out of nothing? We sat back, no longer of the same relaxed mindset.

Slowing down, our driver came to a complete stop in the middle of a busy road. Chris and I turned to look at each other, our minds filled with confusion. At that moment, our "locked" doors were pulled open and there stood two large men wielding tire irons. They jumped into the already-cramped cab and began beating us. Once the armed men were in the cab, the driver took off weaving through traffic.

There was no time to weigh my options. I needed to alert any passersby of what was going on. I pushed my door open and screamed while attempting to kick my assailant out of the cab. He regained his balance, molding his body along the frame of the door so that he was unmovable. Within seconds, he slammed the door shut, locked it, and continued to beat me. I panicked and looked over at Chris, praying to see him winning his fight, hoping he would save me from this nightmare. I saw him slamming the other guy's head into the window multiple times. At this point, the guy who was attacking me moved over to help his friend. The two men fought to restrain Chris. In that moment, I could have jumped out of the cab, leaving Chris. I knew I couldn't abandon him, and so I fought with all I had knowing there was nothing that would cause me to leave Chris, not even my own safety.

If I could just stop the vehicle, we might have a chance to escape. I made my move. I leaned over to the front passenger door, opened it, and screamed like I have never screamed before. I was convinced if people could hear me, they would notice we were in trouble and come to our rescue. I screamed more, helplessly watching as vehicles continued to pass. Nobody stopped. Knowing I couldn't count on the outside world, I reached for the emergency brake and pulled. The cab kept moving. Shit. I fought the driver's hands and slammed my fist on the horn, no sound. I rattled the blinkers, no lights. Desperate, I grabbed hold of the steering wheel and gained control. I wrenched the wheel to the left toward oncoming traffic, thinking if I could somehow stop the cab we would, at the very least, be surrounded by people and perhaps have a better chance of surviving. I felt someone take hold of my hair and pull hard. I sensed no pain. I only saw clumps of my hair in his hands as he yelled at me in a language I didn't understand. As we struggled, I noticed the other man sitting on Chris, covering his mouth. My hope diminished and I was quickly overpowered.

The vehicle crawled along the deserted roadside, no longer in the city. Moments later, we stopped. The men explained the "rules" to Chris in Spanish and he relayed them to me. He summarized: "Naomi, you have to be quiet. Don't say anything and we will be okay." I remember hearing a dog barking. I held onto that sound. The minutes felt like hours. Every second was torture. I lived in the unknown. I had no control over what was about to happen.

They ushered us into the house and threw us face-first onto a dirty mattress. We were wrapped in a blanket, fabric tied around our heads, covering our eyes. I could hear the men talking in hushed voices. They sounded angry. A while later, they moved us side by side. They assaulted Chris as they spoke to him. I hated myself for not having a better command of the language. I wanted to know what they were saying, what our fate would be. I could hear their anger and feel their disregard.

I was unsure of the number of men in the room, but a few of them came over to me. Their hands were all over my body. Some were sitting next to me while others were standing around. I could hear their whispered chuckles. They lifted up my top and began to explore, taking note of my tattoos and enjoying them. I could hear them making what I can only imagine were crude comments during the process. I heard the sound of a camera going off and winced.

There seemed to be a ringleader orchestrating this violation of my body. I remember his voice. He stayed by my side giving permission to others to explore, but only to a point. His stale breath was hot against my ear. His hands covered my body. They were not the hands of a lover, but those of a greedy man touching me. I felt violated, but feared more what was to come. I then felt fingers sliding down my stomach, underneath my panties. I slapped his hand away, getting caught by a swift punch to the side of my head.

They punished my continued attempts to push them away by beating Chris even more viciously. I stopped fighting. During a brief break from their violation of my body, Chris whispered, ever so lightly, "Naomi, they asked if we were married and I told them yes. I told them we left the rings at our hostel. They are looking for condoms." He paused, I could feel it coming, although my mind was fighting it. "They are going to rape you."

I choked on my breath. "They're going to rape me?"

"Yes," he replied. "I'm so sorry."

He didn't say anything more after that. I couldn't stop thinking about what was in store for me. It was at this point I feared that my life might be taken, with no body to be found. I desperately did not want to die. I risked speaking and whispered to Chris.

"We have two choices. We can either let them rape me and possibly make it out of here alive or we fight them right now and possibly die, tonight. I can handle both, but I need you to decide."

He was unable to choose. At this point, the thought of dying at the hands of these men was terrifying. My childhood death wish was no longer where I found solace.

My thoughts turned to what I could do to avoid what seemed to be the inevitable. Perhaps if I made myself as unattractive as I could they wouldn't go any further. I had never hated being cute and petite as much I did at that moment. I remembered some of those high-school parties and the girls who were the sloppy drunks, who after drinking too much and crying their eyes out had vomit all over themselves and mascara running down their faces. I remembered how they looked and smelled. Maybe I could be one of those girls tonight. Maybe it would save me?

I knew I couldn't shove my fingers down my throat without them noticing, so I went to that place in my mind and I forced my stomach to empty its contents all over my clothes. When they brought me a plastic bag, I made sure to get as much vomit on me as I could, and when I could force no more out, I poured the contents of the bag onto my pants and shoes. In the small, humid building, the smell was horrible. In that moment, I took some of my power back. I thought that maybe I'd saved myself from being gangraped.

Once they realized we didn't have that much money — they'd already taken everything we had — they pulled us off the bed and led us to the vehicle. While walking me to the car, the ringleader placed his hands underneath my clothes. I pushed away his advances, no longer mindful of what would happen to me. I didn't think he would risk making any noise while we were outside the building. And the truth is, Chris and I didn't risk making any noise either. We both wanted to live.

After a short drive, the vehicle stopped. They pulled us out of the car and had us lay facedown on the dirt road.

After whispering some instructions that I was not able to understand, he parted with a single word: "Ciao." He said it in a way that showed no emotion, no care for what had transpired.

I asked Chris what "instructions" the men had given us before they left. I asked if he was able to run. Could we get up? Would we be okay? With tears streaming down his cheeks, he nodded. I grabbed his hand and we stormed down the road looking for some sign of life, a glimpse of hope in this fucked-up night. He spotted a car in the distance. I told him that once we started running, we could not stop until we made it to that road. I told him to run as fast as he could, to run like he had never run before.

We survived.

Eight months post-Peru, I was a student at the Evergreen State College and answering calls for the local suicide crisis line. This was a significant step in helping me take my power back. Using what had happened in Arequipa to fuel my recovery, building strength with each passing day, speaking to others on the telephone who were contemplating taking their lives, I started looking at each situation as either a blessing or a lesson. This viewpoint widened my scope of reality, quieting the victim within, and empowering the wise Warrior Goddess that I had always been. I had, in essence, become my own superhero.

My transformation continued as I started listening more and more to my intuition, letting it guide my recovery. I wholeheartedly committed to healing my mind, body, and spirit, knowing that my suffering was more than living with PTSD. Prior to Peru, I lacked a strong social support network, I had a weak connection to a higher power, and I was unkind to my body. These things all changed. I shifted my energy to feeding my mind, body, and soul every day.

As I noticed the shift within me, I continued to listen to my gut. I stopped caring what anyone else thought about me. I was finally at a point in my life where my healing and my recovery were my number-one priority. I began collecting crystals that called to me, starting with black tourmaline. I explored intuitive healing techniques, slowly learning more about working with moon cycles and earth elements. Finding sanctuary in mystic and shamanic literature, I listened to the call to get primal, to connect to nature, and to let go of the fears that still haunted me. Drawing on the power of my ancestors, the warrior women who had come before me, I stepped fully into my power.

Despite the horror of Peru and Tanzania, I have deep gratitude for these experiences. They made me who I am today and set me on my divine path. I've learned through my lived experiences that I am resilient and can survive whatever comes my way. I also learned it's perfectly okay to feel "not okay" as long as I'm not permanently living in that space.

Through my higher power and the divine feminine, I found my true, authentic self and am living a life I never dreamed possible, a life as a conscious, ever-evolving woman.

I'm free.

Katie Seriani Bowell is an energetic and outgoing woman with a joie de vivre. Believing a global movement is afoot, she knows it's imperative for all women to slow down, practice self-care, and embrace a little solitude in order to hear their inner whisperings. Katie works with children and at-risk youths as an educational assistant, connecting with them by sharing her many "Katie stories": fun, sometimes shameless, dysfunctional and yet hilarious accounts of growing up in her Irish/Italian family. Katie lives on Vancouver Island, Canada, with her cat, daughter, and husband. Follow her on Facebook @KatieSBauthorcontributorsimplywoman and Instagram @shesawthiscoming444.

Three Eleven Elizabeth

KATIE SERIANI BOWELL

•

*i*n early fall 2017, I planned a trip to Los Angeles. A friend, who has always believed in me and encouraged me to be myself, posted an Anthony Hopkins quote on my Facebook wall. It said: "My philosophy is: It's none of my business what people say of me and think of me. I am what I am, and I do what I do. I expect nothing and accept everything. And it makes life so much easier."

I'd been unraveling my life for the past fourteen years, but when I read that quote, something inside of me split in two. It was as if the remaining bits of my shame, self-doubt, and self-consciousness vanished.

The night before I left, I looked up at my bedroom ceiling and said, "Universe, I am open to infinite possibilities on this trip!"

The next day, in LA, I sweetly bothered a nearby dinner guest to take a photo of my friend and me. That older, sun-glassed photographer was none other than Sir Anthony Hopkins himself! In the flesh.

• • •

I am the baby of five. I gave Dad his first heart attack, they told me, when I was seven months old. I was colicky and screamed long into the night. Dad would leave at 4 a.m. having had hardly any sleep and stagger down the road to his job at the mill. My eldest siblings were sixteen, fifteen, and eleven. They went to school exhausted every day. My brother, Fred, was three and none too happy that I took his place as the baby.

It was 1969 when Fred turned six and started grade one. I was three and had Mom all to myself! Mom and I would walk downtown, hand-in-hand, and sit at the Woolworths' counter, on Commercial Street in Nanaimo, BC, and eat a burger and fries. We'd walk to the Catholic church, or we would visit her friends or relatives. I loved sitting at the dining room table with Mom trying to spell or sew clothes for my Barbie.

Soon after I started kindergarten, Mom left the Catholic church and deteriorated quickly into her mental illness. She believed God was punishing her, and she alienated herself from her Irish sisters and friends. She would sit still in her chair for several hours, and we knew we were not to bother her. She told us that if she sat still without moving a phone call would come and free her. I walked into the house one day after kindergarten just in time to see my dad, cousin, and doctors struggling to put her in a straitjacket. She was screaming, and her eyes were wild. Someone clapped their hands over my eyes and carried me away, down the hall.

They took Mom away for a short time, but I don't know that she was ever diagnosed. My father and oldest sister told me early on that this was not God punishing her, and my already-developing sense of innate self trusted them on this.

At age five, as well as being a funny, bright child, I was incessantly chatty, feisty, and bold. I'd strut my chubby little body up and down our street, busting boundaries with friends and frenemies. I would argue and say awful things, jutting my chin out defiantly, hands on my hips. I remember wearing my bathing suit, my towel slung casually over my shoulder, and peering over my neighbor's fence, watching them in their pool. I shouted, "Hey, are you going swimming today?"

A neighborhood man handed out ice-cream bars to everyone but me, saying I was a bad little girl and didn't deserve one. Years later in therapy, we traced this to the origin of my "no good" button. By age eight, I was smoking cigarettes, cursing, and I'd had my first fight.

Mrs. Mossy, my teacher at school, looked out for me and my siblings, though. She once knit Fred a toque when he had lice. Plus, she knew Dad was hard on him. She told Mom to start standing up for Fred or she'd call the ministry (which worked). I used to go to school early and sit with her and read the Bible.

Mom's mental health improved somewhat over the next couple of years, but by the time I was in grade two, she slid again. She sat in her big brown recliner for several hours not moving, waiting for the call from God that would free her.

My eldest sister, Diane, had already left home, so when Mom got bad again, it was my second-oldest sister, Debbie, only a teen herself, who took over her duties. By the time I was in grade two, Debbie had dropped out of high school to take care of Fred and me. She was also doing most of the cooking and laundry. Then one day, my dad, who had quite a temper but was too afraid of Mom slipping deeper into her psychosis, literally pulled her out of bed by the shoulders and shook her, yelling "Get with it, or I'll have you committed!" She got out of bed and started, slowly, to function.

Around the same time that Debbie took over, Danny, my oldest brother, was recovering from a bad acid trip. He was never himself again. He was twenty-two at the time and a popular guy — he'd inherited my dad's movie-star good looks, plus he was hilarious and smart. He always had girls hanging around him. Danny was a wicked soccer player and could easily have been the next David Beckham, but he never fully recovered. Damn those drugs! They made Danny nuts and unpredictable.

Danny hated Mom sitting still and being quiet. He blamed her for his addiction and thought God must be punishing him, too. One day when Mom refused to give him money, Danny went into a rage, and he broke her nose with a running shoe and booted the glass panels out of our interior French doors.

When my dad came home, he attacked Danny. Dad was tough. He was a former boxer, with Golden Gloves status. Fighting became a regular occurrence. Danny would tease and scare us younger kids and strike Mom's swollen, painful legs. Then Dad would come back home and attack him. On one particularly ugly evening, Dad tried to break Danny's arm and put him through a window. Dad was angry at the shame his firstborn son had brought on his decent Italian name, but he regularly picked fights with Danny, who often came home stoned. Danny was afraid of Dad and wouldn't fight him back.

When I was seven, Charlie, a boy our family knew in the neighborhood, would sometimes hang out at our home. He was ten and would occasionally grab me when we were alone and dry hump my backside. I was grossed out, but he thought it was funny. I was afraid to tell, for one thing. I thought Mom might think I had encouraged it. He was from a pretty messed-up family, too. When I was ten, and he was thirteen, he hadn't done it for such a long time that I was so surprised and angry when he cornered me in the laundry room of my own house, pushed me against a cabinet, and tried to hold me down as he humped me. I turned, shoved him away, punched him hard in the stomach, and screamed.

My mom asked from down the hall what was happening. Of course, Charlie was terrified, and I saw this. He was relieved when I lied and said that he'd pinched me. Then I leaned close to him and whispered fiercely, "If you ever touch me again, I will tell, and my dad will fucking kill you."

His eyes widened, and he knew I was serious and probably right about Dad killing him. Charlie never bothered me again. I know this made me become even more feisty and stand up to others.

Life got worse when Danny got braver. I was now in grade seven. Dad was hitting him in the laundry room, and Danny was cowering and begging him to stop. Mom, Debbie, Fred, and I were nearby in the kitchen shouting, "Stop it, Dad — fucking stop hitting him!" But Dad wouldn't stop, so we switched tactic and instead started yelling, "Danny, hit him back!"

Danny swung at Dad's head, connected, and knocked him flat on his ass. Dad was stunned and never bullied Danny again, but that didn't stop Danny from attacking Dad a few years later while he was recovering from a cancerous-tumor operation. Danny was then sent away to live in a group home. (He eventually regressed into a gentle, happy guy and has been more stable and nonviolent since.)

Despite our troubles, our family consistently gathered at suppertime and enjoyed beautiful home-cooked meals and Mom's heavenly baking. Fred's delinquent friends, some of our misplaced relatives, and later on my friends, were squeezed in around the dining room table with us most evenings. In the background, there were all kinds of different music genres blaring. The best music was coming from Fred's room. Fred's tastes ran from Rush, Queen, Blue Öyster Cult to Aerosmith and greatly influenced my love of rock. Mom also loved to sing and was pretty good at it.

The truth is, our house was crazy and manic, and yet somehow everyone loved to visit. In many ways, it was a teenager's paradise. Fred's friends loved my parents, and my parents treated most of them like their own. Mom would listen for hours on end to everyone's problems. She was a kind soul. Years later Mom would recount at least forty-four people who had stayed briefly or had boarded at our house at 311 Elizabeth Street.

The welfare department called my mom and said, "We hear you take in all these kids for free. Want to get paid for a real foster child? He needs his own room until he turns eighteen in April."

"Sure," my mom said — and she gave him my room.

I had to sleep on the couch with people coming and going all night, including my exhausted gambling-addicted father (whose addiction almost cost us our home). I was just a few months away from turning thirteen when I started hanging out with a tough older crowd, smoking pot and skipping school. I had grown a few inches and lost my "baby fat." I was dating the fifteen-year-old younger brother of one of Mom's unofficial foster girl's boyfriends. Good Lord!

When he hinted for sex, I broke off with him and gained thirty pounds, learning in hindsight how I protected myself from sexual advances and promiscuity by altering my appearance all through high school. I was boy crazy but would only fool around and not go all the way. My parents had suffered enough shame, and I was careful not to cause more. This and the incidents with Charlie would be the root of my anxiety and eating issues that my therapist would help me resolve in my thirties.

I was into the party scene throughout high school, sneaking into the nightclubs with my fake IDs. I smoked cigarettes and pot, and drank booze. I sometimes even partied with my brother Fred and his friends but refrained from harder drugs and chemicals due to early experiences with my brother Danny. He was the poster child of our town: "Don't do acid or you'll turn out like him."

As I was nearing senior high, our family was healing.

In 1984, I graduated and soon left home, despite Mom's pleas and guilt trips to try to get me to stay. Fred and Danny still lived there, so I knew I had to leave in order to grow.

Without Mom's cooking and baking, and everyone saying "You'd be so pretty if you slimmed down," I lost forty-five pounds and became a little hottie. I received more attention than I knew what to do with. Not just from boys. Job opportunities, too.

As it does, some of life's lemons started hitting me in the head. I realized I was reaching for food for comfort. I was overeating, and I was not going to go back to being a fat girl. I started to make myself vomit to keep the weight from creeping back up. I knew it was wrong, but it was working: I was keeping my weight down. I struggled with this for twelve years, asked my doctor for help, and thought I had fixed it.

My dad walked me down the aisle in 1999. That summer he died from his ninth heart attack, at age seventy-nine. My mom was heartbroken but lived to meet my beautiful daughter, Talia. Mom passed away eight years later, at age seventy-nine. She had swapped her illness and issues with God for shopping and had become an organized hoarder by the time she died. She was troubled, but happy and loved by many.

With the birth of Talia, things started to shift for me. Although it was an exciting new chapter in my life, the stress of being a new mother triggered my eating disorder. Bulimia came roaring back as I tried to cope with my years of stuffed-down shame and lack of self-acceptance.

This was the start of fourteen years spent peeling my onion. I joined an eight-week group therapy session for women with eating disorders. From there I started to read anything positive that would help to shift my consciousness and free me from the shame that bound me. The shame had a lot to do with how I felt about my body. I had carried that extra weight to protect myself, but I didn't know that at the time. I wanted to be thin but could never get there because I was afraid that if I were too good-looking, I'd get myself into trouble. I was "funny, chubby Katie," and this kept boys from liking me too much and from getting too intimate. I knew my parents had enough shit going on, and I didn't want to add to it. I tried to make them proud.

Hypnotherapy helped me set healthy boundaries with some of my siblings (survivor's guilt was significant for me!). I read books by Eckhart Tolle, devoured *Oprah* magazines, and pored over Barbara Coloroso's parenting guides. I was so inspired by learning more about parenting and connecting it with my past that I left my job as an insurance broker and headed into a career working with at-risk youth. I learned about detaching from behavior and enabling kids to make their own empowering decisions.

I tried to "dim my light" so I would fit in with other moms and co-workers, but it didn't last long. I realized I was not meant to keep weight on or conform to a "mom" dress code. I liked to play up my looks, wear beautiful things, and rock out to loud music. Not everyone could accept this, and my newfound confidence seemed to grate or threaten some women, leading to some unexpected confrontations. I was initially very hurt and confused, but then I got angry. What shakes you up sometimes shakes you out. I sought consolation from close friends and my husband. That summer I lay in the sun and read Billy Idol's biography. Want to learn about the law of attraction? Read some rock bios!

In Billy's book, he talks about his early days, when the lead singer of his band freaked out on him for showing up with platinum-blond hair the night of their punk show. Billy hadn't planned on keeping the blond. He had stripped it to have it colored black and blue, but his girlfriend forgot the dye. After the lead singer's adverse reaction, Billy decided to keep the blond hair and, of course, that's one of his famous trademarks.

That inspired me! Not only did I decide to keep my blonde hair (which I'd been criticized for), the following week I asked my hairdresser to add more blonde. In the weeks that followed, I started an even stronger march to the beat of my own drum, not caring or worrying anymore if others didn't care for me shining my light too brightly, being weird, or acting silly.

*   *   *

By the time I hit LA early fall 2017, this energy was radiating from me, and I attracted all kinds of powerful connections into my cosmic sphere, including the coolest star on the planet, Sir Anthony Hopkins. I caught a famous director taking my photograph, and I laughed with him. I partied on Sunset Strip. The hot lead singer of a Canadian band hopped down off the stage and danced with us and sang directly to my daughter. Everything just felt on point.

That little voice that used to annoy me by telling me I was placing too much importance on my looks, or talking too much, or being too pushy had vanished. Somehow that Facebook quote resonated with my inner core. That Facebook post tapped into a belief I already had but had not fully absorbed or owned. The veil of shame that kept me wondering whether it was okay to be the vibrant, enthusiastic, chatty Katie that I am has burned up in flames, and the real me has risen from the ashes like a Phoenix.

I now feel so liberated and free, energized as if struck by lightning, and open to so many opportunities. Just like that Aerosmith song, *I don't want to miss a thing*. I realize it is pretty fucking cool being me! I look back at the crazy times we had in that house on Elizabeth Street, and I know that home is what both rooted me and helped me soar.

I feel I'm close to fulfilling my life's purpose. Many mornings before getting out of bed I stretch out like a starfish and yell "Thank you, universe! I accept it all!"

Karry Ann Nunn is a master empowerment coach who helps women find their voices and live their truth. After working in libraries across Canada, she has finally fulfilled her dream of having her name on a book on the library shelf! Karry Ann keeps it real by spending long days enjoying her animals on her gorgeous farm in Saskatchewan, Canada. Her biggest accomplishment, she says, is raising four wonderful children whom she is so proud of. She lives with her partner and two dogs and can be contacted at KarryAnn.com.

The View from the Top

KARRY ANN NUNN

•

i stood on the rocky banks of that rushing mountain river with tears streaming down my face and despair eating a hole in my heart. I felt like throwing myself into that freezing water. As I looked across the rapids and into the evergreen forest on the other side, I found my eyes wandering up the mountain and up to the icy gray sky. A voice in my head spoke loudly and clearly to me: *Sometimes, the hardest mountains to climb have the best view.*

I knew exactly what hard mountain I had to face. The awareness hit me hard, and I dropped to my knees on the pine-needle-strewn forest floor by the banks of that icy river. As the mountain water rushed and loudly crashed over ice, rocks, and old snagged tree trunks, I cried. For the first time in a long time, I let it all out, my loud sobs competing with the crashing water.

Alone in the wintery beauty of the mountains of British Columbia, Canada, I felt the release, and I cried for all the years of hurt and pain that I had let build up inside me. I cried for the way I had let my life play out. For the pain of a date rape at age eighteen and the shame of a termination of a life. I cried for the mess I made of my marriage, and then my divorce and the shame of leaving the church I'd been raised in. I cried as I saw the judgmental eyes of those who blamed me for "living in sin." I cried for the time when I was so desperate I attempted to take my life, leaving my poor little children to be cared for by other families while I spent time in a mental health facility trying to find my feet again.

I cried the most over the hurt that my relationship with my partner had become, and how much I was hurting because we no longer talked. This was too big. I had let my pain get to be more than I could live with any longer. I was in the dark, icy winter of my soul, and I had allowed my pain to become a mountain like the cold Purcell Mountain range in front of me.

As I walked back to my pickup truck, I knew what I had to do next. I climbed into my vehicle and sat looking out of the windshield, not really seeing the trees and mountains in front of me. I flipped back my coat hood and took off my mittens, and then unzipped the pockets of my thick down coat. I took out my truck keys. My breath came out in bursts of fog. I knew I had to call my partner as soon as I found cell service. I had to tell him that I wouldn't be coming home. I had a past to reckon with before I could move forward in any healthy manner, with or without him. I knew I deserved a better future. I turned the key in the ignition. The engine roared and I took a deep breath and drove forward.

I was raised in what many would call a loving Christian family. I was forty-eight, and I had everything a woman of my age could ask for. I was healthy, and I had friends. My four children were grown up, and they were all doing a wonderful job of looking after themselves in the big world. I was a perfectly ordinary woman whose life seemed just fine to others.

There I was alone in the mountains with tears streaming down my face. I was using a trip west to visit my ailing father as an excuse to leave my beautiful home in Saskatchewan, again. I had let all the years of pain, shame, blame, regret, and anger build up. I was running away. Again.

I wiped my eyes and pulled onto the highway. I knew where I was headed and turned left, filled with a new determination. I drove on up the mountain and into a new future. I didn't realize that the moment by the river would be such a pivotal moment in my life. I didn't realize that the seed that had been buried under so much pain was sending out shoots and finding a new life for me.

I was on my way to my parents' home in the warm Okanagan Valley to spend some quality time with my dad before his health deteriorated further. Though my parents had always done their best raising me, I felt like I had disappointed them. I was living my life in a manner that they did not agree with, and no child wants to feel like they disappointed their parents, especially when a parent is dealing with an illness that is quickly shortening his life. I had been raised in a strict religious family, but in finding my path, I was not in a place that my parents approved of.

As I drove over the snowy mountain passes, my mind wandered back to my childhood. I saw myself: taller than others my age and farm-girl strong; blonde and freckled with a big happy grin. I was a lucky little girl. Blue, our Blue Heeler dog, was my constant companion. And I had my horse, Dancer. I would saddle up Dancer, and we would go for long rides through the fields. The three of us would go on grand adventures that would take us way past lunch and into the long summer days of northern Alberta, where we would wander for hours until the sun started to set.

It was an idyllic childhood, yet one with strict expectations from both my parents and their religion. That religion kept my family separated from the struggles of the "worldly" people. We were a clean-living family with no TV, and no drinking or dancing allowed. The women were "Godly," so they did not wear makeup or cut their hair, and they always wore dresses. The women worked just as hard as their husbands did — in the home raising children and keeping house, and out in the fields or at work in town — but it was faith that kept them in their place in the home.

For some, this works. For me, it was a struggle. I could not see myself living the controlled lives of those women. I would often question and push against the barriers: Why can't I go out and have fun with my school friends? Why couldn't we watch movies or listen to other music?

I wanted to cut my hair. It was so boring having it long all my life, and it got in my way. I wanted to go to the beach and hang out with my friends. I had bigger dreams, dreams of being someone other than just a wife, which was the traditional role ahead of me. I do believe in my Creator. I do not doubt that there is a higher power, and I respect that with all my heart, but the restrictions that made little sense to me sometimes caused me to question the faith and the way I was being brought up.

As I drove through the snowy mountain passes, toward my parents' home, my thoughts headed back to a particularly dark time of my life. I graduated high school at age seventeen and had moved out to central Alberta to help my cousins on their grain farm. Then I found a job that was closer to home and moved back. I was eighteen, and a boy had asked me out. I was on top of the world with excitement. I was excited to be able to go out and have some fun with someone my age. With all kinds of nervousness, I asked my parents if I could go out for supper with this young man. For the first time in my life, they said they thought it would be all right. And off I went.

The first thing that felt off was that this nice young man had brought his young uncle along with him. Even though his uncle was kind enough, it just seemed strange. Perhaps my sheltered life had blinded me to what could happen in this situation, so with no worries, I got into their car and went happily along.

We went to a bigger town for supper — I don't remember what we had or if we did go out to eat at all. What I do remember is being pressured into having sex with two young men. My parents had been trying to warn me about and protect me from just these kind of things — these were the sins and injuries — but somehow along the way I was never given the tools I would need to deal with these situations if they arose. How to say "no" and how to walk away from a situation that puts me in danger. Why does a young girl go ahead with something that she doesn't want just to feel like she is liked and part of the group?

There was no gun held to my head — it wasn't done angrily — but when two young men have an innocent young girl in their control, things happen that shouldn't happen.

In the backseat of a car, I was taken advantage of by both of them.

And then they laughed.

And I felt the shame.

I realized this wasn't about a young man wanting to spend time with a young lady. This had been an opportunity for two boys to have their way with an innocent girl.

Afterward, I tried to carry on living as I had before and put it out of my mind, but then a month or so later I found out that the rape wasn't the end of the horror. I went to the doctor, and he confirmed my suspicions: that I, a young girl with my wide-open future ahead of me, had just taken a deep detour down a road I had never expected to travel.

In my shame, I could not tell my parents, but my mom found a prescription for prenatal vitamins that the doctor had given me. She asked me why I would need them. When I told her what had happened, she asked me what I was going to do about it. I remember sitting there in my teenage bedroom in my parents' house speaking to my mother but feeling so detached. I felt like I was watching myself in a movie. I was managing to talk, trembling as I did. I had a lump in my throat that felt like a boulder. I felt dizzy, yet the words came out. How could this be happening? What do I do now?

All I knew were all the biblical rules: We are not to take a life. Abortion is a sin. One should not have sex before marriage. I didn't know what to do. I didn't love the father. I wasn't even sure which one of the two it was.

In a time when a young girl needs understanding parents, my father stopped speaking to me. He would leave the room when I came in, and my mother became worried and would put pressure on me to act normal. She was worried people would find out and didn't even want to think about what they would say about us. I had been raised to keep the family name clean, and this wasn't the way to do it. There was no way I could have a baby out of wedlock without shaming my whole family. We were an upstanding family in the church community, and my mom was under pressure from my dad to keep it that way.

She suggested that I make an appointment.

I was desperate to turn back time. Desperate to go back to the time when I was still innocent and pure. Desperate to get back into my parents' good books. Desperate to have my father speak to me. Desperate not to be looked at and judged. Desperate to keep the family name clean.

That desperation found me lying on the floor with an unraveled metal coat hanger in my hand. Terrified, I plunged the thin metal inside me, trying to undo what had been done. Desperation and shame made me treat my body with hate and loathing.

Afterwards, for a short time, I left home and took a job on a ranch in the beautiful foothills of the Rocky Mountains. But I still had a ticking time bomb growing inside me. I hated it, I loved it, I wanted it, I couldn't figure out how I was going to keep living with it. I had no one to talk to about it. I could feel my body changing. I knew time was getting shorter for me to figure out what I was going to do. I was scared of the damage I may have already caused my body. I worked hard, lifted heavy things, and did all kinds of work that might make my body void the baby on its own. It wasn't long before I got a call from my mom telling me to come back home.

"It's time to have this looked after," she said.

I flew back home and noticed I had started to bleed as if I were getting my period. My mom picked me up from the airport and took me straight to the hospital. She did not talk much on the way, but when we got there, the nurses matter-of-factly explained that I was to have a "routine D & C."

I had my womb scraped clean. I could now look forward to an unblemished future, and my parents could continue to hold their heads up in their community. I was now "as good as new." The doctors did not ask about the bleeding that was obvious before they even started the operation. There must have been evidence of my attempt to take care of this myself. I was too scared to ask, but to this day I still wonder which abuse on my body actually ended that little life.

When I woke up from the operation, I wondered out loud how much weight I had lost. After all, it felt like I had been carrying a whole big life around inside me. My mom's answer was "It was nothing."

Why did it feel like it was so much more?

It was nothing.

It was a wee little life, my first child, their first grandchild.

It was nothing.

After the operation, we all went back to living our lives like nothing happened. We never mentioned it again. I got married. I had my four sweet babies that I had been afraid I might never be able to have. I watched them grow up and enjoyed every moment with them. But there were times when I would think about the one who was missing. The one I didn't have.

I began to let that pain hurt other areas of my life. I tried to take my life in a fit of anger and helplessness that I had let grow into something bigger than it should have. I broke up my marriage and put my children through pain. I left the church because I could no longer live with the judgment that I felt from the people who professed that "love is the first and only commandment." I found a different partner and I tried to start over again. I was trying to run away from the pain, but I couldn't get away. I didn't know it then, but the winter of my soul was starting to freeze up my life.

How many of our sisters, mothers, aunts, and even grandmothers carry pain and blame and shame like this? How many women who walk among us are hurting like I was, and we never realize it? How many relationships are broken because of it? How many families are destroyed? How many women are lucky enough to find themselves at the bottom of that winter mountain beside that icy river asking the big questions? And how many of those women find the solutions? How many figure out their answers?

After I hit rock bottom, I was able to climb my way back up into the sunlight and find answers and help. In talking about my story and sharing it with others, I have been able to heal some of the pain and move past the shame and guilt. Although my parents did not talk about the pregnancy and the termination, I gently confronted my mother once I felt comfortable in my journey of healing. I can now see her point of view, and she is now more aware of how it impacted my life.

Now that I have climbed the beautiful mountain of self-forgiveness and love, I am seeing my dreams coming true. Yes, even at fifty, dreams can still come true. The best part of my journey is my healing, I am healing my relationship with my partner, too. We are finding a new peace that is much softer and more open and kinder than it was before. I hope in finding my way out of the darkness, and by sharing parts of my story, others might be encouraged to find their way out, too. Maybe in my healing I can also help my children find peace in their past.

There, by that snowy mountain river, I found a new beginning. By doing that hard work to understand myself and what was keeping me unhappy, and by forgiving my family and myself for things that harmed me, I am now so much freer. From this vantage point, I can hug myself and accept my past.

Now I can say, *Yes, indeed, once you climb your hardest mountains you'll find the best and most astounding view*.

Lucy Devi Hall, the founder of Deeply Woman, is a well-sought-after women's empowerment coach. Through her workshops and coaching, she works with women to create more fulfilled lives. She is also an authentic and inspiring speaker, and loves to show women change is possible. As a passionate singer and songwriter, she has contributed to three albums from the Humaniversity Sound Studio based in Holland. She is currently working on the fourth album called The Gratitude Meditation, which is due for release December 2018. Lucy lives in London, England, and can be found at deeplywoman.com.

Love Is the Answer

LUCY DEVI HALL

•

*t*hree years ago, I flew from England to attend an Awareness and Understanding Meditation Intensive in Holland's Humaniversity. During the "explore your sexuality" stage of one of the meditations, I danced with a gorgeous man with dark-brown hair and sparkly greeny-blue eyes. His tight white tee-shirt showed off his defined muscles. The electricity between us was palpable. I am generally cautious when it comes to men, but I was caught up in the freedom of the meditation, and the spark between us was undeniable.

After the dance, I turned to a friend — a therapist who worked and lived at the venue — and asked, "How old is he? He looks kind of young. Do you know his name?"

"Yeah, that's Dhiren. He's in his twenties."

"Um ... Oh God, he's half my age! I'm forty-two. That's too much of a difference for me!"

And, naturally, I ran off.

But he stayed in my mind, and a year later I saw him when I returned to Holland for more training. On my first day back, I walked into the kitchen to make a cup of tea and stopped in my tracks. There he was, chopping vegetables while chatting with the others in the community kitchen. I'd never seen vegetable chopping look so sexy. When he glanced up and saw me, a huge cheeky grin slowly spread across his face. He deliberately put the knife down and strode across the room, coming up so close to me ... too close. For a moment, I couldn't breathe.

"Do you remember me from that dance?" he asked.

I noticed that although he was Dutch, he had a slight American twang.

"Uh huh, yes, yes. Of course I do," I said, giggling like a schoolgirl.

"Shall we have another dance later?"

"Definitely!"

Oh, my God, what was I doing? I knew his age, but I didn't care. And that was the beginning of our relationship and the next phase of my life.

I hadn't had a serious relationship for some time, and this one seemed perfect, particularly because it was long distance. I know it's not what most women want, but for me it was right. It meant we could get to know each other at a pace that felt safe to me. We spent a lot of time chatting on the telephone, on Skype, and flying back-and-forth between Holland and England to see each other. We had so much in common that we laughed every time age was brought up, as it felt so irrelevant to us, and yet, it was what almost prevented me from allowing him into my life. We both shared a love of laughing and movies, and we're committed to personal development and learning. And with all the work I had done getting myself to a healthier place physically, I couldn't have been happier.

Six months later, we were at the Humaniversity again, attending their month-long summer retreat, together. Nearing the end of our stay, we had our first almighty argument. It ended with me saying something along the lines of "I'm never going to talk to you again" and him returning with "Well, I don't ever want to talk to you again, either." Off he went in one direction and me in the other.

The next morning I was having breakfast at the table with some of my friends. In exasperation I practically yelled out "Bloody men!" They laughed, and all nodded in agreement. We were in the midst of our "bloody men-ing" when Dhiren came up behind me and tapped me on the shoulder.

"Can I talk to you?" he asked with not a hint of warmth on his face.

I nodded and followed him outside.

"Let's go to the top of that hill," he suggested without looking back.

My mind was racing now. The top of the hill ... sounds serious. That means it's going to be one of those conversations where he says, "It's been nice, but I don't want to be with you anymore."

As we climbed the hill, my inner chatter was going crazy. *Go on, Lucy, tell him you're sorry for shutting down. Say something, for God's sake!*

Instead, I just stood there, waiting to be dumped.

And that's when he got down on one knee, fumbled around in his jacket pocket, and pulled out a little blue box. He opened it and asked, "Will you marry me?"

I looked into those sparkly greeny-blue eyes and squealed, "Yes, I'll marry you!" and threw myself into his arms.

"Oh, there's just one more thing," he said with a grin. "I've arranged the wedding for tonight!"

I loved this crazy man! I laughed with delight, being with someone so fun and generous was so new and exciting for me. Later that evening, we got married with so many of our dearest friends gathered around. He'd planned everything.

As we headed to the honeymoon suite, I felt a little nervous twinge. We undressed and got into bed, kissing and touching. We started to make love, and suddenly I started feeling sick to my stomach. I felt this tight burning sensation rising through my chest, through my throat, like vomit. And then the voice in my head started again ... *He's a fucking man. He's just using you for sex.*

Feelings of shame and anger overcame me, and I lost it. Full of rage and hate, I pushed my brand-new, beautiful husband away.

"You get off me! I hate you. You're just using me. You're just like all the other men."

The sparkly eyes that had been filled with so much love were now filled with pain and confusion. "What have I done? What have I done?" he asked. "I just want to love you. I just want to love you."

Seeing the fear in his eyes made me cry. I didn't understand what was happening to me. I felt like my mind was betraying me. Or was it my body? Maybe it was my spirit?

I thought I was through with this suffering. Through with this story. Through with all the abuse. Despite over twenty years of therapy, rehab, meditation, and bodywork, I saw that if I wanted to live a truly healthy life — with or without Dhiren — I had more stuff to heal.

My helplessness against my body's response soon turned to anger. *How dare these other men come to my wedding bed!* I thought. *I want my special night to be for me and my husband, not those abusers!*

My young, confused husband looked at me with so much sadness and concern. I knew I had so much more healing to do and my marriage ... and this man ... and I ... deserved it.

• • •

Pain and more pain is all I remember about my childhood. By the time I was ten years old, I had experienced multiple rapes from one man, sexual molestation from another three men, my father had left, and my mother had died. I was left with my older brothers, and I had an eating disorder.

As a teenager, I found drugs numbed the pain. That's when I started to tape razor blades to the inside of the skirt of my school uniform. It wasn't a conscious thing. I didn't know why I was doing it until the day that I decided that I'd had enough. I left the house and went into the back garden, I untaped the razor blade from my skirt, took it in my right hand, and made cuts across my left wrist, slicing me open. I could see my veins. I knew that if I wanted to die, I had to sever them. I sat there with the blade in one hand, staring at the tiny incisions I'd already made across my left wrist and had a conversation with myself to see if I was sure I wanted to die. I was. So I sliced once more. Deeply.

The bully in my neighborhood found me and took me to the hospital. That day he was very caring and compassionate, and he kept me from passing out when all I wanted to do was not wake up. I was shocked at his care, and it was just enough to decide I wanted to live. I didn't realize it at the time, but him dropping his armor of bullying revealed a loving person. Again, something I wasn't used to seeing.

I was embarrassed by the drama I had caused, and once I was home from the hospital, I ran away, convinced that my brothers hated me. I managed to finish high school, but I had no idea how to interact with ordinary people. I was anorexic, using drugs, and full of self-loathing. I would do anything to show my body how much I hated it.

Finally, at twenty-one years old, I walked into a psychiatrist's office and said, "Please help me. I'm not going to
survive another day out there." The doctor took one look at
me, and a few hour later I was admitted to the psychiatric
ward of the University College Hospital in London.

On my first day in the hospital, I met Jane, a forty-year-
old anorexic woman who was less than 100 pounds and
looked like a twelve-year-old child. She had been in the
hospital for three months and was getting ready to leave.
This was her at a healthy weight, she said. I felt a little bit
hopeful seeing someone leaving, which meant these doctors
wanted you to get better. They wanted to help us.

Three months later, as I was getting ready to leave, feeling much better than when I arrived, Jane was readmitted.
She came in screaming and had to be restrained. The nurse
told me she had been in and out of hospitals for almost
twenty years. I was so shocked. Was this what lay ahead
of me?

It was then I made the decision that I wanted to create a
better life. I didn't want to be in and out of hospitals for the
next twenty years like Jane. I knew there had to be another
way. And I was going to find it.

I started group therapy at the Women's Therapy Centre
in England, and although I felt scared and uncomfortable
being around people, I knew that if I wanted to heal and
transform, I would have to put myself in uncomfortable
situations. After a while, I found it comforting. I was among
women who were similar to me, who had experienced abuse,

racism, and eating disorders. I felt at home, and I could begin to open up and share myself a little.

But after seven years of therapy, I realized I had only really scratched the surface of my pain. I still felt deeply unhappy inside. My eating habits were better, meaning I could go a whole day without making myself vomit. It was a big achievement for me. Then out of the blue, my therapist decided to end our group. She was moving away, but she also felt it was time we all moved on to something new. I took this as a huge rejection, and it triggered deep feelings of past abandonment. This confirmed that I was not wanted, nor had I ever been wanted. It confirmed that like my parents, anyone I trusted would leave me.

Swelling with feelings of self-hatred and anger, I started to use cocaine. At first I thought I'd found the answer to all my problems. Cocaine made me feel the way I wanted to feel. Confident. Strong. Fearless. I could speak to people. I wasn't scared anymore. The pain was gone. I felt happier.

But, of course, the good feelings didn't last. I needed more cocaine to feel just normal. And then eventually, the drug stopped working at all. Instead of making me feel like I could conquer the world and anyone in it, it made me feel paranoid, as though everyone hated me. The more I used it, the more I hated myself. Besides the fact that I knew I was breaking the law. But I was addicted. And like any drug addict, I kept taking more and more, hoping that I would get that old feeling back. I felt so out of control. I knew I needed help.

Why there was one of those free community magazines on my bedside table, I still don't know. I never kept those things lying around. But I opened it and saw an advertisement for a spiritual center. I phoned them and went for a weekend, which turned into six months, which turned into me heading to Humaniversity, which turned into experiencing some of the best things and meeting some of the best people in my life — including my husband.

I would spend hours in sessions, screaming and hitting pillows, getting angry at all the men who had hurt me, raging at my mother's death and all the racism I had experienced as a little black girl growing up in Scotland.

After the anger came the pain. There was so much pain. I didn't even realize how much pain I'd held on to for so many years. I cried and cried. Slowly, I emptied out the past. And over time I started to feel again. The feeling was huge. I started to feel joy and happiness. I started to feel laughter. I started to feel love. I started to feel loving. It was like my heart was defrosting and I could give myself the love I needed. Finally.

And that is when I met Dhiren. I was certain that after our long-distance relationship of talking, laughing, and learning about each other, I was ready to be in a loving relationship. I'd done a lot of healing. And I'd met my husband in an environment where I trusted those around me, including him. I knew that if I wanted this relationship to work and last, I was going to have to jump into the abyss and deal with the part of the mess I had ignored: my sexuality.

I remember my friend had told me about something called "orgasmic meditation." At the time, I'd thought, *That sounds weird. I'm never doing that.* But to keep Dhiren and to heal our marriage, I was willing try anything. I went back to London to find a practitioner of this orgasmic meditation thing.

What I would come to learn is that our sexual energy is an important source of energy for our lives. Because of the abuse I'd gone through, I had turned off my sexual being and blocked my sexual energy. I had always believed that men had abused me because of this energy that came from me. I was afraid of my sexual power. I hated my body — especially my genitals. I would often think of taking a knife and stabbing them. I wished they weren't there, believing that if I didn't have genitals, then none of the abuse would have happened. Two of my childhood sexual abusers had even told me that the abuse was my fault, that something in me was making them do it.

Through the meditation process, I realized that my heart had defrosted but my body hadn't yet. I learned that what those men did to me had nothing to do with me. It was about them. I'd hated them.

I meditated almost every day for four months, and every time I would cry and sob, sometimes I would wail and scream. Fifteen years of abuse came flowing out of me, almost as if it came out of the most beautiful womanly part of me: my genitals. After four months of crying, I could feel the warmth of my heart spreading into all of my body, even the parts I had previously disowned.

Alongside all this, Dhiren and I started "relationship as practice." Instead of relying on being in love to fix everything, we used our relationship as a place where we could bring everything in and work on it together. All parts of us: the good, the bad, and the ugly. It took me a while to trust this. It was a commanding and confronting position, and it challenged me profoundly. Many times, I wanted to run.

At a couple's communication workshop, we were taught to listen to each other, to step into the world of the other and see what was going on for them. As Dhiren sat there and opened his heart to me, I saw, probably for the first time, how my behavior was hurting him. My rage and lashing out was hurting him — not the abusers! It was a painful realization. I felt ashamed but also so grateful that he had faith in us ... and in me. I decided to stop pushing him away when the trauma hit. Instead, I would share it. Ask him to hold me. I allowed his love to cocoon me. I allowed his love to comfort me, and I accepted the safety of his heart and arms. I didn't fight it. I let him in.

The more I opened to him, the more I could see him as the beautiful man he is. His love. His care. His commitment. His patience. He wasn't an abused person. He didn't have all the work to do that I did. He may have been half my age, but he had more wisdom and maturity than I did. He would tuck me in on the sofa and choose a movie for me. He perfected my cup of tea: piping hot, with medium milk in my favorite mug. I had to learn how to love. I was relearning what I knew innately as a tiny little girl before all the abuse: I was loveable.

I loved him so much. And it felt good. It felt good to open all of me to this wonderful man. At last, I was allowing a man's love into that deeply hidden part of me. And it felt beautiful.

It's taken me a long time to get here, but now I can say I love my body. I love my genitals. I love being a woman. And I deeply love a man: my beautiful husband, Dhiren. To have gone from such self-hate and rage to self-love and loving a man sometimes feels like a miracle. And it is!

Giovanna Capozza is a transformational coach, *speaker, and host of her weekly podcast, She Rises. As both a trained alternative medicine doctor and spiritual teacher, this self-professed nerdy girl bridges the art and science of alternative healing concepts and deep coaching to support successful women seeking to find their next level of meaning, purpose, and vitality in their lives. Get ready for her first full book,* Unsettled: A Restless Girl's Journey to Life on Her Terms *(to be released November 2018). Visit giovannacapozza.com.*

Dissatisfaction: The Quiet Killer

GIOVANNA CAPOZZA

•

We were all eating at my parents' kitchen table, exhausted from a day of condolences and standing in a line receiving my mother's mourners. We were eating in her kitchen, but she was missing. Truth is she hadn't been there in months. Instead, she'd lain in her bed and fought her losing battle with cancer.

That night I got up from the table in a daze, wandered into my mother's room, and lay down on her bed as if beside her. I clutched her shawl. It still smelled like her, a sweet combination of Oil of Olay and Red Door perfume. I breathed it in and sobbed the deepest and most guttural sobs that had ever come out of me. My sisters ran in to see if I was okay. "Who is going to love me now?" I asked.

. . .

For as long as I can remember I have felt unsettled. I started my search for a more fulfilling life early. I'd suffered from perpetual dissatisfaction since I was a child. I remember my mother getting frustrated with my constant mantra "I'm bored!" As I got older I noticed that many of those around me, including my parents, lived lives of quiet dissatisfaction, filling the empty void with eating, shopping, TV, empty relationships, gossip, and other fillers to numb out and forget deeper desires. The newer generations have social media as our chief numbing agent, but the effect is the same: a life half lived and filled with nonsense.

I remember how I desperately did not want to become my mother.

I grew up hearing my dad chant "be happy with what you have."

This was not his stand for gratitude, mind you. It was a squashing blow to my want for more. My father carried a fearful mentality when it came to taking risks or following your dreams. When I would talk about being my own boss and traveling the world, he'd scoff. Instead, he believed I should have a solid education, a secure job, and a husband, while saving every penny I made.

I remember sitting at our large sunlit kitchen table one spring. It was just before my birthday, and I was leafing through a catalog and circling everything my little heart desired. I heard my dad coming up the stairs, and I was so excited to show him all the stuff. Unfortunately, and in my dad's defense, not maliciously, he huffed, "Oh, what's this? *Ahhh*, you want too much, kid!"

It cut like a knife. Suddenly I was questioning my worthiness. That coupled with the "settle for what you have" poverty mentality left me feeling small, shamed, and shut down. *Who was I to want more for my life than what I saw around me?*

* * *

At fourteen years old, I found myself standing in my bedroom wearing a puffy purple taffeta dress and staring at the ceiling, pondering my third sister's upcoming wedding. *Is this it? Like was "this" life? Was I just going to get married, live with someone, and have babies and die? How could "this" be it for me?*

I could not accept this reality. I felt the sky falling on me, the weight of thousands of years of unspoken cultural inheritance and expectation. This is what the women in my family did and had done for centuries. This is what my mother did: She put aside all her dreams to do what was expected.

As kids, we don't always see our parents as people, let alone people with dreams. I remembered sitting at the kitchen table with my mom. She told me how much she had wanted to be a fashion designer but that my grandfather had forbidden it. My mother was already raising her brother and sisters. She was already obligated to the family, and the idea of following her dreams was nonnegotiable. That was the moment I saw my mother as a woman who did dream and wanted more for her life. It broke my heart to hear her reminiscing longingly about this and all the other things she hadn't gotten to do.

As I stood there in my itchy and very purple bridesmaid dress, contemplating my future, my heart in my throat, the resolution bubbled up like a shaken bottle of champagne: *I don't think so!*

I thank God every day for my mother and the women who came before her. She's the reason I can choose differently and to create a life on my terms. But as much as I didn't want to repeat her choices, I still wrestled with questions: Was it allowed? Could I break the mold and be different? Would I still be loved?

The internal conflict was deeply entrenched. I wanted to be different, but I needed my family and I wanted to be included. As a rebellious teen my motto had become "Never settle for less." It was my war cry. My mother, although stuck in her ways, urged me to "Go do the things that I never got to do, Bella. You're strong. You can do it."

I realized that as much as I didn't want her life, she didn't want it for me, either. I am forever grateful for her recognition of my strong will and permitting me to be this way.

•   •   •

By the time I started college, I wanted nothing to do with tradition or cultural confines. I started with small things: I told my parents I wasn't getting married in a church. I've never seen my mom make the sign of the cross so many times in a row. I think I got a slap on the back of my head, too!

The thing is, the environment you grow up in can't help but rub off on you. For my parents' generation of Italian immigrants, they had to work hard, keep their head down, save money, and not ever, *ever* risk anything. Their dreams were irrelevant. They had to think of the family and their responsibilities. Personal desires were buried deep inside, and they kept going.

These outdated models crept into my generation like a thief in the night. I'll never forget a day toward the end of high school when I was on the phone with a friend discussing college options.

"I just want to get married and have kids and be a housewife like my mom," my friend said to me.

"Oh my God! What? Are you insane? Why would you say that?"

I think I choked on my gum and fell off the couch right then and there. I was dumbfounded. *Was* she insane? Clearly, she drank the cultural Kool-Aid, and I couldn't save her.

I realize that this is a very valid and fulfilling choice for many women, but what about those of us for whom it's not? While many of my friends were planning their weddings and how many children they would have, I was dreaming of travel and owning my own business.

So, with my intense early onset war cry of "never settle," how did I end up with a big house in the burbs, and a husband-to-be?

Here's the thing with cultural and familial expectations and traditions: If you're not paying attention, they creep up on you. In the book *A Course in Miracles* by Dr. Helen Schucman, it says, "What you defend against, you create," and create I did!

Suddenly, like slipping into a warm bath, I had the big house, luxury cars, granite countertops, a fiancé, a career, and I was 220 pounds — the side effect of drowning in despair!

As much as I resisted settling I found myself right there, in Suburgatory hell. *Settle-ville ... I had arrived!*

I was unconsciously still trying to fit in with the rest of the herd, and as a result, I was dying a little inside with each passing day.

A person will sometimes do whatever it takes to hang on to her sense of identity, even if it's toxic or sabotages her dreams. For some of us, it takes a "rug out from under you" moment to wake you up to who you truly are. My mother's death was that for me.

A year later, I looked at my fiancé across my granite countertops and hardwood floors and I knew, if I stayed in this life, I was going to die just like my mother did.

I got up, gathered the destination wedding brochures I had started to peruse, and put them on the magazine rack in the bathroom. I was done settling.

I remembered my war cry, my chant for freedom!

•   •   •

I had no purpose, passion, or meaning in my life, and was far from feeling fulfilled. I didn't even know what fulfilled looked like. Worse, I didn't recognize myself in the mirror.

I tried to keep it together and to make it work for a long time, but I was slowly dying.

I finally woke up.

In the next few months, everything would change. The details of breaking my engagement and leaving what appeared to be a perfectly put-together home in suburbia are not as important as the fact that I looked around and admitted that this was not me. I let go of the shame and embarrassment of appearing ungrateful, and I took a stand for myself — for my very soul. I had no idea what I wanted, but I knew what I wanted to feel — *happy* — and that's the most important compass you can follow.

After seven years as part of a "we," I began to learn how to be "me." Just over a year after my breakup, I was on my own, sixty pounds lighter, starting to live my life again.

This is where I'd love to write that immediately afterward my life became perfect, and I met and married the man of my dreams — who was not only my partner in life but also my partner in a global mission to uplift human consciousness — and that we're abundantly wealthy and living and traveling to beautiful places around the world.

I would love to write that ... and, someday, I will, but that's not how life works. That's how movies and romance novels work, that's how clever marketing and BS on social media works, not how real life works.

After another devastating breakup, I decided enough was enough, and I made a radical shift. I closed down my alternative medical practice, put all my stuff in storage, rented out my place, and moved to Mexico where I enjoyed my new body and all the attention that came with it. I created a new life, did things differently, and reinvented myself.

From trekking through the jungle to hiking up ancient pyramids, to yoga teacher training and a hot, albeit short, affair with a much younger man, I was going to find out what *not settling* looked like for me.

Did I have moments of fear? Of course, but what I learned most is the depth of resiliency and resourcefulness that had been hiding inside of me the whole time. I'd bet if you adventured away on your own you'd discover the same!

You have to be willing to become unsettled in your journey to find what truly fulfils you. You can't live in your comfort zone for this part. You can't do this from the safety of sameness and status quo. You can't do this with financial security and certainty being your number-one driver.

Ultimately, the search to live a more fulfilled life always comes back to you — it has to! It's the way it works!

If you've been living your life for someone else or from someone else's rulebook, chances are much of this is resonating with you. Why not ask yourself: *What would make my heart sing?* Allow yourself to sit with that query. Allow it to sink into your soul and see what bubbles up.

Asking this question and making the answer my compass are what led me to move to Mexico. And that is what started an amazing, fulfilling, five-year journey back to myself.

After years of travel, adventure, a new business, love, romance, pain, grief, and finally complete reinvention, it dawned on me that the word "settle" was a bit of a paradox. It took my mother's death and all of these experiences for me to realize that while I didn't want to settle down, I did want to settle into who I am and who I was meant to be.

I know now that none of this has to do with compromising for less of a life, but with settling into who you are — the same way the snow settles down in a snow globe after it's been shaken.

● ● ●

Five years later, I returned home to Toronto a whole new person, with a deep sense of understanding that home and fulfillment are found within, like Glenda tells Dorothy at the end of *The Wizard of Oz*, "You've always had the power!"

I had finally found the answer to the question I had asked when my mother died years ago: *I was going to love me now!*

There is no love outside of myself, no adventure and no ambition fulfilled that could ever satisfy the deep sense of self that you can only acquire when you go on your own heroine's journey. There is no man, no job, nothing outside of you that will ever bring true worthiness or satisfaction. Sometimes you have to travel far to realize that your home is inside you, that you can design your life how you want it, and that ultimately you can break free from whatever mold has held you captive, and live life on your terms. My gypsy spirit hasn't left me, but I'm not chasing or running away now. I'm finally *un*settled in the best possible way!

Abigail Nadar Nepaul is an attorney and practices law with her husband at their prominent firm in Durban, South Africa. She is also a speaker, trainer, and coach, and has spent over a decade hosting different radio shows on one of South Africa's national broadcasters. The founder of the Abigail Nepaul Coaching Academy, she is currently completing the master empowerment coach certification. A dedicated wife and a mother of two beautiful daughters, Abigail is committed to helping teen girls and women step into their power.

Sixty Seconds

ABIGAIL NADAR NEPAUL

•

*i*t was the beginning of our annual school holiday in December. I was fifteen years old and in grade 10. School had just let out, and I was looking forward to two months of freedom. My mum, dad, and I attended church that sunny Sunday morning, as we usually did. We then drove with the windows open along the promenade near our home in an affluent part of Durban, South Africa. I sat in the back breathing in the sea air and gazing at the crystal-blue water and white sand beaches.

We stopped over for lunch at our favorite family restaurant. As an only child, I was very attached to my parents and saw them as my friends, too. These lazy, relaxed Sundays, full of laughter and gentle teasing, always made me feel warm and close to them.

It was about 6 p.m. when our home phone rang. I was in my bedroom getting ready to shower when I heard my dad answer the phone in our lounge down the corridor. I could hear the worry and anxiety in his voice as he said, "Okay, I'm on my way." I could hear my mother's rushed footsteps coming toward my room.

"We have to go to Aunty Serina's house right now, my love," Mum said, and I could see the fear in her eyes. "Your uncle called and said something has happened to her."

I knew what that meant. It meant he had hurt her again. And hearing the anxiety in my mother's voice made me think that this time it was even more serious than usual. My uncle was an arrogant man. He had created a successful business, but he drank and gambled a lot. If anyone disagreed with him, he would throw the biggest tantrums. He was a strong and powerful man who was also at times very loving and caring. His volatile personality made him a highly intimidating and confusing character.

We arrived, and I saw several familiar cars already parked outside the house. But instead of children playing and people talking happily, there was just silence. The stillness was almost palpable. It made me hold my breath, almost suffocating me as I walked into the large, cold house. Absolute fear and dismay seeped into my bones. I couldn't see my aunt or my best friend Nikki anywhere, and wondered where they were.

I followed my mum, and we found them in a room. They were huddled together, sitting so closely on a bed. They looked at us with wide, frightened eyes. My mum went to Aunt Serina who was like a sister to her and hugged her, then looked back and told us to go outside. I heard my father going up the steps in search of my uncle.

I could hear the men talking as we exited the house, and it wasn't long before we could hear my uncle's shouts. I heard him swear, and I froze. I heard my father say, "But you called us here," and someone else said, "You have to stop! You are hurting her and the child!" and then my dad's voice saying, "We are taking both of them," after which I could hear more curses and things crashing and moving against the floor.

I feared that my dad and uncle were fighting and that my uncle would hurt my dad. I wanted to go back into the house and plead with my dad to leave, but I didn't have to. My mum, dad, grandfather, and the other family members left the house together, my uncle yelling behind them, "Leave my home and don't ever come back here again!"

After hurriedly saying goodbye to Nikki who was waiting outside the house in the dark, I met my parents at the car. We went home, an eerie feeling in the air. I hated leaving her.

I walked up the stairs leading to our apartment feeling defeated. I couldn't imagine not seeing Aunt Serina and Nikki again. The thought was gut-wrenching. Although we had encountered similar experiences before, this time felt final. Angry words were spoken. That night pain, fear, frustration, and stubbornness eroded beyond repair the bond that held us together as a family.

We didn't go back. I wrote letters to Nikki in an attempt to keep our connection alive. Calling each other was not allowed. My friend was the sister I never had. We shared everything: our plans for the future, goings-on at school, new friendships, but most of all our shared misery at the manner in which our family was torn apart. We saw Nikki, Aunt Serina, and my uncle again almost three years later at a family wedding. The tension between the adults had still not dissipated, though, and we left the wedding as broken and tormented as we were before.

More years passed before I saw my aunt and Nikki again. We sometimes met in secret, but those dates were never fun as the fear of my uncle finding out and hitting my aunt again was way too painful. I lost contact with Nikki during that time. We grew apart in a way I never thought possible, but fate had more in store.

Aunt Serina finally left my uncle when Nikki grew up. Before this, when my mother had begged her to leave, she would say, "I have a child, I have to stay." She didn't have any formal education and spent her years after marriage managing the family business. She felt the wealth her husband had created was his and that she and her child would have nothing if she left. But now Nikki was in her twenties, and after yet another episode of abuse, she decided to take the plunge, and she left him.

She moved in with my parents, planning to stay for a few days until she found accommodation of her own. He had tried desperately to convince her to return home during that time, but she would not hear of it. She was tired of the emotional and physical abuse that had spanned for most of their twenty-five-year marriage.

It was a cold, somber morning even before anything tragic happened. It was about 7 a.m. I was asleep in my bedroom after returning home at 3 a.m. from my job doing the midnight show at a local radio station. I was twenty-four years old, and life was wonderful. I was newly married and we were living with my mum and dad until we found a place of our own. I was happy to have my aunt around.

Tears well up in my eyes even as I write this eleven years later. What happened to her that morning would change the course of our lives as a family forever. I always wondered why I was chosen to witness that horrific moment. It spanned about sixty seconds but changed my life forever. It was a moment that was prewritten not just for me but also for our entire family. When something of that magnitude takes place it affects generations and leaves a scar in the hearts and minds of all involved.

"Please, Vikram, no!"

It was my mother's voice, screaming in fear. I jumped out of my bed, disoriented as I had just fallen asleep. Fear, however, takes over your body and moves you. My mother was begging my uncle to stop. I could hear that she was crying as she spoke. The fear gripped tighter.

Please don't hurt her, I thought as I rushed toward the kitchen. Strangely, I already knew it was the end. I knew he was there to kill her.

I raced down the passage toward the kitchen, where I saw Mum still in her nightgown running out of our home toward the entrance gate, desperate to find help. She looked back once as she ran, terrified. I saw my aunt, also in her nightgown, frozen still. I could smell the ginger tea she had been brewing. I saw him. My uncle had forcibly entered our home. He said nothing, but the expression on his dark face said a million words. He wore black and red. To me, it symbolized the rage he felt. He was beyond the point of speaking or negotiating.

As I approached the kitchen, I saw my uncle was holding a firearm. He caught me by my arm and flung me toward the door. As I sailed past her, I saw my aunt calmly kneel on the floor, her face against the cold steel sink. Surprisingly, there was no fear in her eyes. She was beautiful and radiant even then. She looked every bit the angel she was, peaceful, almost as if she were glad she would no longer have to endure such pain. There was silence and then, seconds later, just as I turned back to look at her, he shot her in her head. She was gone.

I scrambled to my feet and ran out the door, shaking. Then I heard the second shot. It was done. The thing we were afraid would happen had happened. An elderly lady I had never met took me into her apartment and tried to comfort me. My mum was still somewhere trying to get help. I didn't know what to think or where to go, and the last place I wanted to be in was our home, which was now a crime scene. Our house quickly became riddled with police officers and paramedics. I was numb. After what felt like only minutes, I left the old lady's apartment and found my mum, dad, and a host of other people, most unknown to me, in the corridor talking with the police.

My aunt was like a second mum to me. In fact, she used to call me her other daughter. She loved me like her own child, and filled my life with love and tons of laughter. During school holidays, I played at her home, and she would invite me to join her in the kitchen to bake delicious cakes or toast rotis. I sometimes accompanied her to the shop that she ran at the time. She was the embodiment of love and passion as a mother and wife.

She loved her family fiercely and chose to stand by them and for them even though her life was far from the ideal I thought it to be. She laughed in the face of adversity and smiled when probably all she wanted to do was scream and cry. She knew no way out. I loved her because she made me feel like I belonged. I was adopted by my mum and dad when I was a month old. I never met my biological parents but was loved and adored by my adoptive parents. My aunt loved me just the same and made me feel truly special.

She listened to me with love and warmth, and cared for and advised me in a way that still resonates with my heart and soul today. She left an indelible mark on my life, and I know now that I had to love her the way I did, I had to feel the pain of her passing and to witness the tragic manner in which it happened, so I could connect with the purpose for which I was born.

The newspapers called it another case of "femicide." It's a known term. It's a term we use to describe death by one's spouse. How ironic that as I write this it happens to be the first of the "16 Days of Activism for No Violence Against Women and Children" campaign that we observe annually in my country.

Over time I have learned that speaking or writing about this incident will not always be accepted in the way I hope it will be. It's extremely difficult for some people to read or listen to stories of this nature. Doubtful of whether I should write about it, I prayed and mediated from the moment I was offered the opportunity. Numerous doubts flood my mind even now, but what good is learning from these experiences if I can't and don't use the message to empower other women? I know my aunt would want me to. She guides me every day. She has taught me to be strong and to speak my truth, and for that, I will be forever grateful. My life changed that day. I knew then that life should be lived to the fullest, celebrated wildly, and lived purposefully, and that I had to do everything in my power to ensure that I did my bit to empower women to stand up against abuse and to choose to live their best lives.

My dear sisters reading this book, know that you are special and chosen! You deserve a life of absolute greatness and abundance. You deserve to be treated with love, respect, and honor. Everyone who knows or is connected to you should be proud to call you theirs, and you should wear your crown with pride and dignity. Love yourself unconditionally and celebrate all you are for you are fearlessly and wonderfully made by a supreme being. Never let anyone hurt or abuse you for you are God's child. Never confuse pain with love or passion. If someone loves you, they will never intentionally hurt you or abuse you physically or emotionally. You were destined for greatness. Go claim your birthright! And as Maya Angelou says, "You may not control all the events that happen to you, but you can decide not to be reduced by them."

Antonietta Mannarino holds a Bachelor of Arts with a major in child studies, as well as a Bachelor of Education, and is a graduate in police technology. She works every day to defy the stereotype of a person living with a chronic medical condition. A teacher and a certified personal trainer who loves to travel, she recently embarked on a six-day solo hike in Spain, trekking over 100 kilometers on foot. A soon-to-be master empowerment coach, Antonietta resides in beautiful Vaudreuil, Canada, with her two cats. You can connect with her on Facebook @Anto-Health&Fitness or Twitter @AntoMannarino or Instagram @AntoM44.

Blood and Independence

ANTONIETTA MANNARINO

•

"**W**ake up, Anto. We have to go and get your blood," he said in Italian.

My father was shaking me, trying to wake me up. He repeated it again.

"Come now, you know we have to go to the hospital today."

I pretended to be asleep, but he kept shaking me.

I sat straight up and looked him right in his hazel-brown eyes. "No," I said.

"What, 'no'? Get dressed, you're making us late!"

"No. I am not going."

He looked at me, irritated and dumbfounded. He looked at his watch again. He knew he was in for a battle.

"What do you mean, 'no'?! We need to go! I'm calling the hospital right now!"

When he left to make the phone call, I grabbed a pair of pants and a sweater from my dresser drawer. I laced up my runners and buttoned up my jean jacket. I quietly closed the front door and left without my dad noticing. I always made sure I wore a tee-shirt under my clothes so my arms were bare for my treatment. Wearing long sleeves bothered me because the nurses would roll them way up to put in the IV.

We lived on the east side of Montreal, Quebec, on a busy street, always full of cars, cabs, trucks, and buses. Many Italians lived in that area. Most of the families we knew had cars, but we didn't. We got around everywhere by bus and subway, so I was familiar with the route to the hospital.

I hiked the backpack higher over my shoulders and crossed the street. I had to run to the bus stop as, luckily, the number 99 bus was already there, pulling to a stop. I didn't have any money, but the bus driver did not seem to mind. I knew that this bus, the 99, would take me to Jean Talon Metro. From Jean Talon, I would take the subway to Berri De Montigny Station —the central station. I knew this connected my subway line to other lines, and that is where I'd get my connecting train to Atwater Station. As I sat on the bus, I was thinking through how I'd handle Central Station. That was the tricky spot because it was easy to take the wrong escalator and end up on the wrong platform. But I was careful. I had watched and learned. And now I was ready.

At age eight, I decided to take charge of my own life.

I entered the Montreal Children's Hospital and went up to the second floor, hung a left, walked through the doors with "Home Care" stenciled on it, and waited my turn to see the secretary. She stared at me in awe and looked around, trying to peer down the hallway behind me.

"Where is your dad?" she asked.

"I don't know," I responded.

She called over my regular nurse, the one who usually treated me. Same reaction, same question.

"I don't know!" I replied, agitated. "When can I get started?"

My nurse led me down the hall to prep me. I figured the secretary called my father as he arrived soon after.

I've always been fiercely independent. Always. Due to my anxiety around getting ill and being worried that I'd be forced to accept the limitations of being born with a genetic blood disorder, I sometimes made it difficult for people to get close to me. I can see that now. I thought that was okay as I had to go it alone. But when things go wrong, they can collapse everything you have built. Turn it into rubble.

When my collapse happened, I had to confront the hardest thing in my life. It was more difficult than managing the public transport system as an eight-year-old who was the height of a six-year-old. More difficult than the time I had to ingest mysterious medication for the purpose of "medical testing," and even more disturbing than when I had a reaction to the blood I was receiving but there was no one to bring me home.

• • •

The genetic blood disorder I was born with is thalassemia beta major. My bone marrow is not able to produce enough healthy red blood cells to carry oxygen to my muscles and the rest of my body. It is a form of anemia, and it requires me to receive blood transfusions every three weeks. It is life threatening. All of my three older sisters are carriers of this illness, but the second oldest was an intermediate carrier. This meant she would only get transfused when her hemoglobin dropped considerably low. She passed away at the age of twenty-eight after having contracted an unknown virus that her body was unable to fight off. I was twenty-one at the time of her passing, and the stigma of living with a chronic illness coupled with my sister's passing imposed a long-lasting vigilance of maintaining a healthy lifestyle.

I began receiving transfusions a few months after I was born, and the last one I had was just last week. I am forty-three years old. That is approximately 730 blood transfusions. I've spent 6,579 hours of my life "getting my blood." This does not include hours spent going to the other medical appointments associated with my condition. I visit a thalassemia clinic once every three months, and once a year I see a cardiologist, a liver specialist, and an eyes and hearing specialist and I also have to get a bone density scan, and an MRI for a ferritin test.

When the doctors sat down and explained all this to my parents shortly after I was born, they also told them I would die before my tenth birthday.

But here I am.

• • •

The hospital visits weren't actually the worst of it. I had to chelate every night before going to bed. This would involve mixing sterile water with a bottle of deferoxamine. I had to shake the bottle until the powdered chemicals dissolved into a clear liquid. Then I would diffuse the liquid from the bottle into a syringe. Once that was complete, I would inject myself with a butterfly needle and its five-inch-long tubing and tape it to my body. Imagine trying to find a comfortable sleeping position with all of that.

I had the option of poking myself either in the legs, arms, or stomach (I preferred stomach). The idea was to pierce the needle into a meaty part of the body. Some nights the needle slid in smoothly and I barely felt anything. Those were good nights. Other nights were torturous. I knew it was going to be a long process when the slight touch of the needle to my skin felt like I was being branded with a burning iron.

My doctors and nurses instructed my mother how to do this. I watched and learned along with her at the young age of seven. I was eleven when I decided I was tired of having her prick me. She came into my room with the tubing, sterile water, medication, and needles all on a tray, and said, "Anto, come and let me prick you." I thought of the last torturous pricking session. I also knew that my mother didn't like sticking a needle into her daughter and hear her whimper and cringe at her poking attempts. I looked up into her dark-brown eyes. She could tell something was up and was about to say something when I interjected and firmly told her, "No, I've had enough!"

From then on, I pricked myself. That is until they invented an "oral chelator," just recently. The bumps and discoloration on my stomach are now gone, but the scarring remains, perhaps as a reminder of thirty years — six to seven nights a week — of "pinch and poke."

As I would sit in the hospital waiting for my blood to transfuse, I would read or converse with the other patients getting transfused. I got quite interested in eating well and building muscles, and was quite motivated to stay as healthy as possible. I would see other patients in the hospital, and I witnessed what happened when they did not chelate properly or they failed to take care of themselves. They developed other complications, like diabetes and heart conditions. Some people's iron levels got so high that their skin turned a deathly gray. These patients lived a short life. I was determined not to end up like them. In my mind, I believed I could beat this illness if I just ate clean, exercised, and chelated diligently.

As I flipped through a magazine, I showed an article to a favorite nurse and told her I wanted to train to become an athlete. I was in my early twenties and full of hope for my health. I'll never forget how she looked at me with so much pity that I felt burned.

"You'll never be able to put on a lot of muscle. You won't be able to become an athlete. You can't because of your condition, Antonietta," she explained.

I froze, the magazine laying open before me, and watched as she walked away. I was absolutely seething.

"Don't call me a thalassemic, or a patient, or a chelator!" I whisper-yelled to myself. "I'm Antonietta. I'm a person first and foremost."

I began lifting store-bought weights at home and immersed myself in reading everything that I could get my hands on about putting on muscle and getting into great physical health. I trained zealously. I even enrolled to become a police officer and graduated with honors in a police technology program. Things were going fine until a dark cloud rolled in.

• • •

Between the 1980s and early 1990s, during the height of the AIDS epidemic, the Canadian Blood Services failed to screen blood from high-risk areas such as San Francisco, California, and inmates in US prisons. It is one of the country's worst preventable public health disasters. Many patients who received regular blood transfusions plus those who received blood products for other reasons, such as for surgery, got infected with either HIV or Hepatitis C. I was one of the unlucky ones: I got Hepatitis C.

I sat across from a liver specialist who coldly stated, "Your liver enzymes have been elevated, and we need to do a liver biopsy as soon as possible to see how much damage there is to your liver. I also want you to start a fourteen-month treatment immediately. Your genotype is the most difficult to treat. The treatment has a 45 percent success rate. If it doesn't work, we can look at other treatments. Since you are young, I would advise you to do this treatment now rather than later. It can be a harsh treatment, but it varies individually."

I stared at him blankly. I could see his mouth move, but the room had gone silent. My throat closed up. I didn't say anything. I took the papers he handed to me, put them in my bag, and left. I worked so hard at being the healthiest I could be with the illness I was born with, and now this? A storm was brewing inside me. I wanted to look God in the eyes. I cursed Him and everything that was around me.

Thalassemia is an immunodeficiency disorder in which patients have a harder time fighting off other viruses. You can imagine what this means when a patient contracts another potentially deadly virus. The odds are against them — the odds were against me.

I reached out to my then best friend. Her attempt to reassure me by saying "you're going to be fine" didn't sit well with me. I knew otherwise. Her lack of time for our friendship at a difficult and crucial point in my life made me realize I didn't need her. I didn't need anybody. I cut off my friendship with her, broke it off with my girlfriend (I realized I was gay in my mid-twenties), and set out for the dark days ahead of me as a lone wolf. I sought solitude during my most despairing time.

The treatment was horrific throughout the fourteen months. I had most of the side effects described in the pamphlet the doctor had given me: loss of hair, dry skin, eczema, anemia, nausea, flu-like symptoms, depression, mood swings, and aggressive behavior.

My family walked on eggshells: I was docile one second, and the next a crying and blubbering mess. Then I'd get angry, loud, and ruthless. I was unpredictable. I wanted to crawl into a cave and have someone block the opening with a huge boulder. I wanted to disappear.

As I stood before a mirror, I felt subjugated by a person I did not recognize. My family did their best to accommodate my moods and symptoms, but it was just too exhausting. My mom was patient but also heartbroken, having lost her other daughter to a similar illness. I knew what a simple complication to a virus could mean to me, as it is what took my sister's life. Mom would drink alcohol in secret to numb her reality ... something that inevitably took her life, too.

After fourteen months of the hellish treatment, the words "you are virus-free" were the finest music my ears had ever heard. I had prevailed. Mentally, however, I was unfit and delicate. Depression swallowed me whole. I pulled away from everyone. But as hard as it was, I found a way to keep my head slightly above water. I was good at that.

My only escape was going to the gym, and although I kept my promise to my body, I was slowly slipping further down the rabbit hole.

That's when something inside of me propelled me to ask my doctor for a requisition to see a psychologist at the clinic near my house. Some part of me knew I was out of resources. Even though my mentality had always been "No, I don't need help," everything inside of me was pushing outward and saying "Yes! You need help. Now."

My "tough girl" days were over.

Anxiety can sometimes move your spirit around, wake you up. It was my body's last resort, letting me know that enough was enough, that I needed to start paying attention to myself immediately.

During my first session with the psychologist, I sat on the edge of my chair across from her and clenched my bag for dear life. My watery eyes darted away from hers, and I was angry and frustrated to have found myself there. *Am I weak?* I asked myself.

The psychologist asked me how I was.

I took a big pause before answering. I may have initiated the help but it didn't mean I was going to do the talking. I looked her square in her big, dark-brown eyes and said, "I'm telling you right now: I don't believe in therapy!"

My psychologist described me as a depressed, angry woman. She helped me understand that I had not grieved for all the pain and suffering I'd been through. My body language, she described, was of a protective nature — I was always ready to bolt. She pointed out that I was looking down, hunched over, in as close to a fetal position as you could be while sitting up.

Yes, I was protecting my life as best as I knew how.

I have to hand it to her: She waited for the perfect time to ease into my world, gently, and ask the right questions. She did it with intention and compassion. I cried — oh boy, did I cry — and I hated myself for it. I would try to prepare myself while driving to the appointment and in the waiting room. I would tell myself that I would not cry this time. This time, I would continue with telling my story without breaking down. But the damage was so embedded within my spirit that any question relating to my life induced hurt, pain, anger, resentment, and sometimes shame.

I learned a lot about myself and my family. I began to understand my relationship with my mother. Although I always viewed my mother as a shero, the sessions brought out the hurt and anger I felt toward her for never having told me that she loved me. Not feeling loved was a prescription for a disastrous and sad life for any child, my therapist explained to me. This truth set me free. Children need to be held and to be told they are safe, they are protected, and they are loved.

I had to accept that although I looked up to my mother as this all-empowering, strong woman who had raised four children by herself while working a full-time factory job and catering to a demanding, narcissistic husband, she did not nurture my emotional health. Simply put, she was not there for me.

I began enjoying my visits with my therapist. It was nice to talk to someone without feeling guilty about my concerns, my needs, and my fears. I did not take well to the end of our sessions. She sensed it and remarked that this was also a form of grieving. I was grieving the end of our time together.

Those fifteen therapy sessions were a pivotal point in my life. They sparked a change in my belief systems about what it means to be strong.

I am a strong, independent woman and I ask for help when I need it.

I am now living a good life, independent of my past, my family, and my circumstances. In fact, this past year I embarked on a six-day pilgrimage in Spain known as the Camino de Santiago on my own. Just me, my trusty backpack, and my legs to carry me.

Seeking help was the best thing I ever did for myself. It allowed me to take leaps of faith, knowing full well that I would be okay in the end. I know there will always be an invisible safety net underneath me if I fall. And I know that everything will always work out just fine because my spirit has led me thus far. My spirit will always lead me to what I need if I choose to listen. Knowing this has allowed me to pursue more, reach higher, and explore my passions thoroughly.

I still maintain a healthy lifestyle, eating clean and exercising regularly, and attend to my much-needed, regular transfusions. I rest when my body needs it and know that it is not a sign of weakness.

I also realize that no one person can take on this journey we call life alone. We are bound to need help at some point. I am cultivating the life I want because I changed my perspective. This, in turn, has allowed me to see my life as a journey filled with endless possibilities and choices.

That is freedom.

Senior editor of Simply Woman Publishing, *Jackie Brown has been a writer all her life and an editor for the last thirty years. She has writ-ten several books for children, including the Silver Birch–nominated bestseller* Sir John A. Macdonald: The Rascal Who Built Canada. *Jackie supports writers through workshops and her coaching practice. She is the proud publisher of* Outfox Magazine, *whose mission is to celebrate, encourage, and inspire kids with autism. She is also the executive direc-tor of Susumai House, which researches and implements new treatment programs for people with chronic depression and anxiety. She lives in Oshawa, Canada, with her four children. You can contact Jackie through jackiebrown.ca or Twitter @JackieBrownca.*

I Know Why the Tin Man Smiles

JACKIE BROWN

•

i went to bed feeling slightly uneasy — I did not like the quiet. As a single mother of four, it was rare for me to be in the house alone. In fact, I realized that this was actually the first time I'd been child-free in so many years. My two daughters were on a camping trip; my nineteen-year-old son, Nehemiah, was at a friend's house; and my second boy, Reggie, just a year younger, had called me saying he'd gotten some last-minute work with James and wouldn't be home for a while.

Leonard and I had been together for a long time, and even after we split up, his son, James, and Reggie continued to hang out together. James had always been difficult to control. He had ADHD plus a learning difficulty, and from an early age he'd figured it was better to be "cool" than "dumb." Although he was as pale as they come and we live in Canada, he adopted his version of a black American accent and did everything stereotypically associated with "urban cool." He then took it even further by joining a dangerous gang.

I asked my boys to stay away from James, but they saw him as their brother. Plus we had recently moved from a small town to the outskirts of Toronto. My sons were shy and had no other friends. James was the only person their age they knew. It was hard to keep them apart — especially since I still had feelings for Leonard and I was afraid of creating a rift that would permanently end our relationship.

Balancing everything as a single mother was difficult, particularly when my way of dealing with things, whether at home, work, or in "love," was to avoid sticky conversations. To let things slide. To keep my fingers crossed and hope that things would work out, without me working them out. I absolutely hated to make decisions that would make anyone upset with me, especially my man and boys. I realized later that this is why I often felt so overwhelmed. I had no idea of what I wanted, only what I did not want: confrontation.

"Be safe," I'd said flatly with pursed lips.

"I know, Ma, I will. I'm only going because he said he really needs my help," Reggie replied. "Promise. I'm just going to do this job then I'm coming straight home. See ya later. Love ya."

I left the radio on as I needed its noise to fall asleep.

I was jolted awake by the sound of my phone. There were no pleasantries: It quickly turned into one of those calls from your nightmares.

"Hello, is that Jackie Brown? I'm calling from the trauma center of St. Michael's Hospital in Toronto. Your son, Reggie, is here. He was in a fight and has been stabbed."

I screamed in shock. What I heard was incomprehensible. Stabbed? Fight? My quiet Reggie? I didn't even know what to ask.

"Is he all right?" I stammered out.

"He was able to talk to the nurse. That's all I can say. You should come as soon as possible."

He did not say "he's fine," I thought. *I can't deal with "real."*

I sat up in the dark and could not pull a single coherent thought. My head felt heavy, full of bricks. I stood up and sat back down. I tried to get dressed, but my legs were leaden. I found it difficult to move. I texted my eldest son, asking him to contact me right away. Then I called my sister, Jessica.

"I'll meet you there," she said, and I finally kicked into action. I was dressed and in my car in minutes, just as morning light was beginning to brighten the summer sky. The usually traffic-packed highway was empty of cars. Everything looked so clean while the city slept. I made it downtown in record time. It was paradoxical that driving to the city was peaceful and without the irritations of traffic and dodging cyclists.

My sister was there when I entered the emergency department. She hugged me as she said, "Jackie, they stabbed him lots of times." She was shaking.

My knees collapsed and I leaned into her. I couldn't imagine that anyone would harm my gentle giant, but I could imagine his loyalty to James getting him into trouble. They told us they'd had to take him into surgery and apologized that they had not been able to wait so I could see him first. A nurse directed us to the waiting room.

Everything felt surreal, and I still had no reply from my oldest son, Nehemiah. I told myself, *It's only six in the morning. He's probably so deep in sleep he can't hear the beeps from his phone. Maybe his phone is dead.*

Jessica handed me a card from the police officer who rode with Reggie in the ambulance. They were now investigating the crime scene on Clifton Street, the officer had told her.

"Clifton Street?" I repeated. Instantly, I was nauseous. Clifton Street was where Leonard's other ex lived. The mother of his son, James.

I inhaled deeply. Of course, he was with James. Why hadn't I said no to Reggie? Why hadn't I risked being impolite and saying something "not nice" that might cause a permanent rift between James's family and ours?

Just as I was about to say something to my sister, a police officer came into the waiting room to talk to me. He took out his notepad to tell us what he knew.

"Officers are at a house on Clifton Street and the occupants are not cooperating. There is blood everywhere. This is a house we're familiar with, associated with gang activity. Do you know why your son was there?"

I nodded yes and told him he worked with Leonard, and I explained that James was Leonard's son.

"And how about the car?" the officer asked me. The car associated with the crime is registered to you. You don't live in Toronto. How did it get there?"

Nehemiah's car! My mouth went dry. *Where was he and why hadn't he answered his phone?*

I explained that my eldest son, Nehemiah, usually drove that car and that I was trying to find him.

"Well, it seems there is a weapon in the car. Can we have your permission to search the vehicle?"

"A weapon?" I was about to say more when my sister motioned from behind the officer that I should stop talking.

I felt like I was in a movie. Weapons and stabbings? This was not my world. Not my children's world! I could barely focus.

A second officer arrived, a woman. She'd seen my sister's warning to me. "Of course, we're going to confiscate the car anyway," she said. "It's better that you cooperate with us. It would be better for your sons."

"Well," I said, "one of my sons in being operated on and the other one is missing right now, so I don't see why there is a big rush. I'll talk to my sister first and then I'd prefer to wait here and pray that my sons are okay."

That little statement was probably the most confrontational I'd been in my *life*.

It amazed me that as I was sitting in the surgical waiting room in Toronto's foremost trauma hospital not knowing the condition of one son or the location of the other that I had to start trying to think like a lawyer.

I knew I didn't want the support of the officers at that moment, especially as it came with veiled threats. And I also knew that I did not know how to handle "judgment." I'd spent so many years of my life caught up worrying what people thought of me, and now that I was in a life-and-death situation, I worried I might lose insight about what was really going on.

It turned out there was no weapon in the car. My son survived being stabbed over ten times, and my other son, who was there to pick up his brother and take him home, ended up witnessing the attack and then was attacked himself. This was my worst nightmare coming true.

Nehemiah was being held by the police, which is why I couldn't reach him. They also held two other boys who were with them at the time — none of them James, who had made sure to disappear by the time the police arrived.

The detective assigned to the case came to the hospital wearing a tight tee-shirt and jeans, with his ball cap turned backward. I spoke to him for a few minutes and then he said, "You don't seem like most of the mothers I deal with. You care for your son. I'm going to really do my best for this case. You've got my word. This is a really special case to me."

I knew what he meant. I grew up in a white area and am highly educated. I don't have an accent or "sound" black. I have used that to my advantage wherever I've had to interact with officials. I knew which mask to wear for this interaction.

I knew to not get upset, as that would make me an "angry black woman" and might give him permission to dismiss me. I did everything "right" so that my sons, hopefully, would be assumed innocent until the facts were revealed, and so that they'd get to the bottom of who did this.

That's when the officer told me straight-out that he didn't care about most of these cases involving black kids because, he believed, so many of them brought it on themselves.

. . .

After a few months, I gave up contacting the cool detective who told me this case was special to him. It became quickly apparent that our case wasn't important to anyone but us. The officer wasn't investigating anything or anyone, even though I had found out where the mother of one of the perps worked, and we had DNA evidence plus witnesses. The detective did nothing.

I wanted to push harder. I wanted to rattle cages. But I felt oddly ashamed. Shame because of the way the incident was reported in the news, and shame because when our kids do dumb things, even when they are adults, it comes down to mothers. And black single mothers are blamed for so much in this society.

So there was my son, hurt, yet I felt shame. Was he less deserving of sympathy and support because he was hurt by someone in a gang? Was everyone thinking he must have done "something" to have deserved it?

When my son was attacked, I reported it to work as I needed time off to care for him. On my return, I told a colleague about it. I don't know why I confided in her. I suppose I thought she was a teammate. I had little in common with her, so perhaps I thought that by sharing it, as she was also a mother, we could find a way to connect.

I told her that when my boy was stabbed, he asked James to call an ambulance. James said to him, "If I call an ambulance, the police will come, too. I can't have that. You have to make your way on your own." And my son said James's mother looked him right in the eyes as he tried to staunch his wounds with the tea towel she had given him. "Just go," she said. And pushed him out of her house, leaving him crying, alone, stabbed, bleeding in the dark.

When I told this to my colleague — her alabaster skin flawless, hair shellacked, fingernails manicured — she said, "*Ahh*, so, she didn't want to get involved?"

Get involved? I thought. *She refused help to a dying boy who was stabbed at her home.* I wanted to explain but, of course, didn't.

Instead, I felt the judgment. I felt the shame. I stopped talking about it, especially to my white friends and colleagues.

•   •   •

I loved Leonard but couldn't talk to him about my fears surrounding his son. So, I pushed him away, too, by just disappearing — not answering his calls. Avoidance was my specialty. I know I should have handled it the adult way, by communicating "I cannot be with you because your son is a danger to mine."

My shame and fear started to paralyze me. I would constantly imagine my children being injured or killed. I would manipulate any circumstance so we were always at home or always together because I couldn't bear those images when my children were away from me. It didn't help matters that my husband had been killed by a drunk driver several years earlier. I couldn't handle the idea of losing any of my children, too.

As a result, I was nervous and vacant at work. I would burst into tears and shake. I was terrified I'd lose my job. But I thought I was hiding it well. I put extra layers on top of the mask I always wore and extended it to cover my whole body. When I visualized myself, it was as the Tin Man in *The Wizard of Oz* — protected by a suit of armor but always smiling.

I'd remove my costume after the kids were fed, when I was free to head to my room and collapse, not sleep, until the morning when I'd start over again.

I was actually relieved when I was let go from my job. But being fired stirred up more shame. And the paid time off gave me time to think about the root of it all. I recalled how, as a child, I felt too obvious: I was the only black kid at the school. No one knew my name — I was "the black girl."

My mother telling me "you have to work twice as hard to get half as far" made me feel judged as less worthy, whether it was true or not. I'd think, *Nancy [my white friend] is better than me*. I'd hear, "Hey, that's the nigger who takes Italian lessons!" Or there were the kids who would smirk and ask,

"What did you have for dinner?" I knew the correct response wasn't "stew-peas and rice," so I'd say "potato chips and hot dogs," which I figured was what they'd had for dinner. There was that mean boy at school, always turning to me and asking, "What's a jive turkey?" To my shocked response of "I don't know," he explained loudly, "They don't even know," and went back to not talking to me. I was tired of hearing "She's trying to be white." Or the continual burning shame of feeling like a fraud everywhere I went — even in groups of black women. After my "white" husband's death, I knew people talked about me as a "black single mother" not having enough money and having checks bounce. It was endless: all the ways I was made to feel like I didn't have the right to make my own decisions.

Shame. Shame. Shame.

I was angry at myself for never standing my ground. I just wanted to hide but being "nice" rather than saying and doing what I wanted to do was so much easier.

So I lived with a lump in my throat, pressure on my shoulders, my fingers crossed, as well as hot flashes of indecision while I tried to figure out what other people wanted. And in doing that I felt I'd risked my sons' lives.

Oh, the guilt of not saying "no" that night. *No, you can't hang out with James. No.*

●   ●   ●

Both of my boys were damaged by this experience. They live with mental illness — a combination of depression, anxiety,

PTSD, and psychosis — and I couldn't find the type of help they needed. So I decided to do something. I created a program for kids like mine, and was inspired by the enthusiastic responses I got from psychiatrists and other mental health professionals.

Rather than looking for a new job, I created my own business.

Admittedly, the decision was also made out of fear of not finding a job. The truth is, I couldn't face being judged as unworthy.

What I can tell you is that I'm stepping up now and creating the life my family and I deserve. One I know I am more than capable of creating. It isn't easy. I still fight with the pressure of shame and being "nice." I'm working on my leadership skills, but at least I've uncovered what I want for me rather than going down the path of least resistance and trying to avoid ruffling any feathers, particularly my own.

Working on not caring whether people judge me has made it possible for me to say no when I need to. It's made me less afraid for my children because I say no to them without guilt. I'm more capable of confronting those who misjudge them, even when it creates more work for me in a sometimes overwhelmingly busy life. It's allowed me to accept and forgive my mistakes. And it means I can work toward creating a less complicated and more honest life.

The best part: Now that I've peeled away the tin costume, the smile you see is genuine.

A writer, artist, entrepreneur, and knitwear designer, Beth Humphreys knows the importance of following your heart and passion. She seeks to live a life of purpose with creativity, wisdom, and kindness. Beth is a student in the master empowerment coach certification at the S.W.A.T. Institute and plans to graduate in 2018. Her compelling articles have been featured in Simply Woman magazine. Beth lives with her husband, their five cats, and a dog on Vancouver Island, Canada. She can be reached through her website at wisewomanempowerment.com and on Facebook @BethHumphreys.9 or Instagram @WiseWomanBeth.

But He Was My Brother

BETH HUMPHREYS

•

*i*t was a sunny day in late summer, and I was driving home from work. I saw the truck coming toward me in the opposite lane. It was a large, heavy truck, perhaps a dump truck or similar utility vehicle, moving at a pretty good clip on a country road. I remember thinking *All I have to do is turn the wheel, and it will be over.*

The idea of ending it was so tempting — no more pain, no more darkness, just oblivion. I had to fight that urge with everything I had as the truck roared past me, leaving me exhausted and frightened by the intensity of that temptation. I had wanted to, but somewhere deep down, I knew I couldn't do that to my daughter, Lorysa. I didn't want to leave her without a mother, nor leave my husband alone

271

without any explanation. That was the day I realized that I needed help and that I needed to tell someone before my secrets and shame destroyed me.

When my husband got home with our daughter a short time later, he found me curled up in a ball, sobbing. I don't know how long it took, but slowly he managed to get me to tell him what had happened and why. My secret started to come out.

The first time it happened, we were on a family camping trip to the East Coast. We got into some bad weather, and instead of two of the kids sleeping in the tent, we all had to fit in the camper, which meant we had to double up on the front bed and two of us slept on the floor. That night, he and I were sharing the front bed while my older sister and other brother had sleeping bags on the floor. I was eleven, and he was fourteen. I remember him whispering to me in the darkness, although what he said is lost in the far reaches of memory, and then he was touching me, quietly in the night. After the first time, he approached me more often, and it continued whenever we were alone for the next four years.

I began to fear being left alone at home with him. I didn't want my mom to go to work because that meant he would probably be the one babysitting, but he was my brother and the logical choice to be there after school before my parents got home.

I think that at one point my parents must have figured something out. I don't know what they knew, but I have a memory of them telling him and me to stop it. He didn't. He just became more careful about how secretive he was and more cautious about not getting caught, which made me feel even more guilt and shame because now I was disobeying my parents. Of course, I didn't want this to happen, but I didn't know how to make it stop. My brother had a violent temper, and I was terrified of him. He had been violent with me in the past, including once when he walloped me across the face so hard that I was thrown across the kitchen. He was older, bigger, and stronger than I was.

I felt guilty and believed that I had started it or brought it on myself. He was fourteen and well into puberty. I was only eleven and had no understanding of sexuality at the time, but I knew that this was a secret. I knew to keep it secret right from the start. The guilt and shame came later.

I remained silent and fearful, afraid to tell him no, and afraid to tell anyone. I felt guilty because I believed myself a willing participant in an act that was horrible and shameful and that made me a horrible and shameful person. What kind of girl would do this with her brother?

In middle school, when they started to teach about puberty and sexuality in health class, I learned about incest, that it was sexual relations between family members and it was bad. I tried to ease the guilt and shame that I felt by telling myself that this wasn't incest because my brother was adopted — he wasn't my brother by blood — so that made it not so bad. That didn't work. My shame grew deeper. Nobody talked about sexual abuse of children at that time.

As an adolescent, I was afraid of any mention of sexuality. I noticed boys and liked the cute ones just as any other girl would, but I was terrified at the thought of talking to a boy that I liked. As my friends started to mature and wear clothing that was more revealing, I was wearing shirts with the collars buttoned right up to my neck. I hated anything revealing and that might make me look more attractive. Of course, I got teased for my style of dress, and this probably contributed to my being an outcast, weird, not part of the "cool crowd." I was bullied by the other girls, and I had few friends (only the other girls who were in the "misfit" group). I was shy and did not want to draw attention to myself.

My second brother, who was in the same grade as I was, was a member of the cool crowd, had better grades, and was athletic — just further proof that I was a loser. In high school, I was invisible. I preferred to be the quiet one who went unnoticed. It was safer than being out there. I watched from the sidelines as my friends had boyfriends, had fun, and went to parties.

When I was fifteen, my parents sent me on a six-month cultural exchange in South America. By the time I got back, my brother had a girlfriend. My own personal hell was finally over. We have never spoken of it since, and I kept his secret for another ten years before I finally told anyone.

• • •

The long-term effects of childhood sexual abuse are known to include numerous ongoing mental and physical health issues including depression, anxiety, post-traumatic stress, autoimmune disorders, and other stress-related conditions. My case is no exception. I have suffered chronic depression, anxiety, and low self-esteem for most of my life. I have experienced flashbacks for years that left me feeling anxious and frightened by their intensity. As a result, I avoided any situation that might remind me of something that I did not want to relive. It has damaged my relationships with others and my confidence in my abilities and judgement.

I spent years living in fear that people would find out that I was not as smart as they thought I was, internalizing all criticisms and fighting any evidence of my value. I am a highly educated and intelligent woman, yet I lived my life feeling like everyone else around me was smarter and more capable than I was and would one day realize that I was stupid. I have sabotaged myself in my career because I did not feel that I deserved to be at the level I was. I have had little faith in my ability to make right decisions. I allowed others to push me down paths that were not right for me because I was so paralyzed by the fear of making a mistake that I could not state what I wanted.

Chronic depression and anxiety have been constant companions in my life. Depression is like a dark fog, which dulls even the brightest lights around you. Even in times when things are going well, and you feel happy, there is a constant anxious feeling that the darkness is there, just outside your peripheral vision, waiting to seep in and engulf you in its darkness.

There have been times in my life when that darkness was comforting in its familiarity, and it was tempting to allow myself to sink into it and not come back up. Depression steals the joy from life. It saps your energy and whispers lies that leave you believing that you are helpless and lost in the fog. It affects your sleeping and eating, which then affects your ability to think clearly and your physical well-being, which can then lead to stress and autoimmune-related illnesses.

I started to have symptoms of chronic fatigue and pain in my late teen years. By the age of thirty-two, I was diagnosed with fibromyalgia — a debilitating illness that is character- ized by widespread musculoskeletal pain and fatigue. Living with this illness forced me to alter the way I worked and the occupations available to me.

The depression, PTSD, and other issues that I have faced has not only affected my mental and physical health, but it has also had a negative impact on the relationships that I have had. I have often reacted to situations with my hus- band out of fear or shame, which negatively impacts all aspects of our relationship. Being a good parent without slipping into the temptation to be too overbearing or over- protective has also been a challenge.

My mother returned to work as a real estate agent when I was eleven — the same time that the abuse started — and worked for a while before giving it up, partly because I was not dealing well with her being away so much. I remember my father being annoyed that I was acting out and Mom had to quit her job to accommodate me. Looking back at it now, I understand why I did not want her to go out. As I have worked through my journey of healing, I came to realize that this had a profound effect on my feelings about going to work when my daughter was young. On some level, my child-mind equated Mom going to work with bad things happening, and that child inside me was screaming at me every time I left my child to go to work.

The conflict between being a working or stay-at-home parent was a significant source of conflict in my life and my marriage as my daughter was growing. This revelation, which only occurred recently, allowed me to let go of the guilt that I felt when I left my daughter in the care of others to make a living, and helped me to understand the reason that I had been so reluctant to return to work after I became a parent.

I had difficulty having a second child, and after several frustrating pregnancy losses and infertility treatments, I finally resigned myself to only having one child. Much of this occurred after my initial disclosure to my husband. I remember the anger and jealousy that I felt toward my brother, who seemed to be living his life according to plan: married, both with good jobs, and two kids ... the perfect family scenario. How was it that he could have all of that, living the ideal life, while I was miserable in my job and struggling to do the one thing that women all around the world should be able to do easily?

Healing from this type of trauma comes in stages. When I first told my husband about the abuse, I had taken my first step. I started to work with a therapist who helped me to understand that this was not my fault and I had nothing to feel shameful or guilty about. From there, I had to begin to heal the deep wounds that I had inflicted upon myself as a result of deep shame and guilt. This was much harder and takes time and hard work. This work can be difficult and painful, but the revelations that occur as you work through the layers can be life changing.

When I first told my mother about the abuse, her reaction made it clear that she had not known what had been happening. My mother was always one of my best friends and confidants, and it helped that this secret was no longer between us. The thought that one of her children had done something like that to her other child was devastating, to say the least, and we had many discussions about it over the years. She once remarked that I had been his first love. I replied that what he did was not love. I was dismayed that she could not see the difference between the sexual abuse that had occurred and love, which never seeks to hurt others. Incest and sexual abuse are not about love, or even about lust and physical attraction. It is about the use of power and control. There are many myths about childhood sexual abuse, including the ideas that the child can say no, that their silence implies consent, or that if they felt a physical response then they must have enjoyed it. These incorrect beliefs only serve to deepen the guilt and shame that victims feel.

About a year before I disclosed my experience, I was at a get-together with friends when one of the women began to speak about abuse. She spoke about the conflicting feelings and confusion that happens when something this frightening and shameful feels physically good. I did not yet have the courage to say anything, but I remember thinking, *Wow, she gets this! Perhaps I am not so alone.*

I think her disclosure made it easier for me to eventually tell my story.

• • •

One of the difficult things that I have had to face during my healing was reconciling my feelings toward my brother. How could I be so angry at the person who hurt me and stole my innocence and yet still care about the brother with whom, as a child, I played and shared so many good family memories and experiences?

The difficulty lies in reconciling the fact that these are both the same person. It is normal to feel anger and hatred toward a perpetrator, and when he is a stranger or someone distant from you, it is easier to remove them from your life. This cannot happen when it is a close family member. For years, I have had to see my brother at family gatherings and holidays, and pretend that all was well. I buried my feelings of anger and hatred, ignoring them and pushing them back down when they inevitably surfaced, usually at the most inopportune moments.

The amount of mental energy that this requires is enormous and taxing on the mind, body, and spirit. I had found that when I stopped fighting the feelings and flashbacks and faced them, I was able to free myself from the self-imposed prison that they created within me.

By telling people about my experiences, I have furthered my healing and freed myself. I have written journals and letters and used other creative methods to name and release my painful memories so that they now no longer hold me prisoner. I can now look back at that time in my life from a more objective viewpoint, without feeling triggered or threatened by the memories of what happened. More importantly, I can now finally think about spending time with my brother without feeling intimidated by him or the memory of what he did to me.

As I have continued to work toward healing and discovered my calling to help other women who are similarly healing, I have discovered some truths.

First, I believe that true healing can only come if you are willing to do the work yourself. While it is important to have support and reach out when help is needed, the only person who can rescue you is you, yourself. Changing the ingrained beliefs that we develop in childhood takes a lot of hard work, but the rewards are worth the effort.

Second, I believe that all of our experiences in life create the person that we become. It includes the bad as well as the good times. I love the person that I am now — what a great feeling to say that — and I am proud of who I have become. I know that I would not be who I am without these experiences (not that I would wish them on anyone to build character).

When trauma happens, we begin to put layers of protection on ourselves to shield us from the world. The problem is that this not only shields you from the world, but it also stops you from shining in the world in the way that the universe has meant you to shine. I have spent many years working to understand myself and peel the layers away from my protection. Real healing can only occur when we are no longer afraid to allow our light to shine brightly in the world.

I won't dull my shine any longer. I deserve all the same love and light and joy that every woman does. But I realize now that until I claim it, it will always elude me. The fact is, #TimesUp.

After a painful childhood, Elizabeth Walsh is living proof that you can transform your life no matter your circumstances. She has received several accolades in her studies of Eastern medicine and holistic therapies, including the Student of the Year Award upon graduating as a holistic therapy practitioner. Elizabeth has practiced in a clinical setting for nine years, healing emotional and physical stress through health and lifestyle coaching. In her free time, she enjoys spending time with her three loving sons. Visit libbiewalsh.com or Facebook @EWalshAuthor ContributorSimplyWoman or Instagram @Libbie.Walsh.

A Mother's Love

ELIZABETH WALSH

•

I t's Valentine's Day 2008. I am holding the collar of my coat together at the neck as the biting winds whip the hair around my face. I'm standing with the other mums, waving off Tyler, my eleven-year-old son, as he slowly moves through the school gates. I look around, startled by the honk of a car's horn, and turn to go home. I nod hello to Nicola, just as I do most days, as she walks past with her two little ones. But today is different because I know that I will see the doctor soon to receive the results of my recent biopsy. The pain in my right breast feels worse than it's ever felt. It is all I can focus on. *What if it is cancer? How will I tell my boys?*

They would be devastated, as the two eldest lost their father to cancer three years earlier. They need me. And I need them. I know how much I needed a mother's love and how the lack of it was so devastating to me. I can't do that to them. I want to live.

• • •

My parents had traveled from Ireland to England to find work back in the late 50s. They made the difficult decision to leave their two-year-old daughter, Bernadette — my sister — in Ireland, as they would not have been able to find lodgings and work as easily with a young child. The decision was made more difficult because the only relative available to care for Bernadette was Bridget, my mother's aunt. My Great-Aunt Bridget had been very cruel to my mum's sister Bridie when they were growing up, so Mum didn't fully trust her to be kind to Bernadette.

Mum became pregnant with me soon after they arrived in England. She told me they had to hide me in boxes to silence my crying for fear of being evicted. Each time it was discovered they had a child, they were forced to move from one one-room apartment to another. There was no way they could get Bernadette until things were more settled.

My parents traveled back and forth to Ireland several times over the years to visit her. Sometimes they would visit individually. After I was born, they would take me with them on these trips. Bernadette would be waiting at the gate every time we went to see her. The plan was to bring her back to England when she was school age. Then we could all finally settle as a family.

Although I was only three, I remember holding on to my father's hand so tightly as we made the final trip to Ireland to bring Bernadette home with us when she was five years old. My father had steady work and enough money to rent a warm place, still only one room. I knew that my sister coming home meant I'd always have someone to play with. I proudly held the huge doll that my parents had bought for her — I wanted to be the one to give it to her. I was full of excitement.

This time the crossing was long, and we were held up overnight due to the bad weather. Back then, there was no way of letting Aunt Bridget know the crossing was delayed. We continued our journey and finally got to the house the next morning. My parents were tired, but we were all excited to see my sister. As the car pulled up outside the cottage, Bernadette was not at the gate as she usually was. On most of the trips, she would watch from the window as the car traveled along the country lane, and then run to the gate to greet my parents whether it was one or both of them. It was always a loving reunion.

We walked down the path. I was holding my mother's hand and carrying the doll — we could hardly contain our excitement at surprising her. As we arrived at the door, we found it already open, and Aunt Bridget was standing in the doorway, her body shaking, her face ashen, tears streaming down.

"I am so sorry," she wailed uncontrollably over and over as she threw her arms around my mother. "Your daughter is dead!"

We rushed past my aunt into the kitchen. There she was, beautiful Bernadette, with her long black hair, laid out on the kitchen table. She was covered in a white cloth with fresh flowers and glowing candles placed around her. She looked like an angel. We later found out she'd died of pneumonia. My aunt said she'd been sick for days but didn't want to take her to the doctor.

A deep sadness settled over us in the years following my sister's death. My father never really recovered. He would disappear for days at a time. I looked up to my dad. He was tall, dark, and handsome. But one of my worst memories was when I was five. I was on the bus with my father. I had an upset tummy, but I was too afraid to ask to go to the toilet or to sit down. I wanted to wait until I got home, but unfortunately, I had an accident. My father was furious. When we got back to the house, he grabbed a hurling stick (similar to a hockey stick) and chased me around the table, beating me with it. He then yelled at me to remove all my clothes. He tossed me into the very old butler's sink in the pantry cupboard. He came back with a large wooden scrubbing brush that was used for scrubbing the floor and Vim (a powerful cleansing powder) while swearing and telling me what a bad girl I was. He shook the powdered bleach all over me, adding hot water, then forcibly used the scrubbing brush on my tender young skin until I was raw all over. When my mother returned home, she was horrified at what she saw. She chased my father out of the house. He disappeared yet again.

My mother also had a fierce temper. As a child, it wasn't unusual for me to have stiletto heel marks on my head, indicators of the times her unhappiness got the better of her. There were no hugs or kisses from my mum. Instead, I would run to my Aunt Bridie — Mum's sister, who lived in a room downstairs — when I was hurt or afraid. She would always save me if she were home. But I was left alone a lot, although sometimes my mother would bring me with her when she went to visit her male "friends."

Once, at age six, I was left with a male relative. When Mum returned from her hospital appointment I gave her graphic details of what he had done to me while he was looking after me. Mum bent down and shook me by the shoulders. "What is wrong with you?" she said sternly. "You could have got pregnant!" I knew that it was never to be spoken about again, which meant I had no protection against him. The sexual abuse continued. Consumed with shame and fear, it took many years of therapy for me to realize that I had done nothing wrong, that it hadn't been my fault.

Despite my mother's desire for secrets, some things were harder to hide. She never knew this, but it was her sister, my beloved Aunt Bridie, who reported my abuse to social services. She secretly phoned them and said, "If you don't do something, this child will be killed!"

I was taken away and examined by doctors, who asked me about the bruises and marks all over my body. I was a thin, timid girl and had been taught to be seen but never heard, so I didn't say much. I was bounced around several foster homes until finally, when I was eight, I was sent away to boarding school for my safety.

Recently a dear school friend told me that on a bus ride home for the holidays, I shook and sobbed quietly throughout the journey. I do not remember that, although I do remember one of the worst times in my teens when Mum had beaten me.

I was fourteen. It was my last day of summer holidays before I had to return to boarding school. Mum typically liked to go out in the evenings, so when I was home, it had always been my job to bathe and feed my younger siblings, who were five and seven at the time, and get them to bed. I was not too happy about it this particular evening, as I still had to hand wash my clothes (we did not have a washing machine), hang them to dry, and then pack my suitcase all in time to leave for my first day of school, the next day. I would never disrespect mother, but I felt it was unfair. I had a few cross words.

She got so angry, she threw a heavy tin at me with great force. It hit me square on the side of my face, and I fell to the floor holding my head, bleeding. She then raced toward me, trying to scratch out my eyes, it seemed. I was screaming and crying. I tore away from her, left the house, and ran through the neighborhood. I got on the bus with blood streaming down my face. I kept my head down and covered my face with my hands and the cardigan I was wearing for the forty-five-minute bus ride to Aunt Bridie's. She patched my gaping wound and insisted I go back home since we knew my mother would have left my sisters alone in the house.

I was making my sisters dinner when my mother came home. She had been drinking. She saw my swollen bruised face, and the ugly scratches around my eyes.

"Don't you dare tell anyone," she warned me before staggering to bed.

The next day, I woke up to a beautiful sunny September morning. I was bruised, and sore, my head was pounding, but sun beamed through the windows, and I felt happy. I was on my way back to school for a few months where I knew I would be safe again. I just wanted to get back to my friends and my new boyfriend who I'd missed over the summer.

Soon after I returned to school, social services got involved again. It wasn't possible to hide the damage done to my face, and the school had reported my injuries. They looked for a suitable place for me to stay as it was clear I could not go back to my mother. In the end, I had many different "homes" during the holidays.

By the time I was fifteen, I couldn't focus at school, I couldn't focus on anything. I dropped out and got a position as a trainee in a hair salon. When they let me go, I had nowhere else to go but home.

Social services surprised us one evening not long after I moved back. They were taking me into their care until I was eighteen. As my young sisters played together, unaware of what was going on, I left with a suitcase and a bag. They set me up in a small hotel nearby until they could find me a suitable children's home.

My boyfriend was so upset when he heard. The thought of me going away broke his heart. He begged his mother to let me stay with them. She did not know me, so naturally she was suspicious of what I had done wrong to be taken by social services. She asked for a meeting. My social worker explained that I had done nothing wrong: "All she needs is a family to love her."

His parents were so kind to me. I finally had a beautiful foster mother and father, parents who loved me. I was grateful and happy. The relationship between my boyfriend and me changed to be more like brother and sister. And until his parents passed, I kept in touch. I am eternally grateful for the deep sense of love they brought to my life.

I moved away from them when I was nineteen and met my first husband. We dated for a few years, and although he had shown how volatile he was, I still married him. He was so handsome and charming — not to mention, he could have had any woman he wanted, but he chose me. On the other hand, however, he'd physically abuse me when he was angry. He promised many times that it would stop, and I kept hoping. We had two beautiful sons together.

One night I was startled awake by a nightmare. The week before, my youngest son had been diagnosed with autism. That night I woke up in a cold sweat. I got up and crept out of my bedroom and quietly walked into my sons' rooms while they were asleep. I kissed them each gently and stroked their soft cheeks. I had lived in fear for so many years but finding out about my little boy's autism made me open my eyes. I had to do something.

My biggest worry was that I was seeing my eldest son's behavior changing. He had angry outbursts like his father, yet he was still a little boy. How much worse would it get if he continued to model his father's actions as he was witness to many episodes in our turbulent, violent marriage?

I don't remember the nightmare now, but I do remember that it shook me so deeply. I always thought of my sons as my world, and it was my job as a mother to protect them. I needed to find the courage to end this marriage, and for them, I finally did.

I set up house with my two sons, determined to undo the damage I could see in my eldest son and provide the safe home they both needed.

In time, I met a kind-hearted, loving man, and we fell completely in love. We married four years later. I prayed that my sons would feel safe and happy. I hoped my new husband would give my boys the loving male role model they both desperately needed. I gave birth to Tyler, my third son, two years into our marriage, and I tried my very best to create the happy family environment I'd always dreamed of. But as my eldest son entered his late teens, his behavior toward me turned volatile. This continued for many years, until we became estranged. My heart was broken, and I distanced myself from my husband. Meanwhile, he had created another life for himself outside our marriage.

• • •

It's Valentine's Day 2008 again, seventeen months since my husband walked out on me. I'm sitting in the oncologist's office. The wind is still howling outside.

"Yes," she says, "I'm afraid it is cancerous."

Over the course of the next nine years, I would lose both of my breasts. I had muscle removed from my stomach to reconstruct the first breast, and then muscles removed from both of my legs to reconstruct the second. And yet the pain of losing both of my breasts — and both of my husbands — didn't compare to the deep-rooted sadness in losing the close connection I had with my first-born son. All I could do was focus on my healing and continue to take care of my two other sons, who still needed me.

I spent years focused on every natural healing modality. I studied Eastern medicine and learned about chakras. I became convinced that the love I'd so desperately needed growing up was a major cause of my cancer. And I was determined to become the loving "mother to myself" that I needed. In doing so, I was able to reconnect with my eldest son in the way that he needed, too.

Fast-forward to 2018: I'm happy, and not only am I free from any pain, I'm free from cancer, too. The best news of all: My eldest son and I have made amends, and he has a happy life. We both know that anger does not serve a purpose for what we've both been through, but that love will see us through.

I may not have my breasts, but I have the biggest heart. If I could offer you advice it would be that self-love is the greatest healer of all.

Born with the gift of gab, Shireen Clark is a natural leader and activist. She pursued a professional career in accounting, working her way up to a senior role before being recruited by her local union. She was recently reelected to serve a second term as union president. Her sense of humor and storytelling skills allow her to rise above and come out on top. Shireen currently calls Victoria, Canada, home. Visit her on Facebook @shireen.clark.5 or Instagram @bowlofcherries7 or Twitter @bowlofcherries7.

Perseverance

SHIREEN CLARK

•

Some mornings I am woken up by an unseen force pushing a huge weight against my chest, squeezing the air out of my lungs. What most people don't know, particularly the men I work with, is that I live with an undiagnosed health condition that has caused me to go into cardiac arrest and lose consciousness. Yet every day I rise and go to work with a fierceness in my step. I need it in order to compete in my aggressive male-dominated industry. I wonder sometimes why I do it, and then I remind myself that I want to feel like a superhero from a movie! I want to be one!

I remember telling my mom that I had a "dizzy neck" when I was three years old. It turns out that my explanation of having a "dizzy neck" was very literal. The two main arteries that go down either side of my neck can't always deal with my erratic heartbeat, which causes uneven blood flow, creating a swirling motion in my neck and throat that made me "feel funny." As a three-year-old, there wasn't much merit put to my funny feeling, but my parents always worried.

At twelve years old, I started having grand mal seizures. After the third one left me unconscious and hospitalized for a long period of time, the doctors said I should expect my brain not to function as well, and that I would never achieve straight As. I would have to accept being a below-average student. They continued to say this each time seizures required me to be hospitalized.

My parents pushed the specialists to check my heart, and although the cardiologist was skeptical, he performed the tests, including a stress test. Three and a half minutes on an intense treadmill and there it was: those "funny feelings" I always had before I lost consciousness. The doctor got me off the treadmill immediately, as he could see my heart was beating erratically and my blood pressure was dropping fast. My parents always pushed for answers ... ones they never fully got.

I didn't listen to the "no's." I never listened to the naysayers. And I still don't. A boy I knew when I was a teenager taught me something about facing fear. He faced his fears head-on to get rid of them. He was so scared of heights that he went skydiving. It always stuck with me, and I felt to really live I had to push the limits and find out what I could handle.

I worked hard to prove to myself that I wouldn't let the opinions of others change the way I saw myself, and in doing so, I achieved top marks in school and even broke records in math and science. In fact, as I breezed through high school, went on to university, and began climbing the ranks in my career, I realized I had a special power: *turning frustration into fuel for my success!*

The good news is that the medication I take now allows me to live somewhat normally. To drive a car. To run across the street without losing consciousness on the other side. Although every so often, without rhyme or reason, I still go down for the count.

In any case, from a very young age, I knew I would need mental tenacity to handle the positions in life that I wanted to reach. As a kid who sometimes got bullied, I would channel each accusation, each berating comment, each assault from both girls and boys into a force that only made me stronger, smarter, and more determined to have my voice be heard. Besides, those doctors were wrong. I could do anything that I put my mind to!

I am lucky that I came from a loving and supportive home. My parents have been a rock-solid support throughout my life, and remain so. I have an older brother who is protective of me. Always having him and his big athletic, jock friends around gave me the courage and strength to not take crap, especially from boys, and to not be physically intimidated by anyone.

The frustrating thing (but don't worry, remember what I do with frustration?) is that from as far back as I can remember, through school, activities, and work, men/boys have always tried to push me down and take over. I refused their sexual advances and didn't cave to their bullying tactics. Ever. I can't count the number of times I've been at an event where drinking was involved and the men thought they could just paw at me and get what they want. I remember in my last year of high school, three older guys crashed a party I was having and they were trying to pick a fight with one of the other guys. I was the only person there who had the guts to go face-to-face with the ringleader, with all the boys hiding behind me, and tell them to get the hell out. Fortunately, I had the willpower that could overcome even a drunken man. I have always been headstrong and courageous when it comes to everything ... except love (but that's another story).

In the late 90s while in college, I attended some monthly business motivational events with my dad. There were two motivational speakers per month. Approximately 500 people attended each time. I noticed that over the course of the entire year there was only one woman at the podium, and she was by far one of the best speakers of them all.

I found out that each man was being paid between $15,000 and $20,000 per speaking event, and yet that woman only received $7,000. It was in that moment I really saw and felt the impact of inequality. It bothered me so much that I made a decision to become not only the highest-paid and most-sought-after woman, but also the top-ranking person in my chosen profession. In other words, the highest-paid person — regardless of gender.

Today, I am the president of my local union. I don't share this position to sound boastful but to help remind every woman (and man) that regardless of your so-called limitations, you can break glass ceilings.

In the past two years, I have grown our local union to representing eight employers and over 1,200 members. We represent many municipalities and several public works employees. And don't kid yourself: I have dealt with so many angry men. I never know what a day or week will throw at me. But I have my super powers! I'm never afraid. Anymore. But it was actually a dramatic physical change that brought me into union leadership in the first place.

Nearly three years ago, I woke up one morning and couldn't move my legs. I was numb from just below my belly button down to my upper thighs. As a single woman living alone, I felt sheer panic. I had to use all my upper body strength to lift and drag myself out of bed and call my family. The pain was excruciating. I waited for my family to come from an hour and a half away.

After an initial visit to my doctor and physiotherapist, I was told it could be a year until I would be able to walk again and move comfortably. On my first assessment in physiotherapy, I had less than 10 percent movement in my body. It was scary and jarring, but I knew there was no way I was going to be like that for a year!

I took the exercises the physiotherapist gave me and did them three times a day. I went to the pool on a regular basis to improve movement. Six weeks later, I was able to return to work, modified workspace and minimal hours to start. I didn't have a huge support system at work, and my condition wasn't easy for other people to understand. But that is when opportunity fell in my lap. An opportunity that may not have come had I not had to slow down due to my illness.

My friend and colleague told me he was going to move on in his career and therefore step down as union president. He asked me if I would consider running for the position. It wasn't something I had ever thought of doing, but after mulling it over and looking at all my opportunities, I decided I could make a huge difference. I felt my perspective — a woman's point of view — was important. I could tackle the issues that affected so many women, issues that too often seemed to be forgotten. At the time, I didn't see the challenges I would face as a woman in the role nor did I expect them.

It's not always easy being a female boss in a male-dominated industry. I play by the rules and try to make others stick to them, too. Regardless, I am still attacked daily — both my integrity and my professional life — and it's frustrating. Sometimes I even feel as though my daily life is made as miserable as possible, all in an attempt to break me down and make me quit. The good news: It ain't happening!

As president I try to lead by example, to be a role model to my members, to the women on my board, and to the women I represent. I want to teach men that a woman is capable of being a terrific leader, one that they can learn from and follow. Most importantly, I want to teach my twelve-year-old niece to be a strong, confident girl. I hope she'll get through adolescence somewhat unscathed and with the tools and knowledge to navigate life without letting boys take advantage of her or put her down. Like I have.

When I am faced with a disgruntled worker who feels unrepresented, I try to face it head-on. Several times, I have gone into all-male companies and answered their angry questions. I have had some men get right in my face. Instead of backing up, I move in closer, nose to nose. If they yell, I yell back. My philosophy has become "meet them where they're at!"

When they realize they don't scare me, my unwavering confidence changes their attitude and approach to me. When we have an issue, instead of creating more division, I try to band them together and lead them forward as a team. This has earned me — "a sassy little 5'3" spitfire" — their respect. But the real reason I do it is because I feel like I am making a difference.

A couple of years ago, I started participating in intense boot camps and trained to compete in the Tough Mudder in Whistler, Canada. Tough Mudder bills itself as one of the toughest events on the planet. People come from all over the world to test their physical limits in extreme conditions. I trained hard for eight months, working out five to six days a week and eating healthy. It was a tough course of ten miles and over twenty obstacles, but my teammates and I completed it in four hours. It was grueling and hard, and at times I wasn't sure I could keep at it, but I did. And although I was a little bruised up, I survived it. It was a huge accomplishment for me. I felt like I could do anything after that.

What I have yet to learn, however, is how to balance this necessary fierceness I have with what it takes to find love and keep it. I have asked myself, *Must I be one of "those" women — the ones who climb the corporate ladder in lieu of love?*

Now, don't get me wrong, I've had lots of partners. I could have taken an easier road long ago. I could have chosen to marry one of the men in my life. I even decided that maybe I was one of "those" women who would give birth by in vitro fertilization. Sadly, I learned that I am unable to have children. That was a very hard blow to come to terms with. But maybe somehow, deep down, I knew I wasn't able to have children and that is what drove me to focus on my career and not on my fertility.

So, I continue to aspire for exceptional on my own. And until I find a partner whose life will complement mine, and vice versa, I am happy to remain single and self-sufficient.

I've recently entered my forties, and I've been having more "spells." They frustrate me. I wonder if these spells could be stress-related, could they be due to age-related changes in hormones, or could they mean my condition is changing? Some days I push it aside and just keep living. Other days

I have no choice but to listen to my body and deal with it despite my competitive drive.

I am not sure what the next year will bring me, but I write this as I prepare to step into battle to prove that I am a true leader — regardless of gender, motherhood, or age. My purpose is to lead and educate this next generation of women and men, and to remind them that equality matters. Women matter.

May the best person win. *Roar!*

Mary Jane Mendes is an award-winning professional photographer and educator. A trailblazer, she started as an electrical engineering technologist and the first female government chauffeur in Ontario, Canada. Her work has featured images of professional athletes (Joe Carter), international celebrities (Carol Burnett), and government officials (the late Benazir Bhutto), and she has also worked for corporate clients (IBM, Celestica). In her spare time, she satisfies her adventurous spirit with travel, music, hiking, and supporting community events, the arts, and charities. Mary Jane is a very proud single mother of her amazing son, Liam, and her dog, Trixie. Follow her on Instagram @maryjanempix or Facebook @mjmpix or LinkedIn @maryjanemendes11.

The Lioness, the Doctors, and the Lawyers

MARY JANE MENDES

•

*a*s part of my ongoing treatment after sustaining injuries from a series of car accidents, I routinely saw a medical practitioner for pain therapy. After so many years, I trusted him. I had been going to him for nearly six years, and we had a friendly relationship that I was comfortable with — at first. But soon the questions started to get too personal. He started making advances, and this increased once he learned I had separated from my husband. He kissed me on the lips in his closed office when I thought he was reaching in to hug me.

Soon he was getting even bolder. He fondled me and pressed his erect penis against me. I told him off, but on the next visit, he went even further. He unzipped his pants

305

and pulled out his penis in front of my face as I lay on the treatment table. I whispered, "stop!" as I knew that other people would hear if I yelled. He continued, saying sexual things to me and suggesting we get together. I said no and told him I was not interested. I was his patient and he was married.

Because we had a prearranged agreement, made through lawyers and my insurance company, that he would get paid once my settlement from the car accidents was reached, I felt I had to continue as his patient. It took a lot of courage to go for my treatments, and I would leave bigger and bigger gaps between them. In order to make his access to me more difficult, I refused to change into a dressing gown. But still, he would manipulate and fondle me. On occasion, his wife was assisting at the reception desk when I was receiving my treatments, leaving me infuriated.

As I lay facedown on the treatment table on what would turn out to be my last visit, he was chatting away. On this day he straddled me again (I had stopped him from trying to force intercourse during a previous visit). I dug my head further into the headrest as I felt him attempting to penetrate me. Other patients were sitting a thin wall away in the waiting room. *Am I dreaming this?* As I lay here, I could hear the receptionist busily taking calls and making appointments. The feelings of shame, betrayal, and mistrust crept up. *How could this be happening?* Feeling powerless, I left the office never to go back and buried yet another secret.

A year later, I had a defense medical examination with the insurance doctor due to this series of car accidents. It was a one-off appointment.

The insurance doctor was very cheery and talked to me as if he already knew me. He sat and spoke to me for about twenty minutes, asking me questions about my career and my ex-husband, and then he asked about my sexual relationship with my former husband. I did wonder what that had to do with my injuries, but I reluctantly answered his questions.

I told the doctor that I used to be quite active, and I was trying to get back into shape. The doctor responded by saying that I had a really good-looking body and that I appeared to be physically healthy. He also told me that I had a pretty face and that I should have no problem finding someone now that I was divorced. He made compliment after compliment. It started to feel like I was on a date, and I felt like he was looking at me in a flirty and sleazy way. I was beginning to feel very uncomfortable, and perhaps he saw that as he started to ask me details of what happened in each of the car accidents. Then he left the room so I could change into a gown. He told me to remove everything but my underwear.

Finally, the examination proceeded. The doctor had me turn around with my back toward him so he could examine my back. As I stood there, in a backless hospital gown, he reached from behind and asked whether my breasts were tender. He touched my left breast first with his fingertips then cupped both of my breasts and asked, "How does this feel?" I took a step away from him as my body tensed up, and he pulled me back, even closer to him.

Inside I was screaming "No!" but the "no" got stuck in my throat. Terrified, I couldn't get those words out. I could not vocalize or scream them out. Why? He was the doctor. I was the patient. The abuse of power made me feel helpless, just like when I was a little girl and someone who I had trusted had taken advantage of me.

The doctor then told me the exam was over, but he kept on talking as I stood in my gown wanting to get dressed and get the hell out of there. I put on my pants, under the gown, as he continued talking, asking me about my sex life and if I had a boyfriend or "anyone steady." I felt dazed and even more uncomfortable and stood there frozen, unmoving.

"Don't worry about me," he said. "Continue getting dressed," and he asked me more questions about my sex life.

I turned my back to him, got dressed, and swiftly ran out of the office, all the while screaming inside. I left the office as soon as I could. Another secret to bury?

I would soon find a way to engage my inner lioness in finding my courage and strength to speak up and be heard.

During my healing journey, I was attending art therapy classes, which I found to be very therapeutic. For people who have a difficult time verbalizing their emotions or journaling, art therapy is a compelling way to express your emotions and feelings by creating art pieces. I relished in my art and through them managed to remove layers of buried pain that I had been carrying. My counselors even had me publically speak at a conference that showcased my therapeutic artwork, and they asked me to talk about my healing process. It was very empowering to be validated by a very large group of people. My art helped build my self-confidence and inner self-worth, and through it, I could process my anger and resentment issues. It empowered me to visually express suppressed demons and emotions buried in my subconscious. My creative art pieces were based on the horrific abuses I had suffered.

The counselor encouraged me to report the medical doctor to the medical board in my community, and years later I summoned the courage to do that. They sent a caseworker to my home to interview me, record my statements, and help me fill out the necessary forms and reports. I filed a case of sexual harassment, abuse, and misconduct against the doctor.

I reported that my rights and personal boundaries were violated as he made flirtatious comments and performed an inappropriate breast exam and did not leave the room while I got dressed.

Years later they were still investigating. I would call several times a year, only to be told that the investigation "was in process." They said they were backlogged. My caseworker said, "You will get justice."

Finally, after five years of waiting, I got an answer: The case was referred to the Quality Assurance Committee for review, and the doctor was only given a warning. Two years later, the second committee mandated that the doctor was to have another person in the examining room — a small victory. Both of these doctors acknowledged that what he did was wrong, but that the seven-year deadline for pursuing a civil suit was up. Therefore, they said, I had lost the opportunity to take any legal action or to sue for compensation.

Who was the medical board protecting but their own doctors? It seemed to me that it was a well-orchestrated scheme to prolong the investigation to the point where it was "coincidently" past the seven-year mark. Once you speak up about the abuse, you have seven years to file a lawsuit. With the 2016 changes, it has now been clarified that no limitation period applies to claims resulting from crimes of sexual violence.

I was furious and decided I would not be silenced and would continue to pursue these doctors. This time I figured I'd seek out a female lawyer, as I hoped a woman would be more sympathetic to a sexual assault case. She had me sign an eight-page agreement regarding her terms and payment conditions, which were written in the typically dense and convoluted language of lawyers. I trusted her and, as I had a better understanding of the complaints system, I read through it and felt safe signing it. She also confided that she had knowledge about the insurance doctor.

The insurance doctor never responded to her letters and I didn't have the money to pursue more legal action. It costs money to seek justice. Slowly, I was gaining strength and the courage to speak up by taking these significant steps to fight back, but I realized I had to give up on this particular case.

The lawyer was, however, very successful in obtaining some compensation from the medical practitioner in a very short period. She stated that it was the fastest and easiest case she had ever resolved. She was glowing about it when she proudly handed me a check. I looked at it and saw it was much less than the compensation amount minus her stated fees. I questioned her about it, and she told me she had decided to pay herself a bonus for resolving my case so quickly and efficiently. She pulled out the signed retainer agreement and went to page 8, paragraph 5. She interpreted it for me: Basically, it stated that she had reserved the right to pay herself a bonus. I went red with fury, and she noticed it. She quipped, "Well, you could have gone to another lawyer to have this looked over before you signed it." Then she turned and walked away.

Coincidentally, a year later, I received my settlement for the car accidents after nearly eight years. The lawyer took a 40 percent contingency fee instead of the initial 20 percent fee we had initially discussed and agreed on. Although I had asked for a copy of this agreement from day one, he never provided one despite my repeated requests. Upon receiving my compensation, when I brought up that he had taken more than we'd agreed, his office stated that they could not find the original agreement. It was conveniently lost.

As thrilled as I was to finally get some justice for the sexual abuses and compensation for the accidents, I felt further violated by their actions. These experiences of white-collar misuse of authority shocked me. We are supposed to be able to trust doctors and lawyers. It surprised me that one of them was even a woman. It was a bittersweet win. I looked at the positive side, reminding myself that I had spoken up and taken action. The lioness was starting to gain some strength. At least I won.

Other times when I had summoned the courage to speak up and go to the authorities, I felt like I was never heard, taken seriously, or even respected. Inside, I felt small and insignificant, like a mouse. I wanted the world to hear the lioness in me roar! I had bottled up so much. My rage, anger, tears, and frustration at all these betrayals were taking a toll on my body and personal relationships. During the reporting process, I had moved back to my parents' home to help care for my mother, who was battling cancer. I had also remarried and gave birth to a beautiful son.

My dad, who was only sixty-seven, had a lot of major health problems. My son was about a year old when my husband left me, and within a couple of months, my mom passed away at the age of sixty-three. My son and I remained at the family home so I could help care for my dad, and my dad could help out with my son when he was able. Years later, I made another career change, this time teaching.

Unfortunately, I needed lawyers again soon after my father passed. I was the executor of my parents' estate, and my siblings contested my father's will. Being an executor is like having a full-time job, except you are also often an emotional mess and grieving. On top of this, I was heartbroken over my siblings' actions. I found the lawyers tried to prey on these perceived weaknesses — but I was ready for them.

At the beginning, I had a couple of good lawyers, but they didn't practice litigious law so I needed to find someone new. Would you believe that I had to take legal action against the next lawyer I retained for overcharging me? It was a formal affair held in a courtroom. And I had to hire legal advice to deal with him and had to appear in court about three times. The lawyer in question did not show up to any of the court dates. He always sent an articling student. On one date, there was another complainant suing him at the same time.

The last lawyer I hired during the mediation phase of the case brought by my siblings made a calculation error that resulted in a loss to me of over $10,000. When I went over the paperwork the very next day after the mediation case concluded and found the error, I immediately phoned the lawyer.

I even went to his office and sat in his waiting room for several hours in hopes of confronting him. When his secretary finally came out and asked me why I was waiting so long, I tried to explain that I needed to speak to the lawyer directly about the errors in my payout, but halfway through I burst into tears. I was crying uncontrollably. I was fed up from over five years of standing my ground on the litigious estate issue, and this error was the last straw. Having a lawyer make a simple calculation error yet not work with me to resolve it felt like more than I could take.

Finally, days later, he agreed to meet me. He threw the blame on me, saying I signed the documents and should have noticed his mistake before signing during the highly stressful mediation day. Plus he was upset with me for embarrassing him in his posh downtown office. Although he acknowledged that there was an error, he didn't attempt to rectify it.

What I have never told anyone until now is that I struggle with a learning disability. Reading and writing have been a challenge since childhood, so dealing with contracts and legal matters has been very arduous. It has taken a tremendous amount of courage and tenacity for me to stand up to these lawyers and medical professionals, people who are so highly respected in our society. I am pleased that I found my voice and stood up to them. I channeled my inner lioness and roared when I had to, even though inside I sometimes found myself quivering. I carried on.

Should you find your trust in influential professionals betrayed, you can and must take action through whatever avenue is available. You can get justice and fairness. And protect yourself — there are some untrustworthy characters among the people we have been taught to look up to.

As I finally reach into the depths of my soul, my inner voice speaks up, and I embrace my strength and perseverance. Hear me ROAR! With the courage of a lioness I speak my truth, I am heard, and I am free.

Janice McIntyre is an eclectic poet *and writer with a love for words and people. She considers herself to be blessed with an observant eye for nature's aesthetics, which invariably manifests itself in all of her creative endeavors. Janice is founder and host of Loose Leaf Poets & Writers, a writing group and performance series. Janice has been featured on U of T Radio and BlogTalk Radio, to name a couple. Having lived coast-to-coast, Janice now makes her home in Mission, Canada, where she focuses on family, writing, and creativity. Join her movement on Facebook @Loose LeafPoetsWriters and @JanicemAuthorContributorSimplyWoman.*

•

The Widow's Peak

JANICE MCINTYRE

·

We leave something of ourselves behind when we leave a place, we stay there, even though we go away. And there are things in us that we can find again only by going back there.
— Pascal Mercier, Night Train to Lisbon

Walking alongside the lake in the dark, the wind whipping my hair at my face, the snow falling steadily, I could see the trees were filled with large crows. Lake Ontario's waves were on a winter high, smashing against the rocks. I reached the bench and sat for a moment. Further down the shore, a man threw a stick for his dog — it chased after it. Snow collected on my coat as I prayed for answers.

I knelt down, my knees digging into the frozen ground, the snow crunching beneath me. I cannot recall how long I stayed like that, but by the time I stood up, I could no longer feel my toes. Watching the snow dance under the streetlights, I slowly got back up and trudged toward my vehicle. The wind picked up as I pulled away from the lake toward my return home and my reality.

Just days later my husband left for Heaven. I, a young mother of two children aged five and seven, was left in the throes of despair. His departure left us devastated. Widow status now afforded me the unfortunate opportunity to define myself: "Without."

"Without" slept in the corners of my mind and kept me awake at night. "Without" often made me late for appointments and make poor food choices. It left beds unmade and fed my kids McDonald's and hours of TV. Draped in a familiar cologne, it hung in the closet along the creases of his shirts. It sat beneath the linen he had folded and wrapped itself in each blanket and patterned sheet. It screamed from bookshelves, the washing machine, the gas tank, and hallways. It overtook every piece of my life.

Antidepressants and sleep aids were my vices. I often woke in a fog, putting my earrings in the freezer and forgetting to take out the trash. I had grown weary of the kind gestures of others, household projects, and the emptying closets.

Nothing would stifle "Without." It stayed on like a bad stain on the carpet. Strangers and neighbors embraced "Without" with compassionate tears, stiff hugs, bad breath, asphyxiating colognes, and imposing inquiries.

Logic dictated that eventually I would leave "Without" behind. However, it had long since attached itself to my skin, its tentacles carving deep scars. "Without" would unhinge every part of me in the years to come.

*   *   *

It was December and I was sitting at my desk on the thirty-ninth floor in downtown Toronto. I was dressed in a plaid suit — a matching skirt and blazer — and a pair of black pumps. Papers covered my desk, and my dictaphone was jammed with a cassette. Schooling, along with four years of working nights in this same firm, had finally paid off.

My phone rang. It was the hospital requesting that I come right away. Although my husband had been admitted the night before — he'd been suffering abdominal pain and bouts of vomiting — he insisted I go to work that morning as taking time off was frowned upon at my firm. I began to stress and cry. One of the senior lawyers came out of his office with a box of Kleenex and helped tidy my desk. He somehow knew how serious things were by my reaction. He got my coat, and we took the elevator down to the concourse. He flagged down a cab on the corner of King and Bay. I thanked him.

Little did I know at the time, I'd never see that lawyer again nor would I be going back to work anytime soon.

The cab weaved in and out of traffic as it traveled the few blocks over to University Avenue, where I got out at the hospital entrance. I stood looking up at the tall buildings, the cold air biting at my tears. Inside, I took the elevator to the fourth floor where my husband waited. The room was fluorescent-lit, the bed was covered in crisp sheets and pink blankets that smelled of antiseptic. My husband sat on the hospital bed with an IV dangling from his arm, his skin gray and his eyes sullen. I was speechless. His legs began to shake, and the bed rails tapped loudly against the green wall. The rattling sound was loud in my head. Bracing his leg and then his hands with mine, I tried to make it stop — the pain, the shaking, the noise. He said he was afraid. I was, too.

The doctor arrived, and I slowly slipped off the edge of the bed and veered toward the door. I just wanted to run away. Gently, the doctor guided me back. "You need to be here ... I am so very sorry ..."

My husband was diagnosed with stage 4 pancreatic cancer and didn't have much time left. We'd been together nearly sixteen years. I don't remember the rest of that day or how I got home.

It was Christmastime, and neighbors, family, and friends streamed through my home as if there were a revolving door. Someone shoveled the driveway, others cooked and cleaned. My family was feeling both hopeless and helpless. All this happened back when people communicated in person and had real telephone conversations dialed on rotary phones that dangled from kitchen walls. But I didn't want to talk to anyone. I despised the sound of that ringing phone. I wanted to disappear. Run away. Instead, I wrote scrambled notes, hung up on tele-sales people, and didn't answer the door. My circle of friends grew smaller.

On New Year's Day, the snow was piled high outside the windows. I made my way to the hospice, where my husband's health continued to decline. There were chemotherapy and radiation treatments, ambulance calls, infections, complications, stent surgeries, port-a-caths, clean-ups and cover-ups sheltering the kids from the many storms that passed through our lives. There were family breakdowns and heart-wrenching talks. The cancer metastasized, and a few months later sepsis affected his brain.

My husband was angry and spent many sleepless nights in front of the blaring TV. Things got broken, words stung, and every day felt like a hangover.

I tried to sleep in the chair beside his bed, but he'd constantly toss and turn, often anxiously undressing. On this particular day, he was down to his boxers, with the call button pinned to them. And although he was too weak to walk, anxiety had gotten the better of him, and he continually tried to get out of bed. I went down the hall for a short rest, only to awake minutes later with a compulsion to return to him. I found him convulsing and bleeding from various parts of his body. I pulled the call button for help and held his hand as he succumbed to his illness. The room went quiet, and I wept in despair.

My husband had died.

Family arrived, the doctor arrived, and the funeral director arrived, and the long hours of that day painfully passed
with questions he could no longer answer. I returned home
with the news. My little son was angry, breaking toys and
slamming doors, while my daughter hid in her room under
blankets, completely inconsolable.

The days and weeks that followed melded. Every routine
was difficult, off-kilter, and short-circuited. I changed my
telephone number and locked my front door. There was so
much to sort and put in order.

Not ready for any of it, I immediately packed the children
up and embarked on a trip south of the equator. I needed to
get away. There on that little bay beside the ocean, far away
from it all, we struggled through the days with unfamiliar
people. My angry little boy, who only a few weeks earlier
had climbed into the silk-lined casket of his father, tossed
rocks in the ocean and furiously screamed at the waves.

Soon after, I reconnected with a longtime pilot friend in
Vancouver. He was welcoming and familiar, and our friendship quickly evolved into something more. That summer we
fell in love. I sold the house and relocated to the West Coast.
We married a year later. It was an exciting time. I discovered I was pregnant, and between the children, house, and
gardens, my life was full. But I was often lonely when my
pilot was away at work. My grief hung on and the shadows
of "Without" continued to visit as I searched for answers
that I was not ready to receive.

In the years that followed, my son would continue to suffer differently than his sister, fighting health issues and emotions long into his life. My daughter, daddy's little girl, remained strong and brave and a little fighter. She forged on and aimed for nothing but perfection. She would go on to compete in athletics well into high school, and eventually study to became a nurse.

September 11 shook our world and my pilot's career. Airline A bought out Airline B, and we transferred from Vancouver to Halifax — clear across the country. Forced to start another chapter, we built a home on five acres beside a lake. Discombobulated, we wanted to be happy but we all found ourselves struggling with the move. It snowed from October until April, with heavy rains and power outages. Hurricane Juan hit hard: There were fatalities, fallen trees and damaged houses, lost boats, and fires. We were without water, septic, and electricity. Luckily, we were able to evacuate before all the roads closed and spent four sleepless nights holed up in a hotel in Fredericton, swimming in the dirty pool of the Howard Johnson and eating at the local diner.

Once we were able to return home, life went back to normal. I still missed my pilot terribly when he was gone, and worked hard to make things better. I joined the gym and took a local hospital job. I found a babysitter to help out at times when I just couldn't do it all alone. I sold Mary Kay, and joined a pottery class. I spent hours listening to the loons on the lake, waiting for the school bus and journaling away the rolls that had accumulated around my waist. Sadly, somehow my marriage stopped growing.

We had survived terrible storms, but extended out-of-our-control separations and unboxed grief were impacting everything. Though we were disappointed about real estate and wary of another move, Airline C necessitated our return to BC. For a third time, we answered to the call for another coast-to-coast relocation.

The baby was now three, and our teens challenged and tested our mettle. We struggled with settling in. I sought a new job and trained in fitness, yet remained insecure about who I was and how I got there. Though my husband was a good provider, we were clearly unraveling. And instead of focusing on how to fix it, in a rash of emotional discomfort I made an absolutely illogical decision that would leave fossils on all of our hearts forever ... I chose to leave the comfort of the home and hearts of those I loved.

The two older ones were already out of the house, and although I had joint custody, I left my youngest son with his father. It was a game-changer that I thought was beyond all repair. I did not know at the time that instead it would reveal my true authentic self and lead me to pathways yet unwalked.

It wasn't until I was involved in a scary vehicle rollover that my vulnerabilities were unearthed. I apologized to my husband and asked for a fresh start, but it was too late. I was old news. He insisted on keeping our son with him. Having barely recovered from the accident and a divorce that I had initiated, negativity nipping heavily at my heels,

I made the decision to leave BC and I ran, again. I'm not proud of it, but at the time it was all I could do to survive. Emotionally drained, I returned to Toronto, alone, where my extended family and roots were.

Toronto was harder than I imagined. I rented a little apartment with hardwood floors and cast-iron radiators in a six-plex on my childhood street above the lake. I took a job downtown and took up with a musician. I ran a poetry group, made new friends, and experimented with speaking in front of large crowds. I forged through seasons, walking up and down familiar streets looking at the houses I grew up in. I visited old schoolyards, parks, swimming pools, libraries, and churches. I rode streetcars, subways, and my bicycle. I cried myself to sleep most nights and worked hard to find the missing pieces I had been searching for.

My divorce was in full swing. There were challenges in all directions. My youngest visited during school breaks but there was never enough time, and it was always heartbreaking. My entire family struggled with my decisions. I had made it hard for anyone to love or understand me. All the while the sorrow and guilt grew.

I often visited the cemetery my first husband was buried in and sat at the foot his grave. I was grieving my life and my decisions. One afternoon, a large hawk flew just above me, its wings clipping my hair. He landed on a tall, weathered headstone in front of me and looked down at me curiously. It felt like even he was asking me questions. *No, it was never my intention to become so separated from my children.*

After much counsel, contemplation, and careful planning, I returned to BC. With the help of a dear friend, I found a small suite to live in. I settled back on the West Coast, taking a new job and filling my little space with the comforts of home. Longtime friends appeared with bed knobs, broomsticks, and love. I was humbled by their friendship.

It would be a year before I could stand on my own two feet again, but I put all of my efforts into family peacemaking, sharing meals with my kids, and cheering from the sidelines. I stood proudly on the sports fields of my youngest son and keenly followed my daughter's nursing career studies and quietly celebrated the birth of a grandchild I have not yet met from a place of joy that came from within instead of without.

Then, quite unexpectedly, I met an incredible person who made me laugh until I cried. He was warm, welcoming, and wanted to hear every story. We often found ourselves finishing each other's sentences and were certain we'd met in another lifetime. He became my best friend and soulmate. He waited at the train with flowers on rainy days and cheered me on through continual life changes. He was kind, humorous, and artistic in ways that filled our days with blessings and love. I am thankful for him every day. I know that if it weren't for all the hard events and decisions in my life, we very well would never have met.

And although it's been a long journey, I have learned survival is not for the weak. No matter how hard you try, people will judge you for what you did or didn't do. Some people will hold grudges, eager to highlight your errors and chastise you for going left instead of right. They will talk behind your back, even compete with you. They will let the door slam in your face. They will take from you, hoping you won't succeed — but you will. From the cries of a newborn baby to the casket of a loved one, you will survive it all. You will survive with certainty and clarity. You will learn to let go of the small stuff, the small people, and the struggles.

And so I choose to live with an attitude of gratitude and accountability for all choices and finding strength whenever "Without" comes knocking — therein lies a special kind of wings.

Journey on, loved ones. If I can learn to fly, you can, too.

Lynsi Anderson is a holistic practitioner, *herbalist, medical medium, and intuitive healer. With over a decade of experience as a healthcare director, a bachelor's degree in business, certifications in NRT, reiki, herbalism, tarot, and EFT tapping, she works passionately to help others reclaim their health and inner divinity. In 2012, Lynsi was the "fans' choice" for local entrepreneur of the year in The LYFE Magazine. Mother to her feline fur baby, Magique, Lynsi dreams of one day spawning her own earthling. Visit DarlynApothecary.com.*

Transcendence

LYNSI ANDERSON

•

from a young age, I could sense people's energy — including that of people who are no longer living. I was an empathic soul and sensitive to the needs of others. Because of this, I attracted people in need. Trouble was, I would get so drawn in that I would often forget about myself — my gift of empathy would become my near demise.

My entire existence seemed a pursuit to transcend my own lot in life. I prayed for years for the type of understanding, joy, and calm that I witnessed others experiencing. I had never known "normalcy" so I didn't know where to start. Unfortunately, that meant I had to hit rock bottom before I let go of my ego and asked my higher power to guide me to serenity.

When I looked at my life, the common denominator in my despair was me and my lack of boundaries ... Only upon realizing that did I learn to put down the crosses I had chosen to bear. The exciting part was discovering the same struggles that nearly broke me were also the ones that brought me to what my shaman family calls a "rebirth of spiritual emergence."

• • •

I was nearly five years old when I first remember witnessing occurrences that affirmed the presence of the afterlife. The first visitation came to me one night after my mother had tucked me in bed. There was a cold breeze, and I asked her to shut the window. She told me it was closed. I saw her check it, but I could still feel the cold air wafting over me. After she left, I got up and went to the window to check it myself. There, I saw a colonial soldier. He was standing outside, looking in. He didn't speak. Terrified, I got back under the sheets and prayed for him to leave. From then on, ghosts were very real, and I saw them often. I would regularly wake in the middle of the night crying out in a panic, "I don't want to die!"

My mother saw nothing odd about these experiences. She accepted my description of the occurrences because she is pagan and clairaudient. She explained to me that I not only shared her gift of clairaudience, but that I was clairvoyant as well: I see and hear spirits beyond the veil. Little did I know these same gifts would be the very salvation that would help right my path in years to come.

. . .

My upbringing was anything but traditional. My parents were very young when they had my brother and me. They both came from homes that others would describe as dysfunctional. They had the typical problems of those who take on adult responsibilities too soon. They chose to solve their altercations through shouting matches. As soon as the arguments began, my brother and I would be sent to our bedroom, but it would often escalate to the point where it felt they were in the room with us.

My mother sought help for the troubles in our family early on. She wanted stability and security. She learned to stop enabling my father's irresponsible behaviors. She gave him an ultimatum to get his shit together or she was leaving.

After several bounced checks and lost jobs, he came home having joined the military and was assigned his first duty station. My father leaving, I would later understand, was what my brain registered as my first period of abandonment. I was eight when we began to travel around the world, following after him. We moved every three years or so, and I adjusted to each new location without ever planting roots.

. . .

By the time I was twenty-seven, I was living in California but had decided to move to Florida. I had grown up a military brat, traveling the world, so this cross-country move wasn't a risk to me. In the coming months, a new unfamiliar world of chaos and self-destruction would be.

I met and started dating a man who I'd later learn was a cocaine addict. He was Cuban with dark eyes, tan skin, and raven-colored hair. He was charismatic and intriguing, a "ladies man," and it seemed everyone in town knew him. Many of the stories he lived or drummed up were exciting and fun. He was unlike anyone I had ever met.

Despite the upsets in my childhood and many experiences of my youth, I was a naively trusting young woman. It was clear from the start he drank a lot when we went out, but I chalked it up to the fact that he was showing me the town and just enjoying himself. As we grew closer, I saw that it was more than socializing: He was an alcoholic. His addictions combined with manipulation and lies made me continuously doubt myself. For example, I saw him regularly with a woman who turned out to be his ex-wife. When I asked him about her, he told me she was just his lesbian friend who he shared an apartment with. Oddly enough, I also learned that he and his ex-wife were wanted for fraud and theft. A Google inquiry of his name showed them linked to activities that should have rendered them both a permanent jail sentence. They seemed to evade the law on numerous occasions.

This man soon went from Mr. Charming to disappearing for days and then reappearing as if nothing had happened.

When I mentioned my concerns, he would dismiss them or tell me I was imagining things. He would try to hide his cocaine use, but it was obvious: He'd become dangerous, threatening, and sexually aggressive. Even with the deceit, I remained an eternal optimist — the fixer — but now I was in a situation far beyond my control. I lived in complete fear of him: emotionally, physically, and psychologically.

One night after a three-day binge-drinking bender, he came home and lunged at me during an argument. I could smell the alcohol emanating from the pores of his skin. His wild eyes and extreme aggressiveness made him all the more terrifying.

During this fight, I blacked out. When I came to, he was cowering in the closet that he'd attempted to corner me in. To this day, I don't know what took place during my blackout, but whatever it was, it was enough to frighten him from touching me again.

I left him and moved back with family in Alabama. I sank into depression and began eating my emotions. Food would become my addiction.

•   •   •

Despite my grief, I found a job and became obsessed with working hard to save money to start my own business. For the next five years, I focused on self-sufficiency and financial security. Focusing only on my career kept me from dealing with my trust and anger issues. I worked my regular day job, took a second evening position, and spent hours network-ing to build my business. My body was exhausted, my mind fogged, and my spirit broken. I was previously diagnosed with rheumatoid arthritis, and I'd just survived a horrible vehicle fire that sent my PTSD spiraling: thoughts of dying alone were ever present.

I wanted to love and be loved, but I still felt too vulner-able. I figured I was safer alone, even though I longed for a special someone to share my life with.

•   •   •

When I was thirty-two, I met my next addict, who would bring about my awakening.

I saw this woman across the room at a business event and fell for her immediately. Again, tan-skinned, dark-eyed, and raven-haired. My spirit guides told me she'd be a part of my life. I was still afraid. Yet the more I tried to deny it, the more I wanted to know this woman.

She was a recovering heroin addict who had seemingly found a twelve-step program. I desperately wanted to avoid repeating past mistakes, but I also wanted to support my girlfriend in her recovery, so I attended my own meetings. I learned a lot about myself, my past, and my parents.

When things turned tumultuous, instead of listening to my intuition, I stayed. I was hyper-vigilant to make this one work. I'd been successful in every other facet of my life except a loving relationship. *Maybe it's me*, I wondered.

Maybe there was something I wasn't seeing and needed to change about myself. So I tried harder. More meetings, more counseling, more workshops and self-help books.

Years later, I found prescriptions for Suboxone. She lied and denied they were hers, rather than admit she'd had a relapse. We would have screaming matches that reminded me of my childhood. With each argument, my arthritis would flare up and I'd be bedridden for days. We'd both be so worn out mentally and physically, we'd plead for a reprieve.

My endocrinologist knew of my dreams to have a child someday, and told me that with my age and ailments, I had a decision to make. Our environment was not conducive to nurturing a child or conceiving. We were nearing an end, but I struggled to let go until I came home to her lifeless body. Her mouth was gaping open, her eyes were sunken in, her limbs hung off the couch, with no signs of breathing. I feared checking for a pulse. Thank God that as I walked into the room, she came to. The scare, however, was the last straw. I was done.

It was then that my spirit guide sent me a vision of my future child, a little girl. *What kind of mother would I be if I carried on this way?* Instead of fighting to make it work, I realized I was enabling behavior that I'd never want my children to witness.

My mother had enabled my father, and I swore that I'd never repeat their patterns. It was my turn to set boundaries and get out. I summoned my inner strength to break the chains that bound me to people with addictions, drama, and dysfunction. I had to heal my legacy.

I was diagnosed with Complex PTSD and Lupus. I was fifty-five pounds overweight, in excruciating pain, walking with a cane, and sleeping on a heating pad when I left her.

But with this new start, I had more knowledge and new tools. Spirit was telling me this was my chance to build the next half of my life, out of the ashes and into the light.

Fate would have it that, after prayer and meditation, I received a customer's online order that would send me directly to my place of salvation and healing. While researching vendors for materials I would need, I came across information about a treatment I had not tried before. The very first review seemed as if the customer had written my own story. It detailed her fears of being a mother suffering from rheumatoid arthritis, and her distressing experiences with the ailment. She went on to explain how a specialist helped her with only whole-food nutrition and organic supplements.

After the first few weeks of treatment, I was able to stand upright and walk with only a back brace. My intuition, clairaudience, and clairvoyance were resurfacing. I noticed that the cleaner I ate and the fewer prescription medications I took, the more my body and brain responded. Veils lifted as I followed my new health regime, living in faith.

My new mentor suggested I use my experience to obtain my license and help others as she was doing. My path was crystal clear. In a full-circle moment I realized *my destiny*: My mother had always taught me ancient rituals and herbal remedies. I have embraced them as my own.

I am a Pagan Solitary Green Witch and Holistic Practitioner. I have answered my divine calling to help others mend with whole-body healing practices.

Holding many certifications and a graduate of Cascade Business College, Toinette LaShawn Benson has mentored homeless youth for years while also working with autistic children at Consumer Advocacy Projects. In addition, Toinette has been personally mentored by many industry-leading experts. Upon learning of her brother's horrific death, she felt a flame ignite in her to pursue her passion: coaching women, men, and children on love and forgiveness. Despite all of her accolades, her most precious gifts are her two children and five grandchildren. She lives in Scottsdale, USA, with her husband, Rick. Visit Toinette at loveandforgivenesslifecoach.com.

The Remains of Love

TOINETTE LASHAWN BENSON

·

ometimes life-changing moments occur when you are doing the most mundane things.

It's September 1986. I'm standing at my kitchen sink, plump and pregnant, washing dishes when the phone rings. I wipe my hands on a towel and reach for the receiver. It's my brother.

"Todd, it's great to hear from you! How are things in California?"

"Not so good. I'm leaving."

"Why?"

"I don't have much time to talk right now, but I can tell you this bitch stole my money and stash. I'm screwed. These people will not understand or care. I know. There's going to be a contract out on my life."

"What are you talking about?"

Todd said he had been partying at a Nevada casino with a woman. When he woke up the next morning, she'd stolen $5,000 in cash and a stash of cocaine he'd been holding for someone. Neither the money or cocaine were his, he said. And now he was in serious trouble.

I could hear the fear and desperation in his voice. He was emphatic that I not try to contact him, either by phone or on his pager.

"Don't come looking for me, and don't call," he urged, adding he would contact me as soon as he could. "I'll call you first and let you know when I'm coming back to Seattle."

I trusted what he said, but I also suddenly felt afraid.

"I have to run," Todd said quickly. "Love you, Toni. See you soon."

Soon never came. As days turned into weeks and weeks into months, my mother and I became very concerned. She filed a missing person's report.

I never told my mother about Todd's phone call that day. At that time in our lives, we were all somewhat disconnected. It was safer for me to talk about what may have happened to Todd with friends who did not know him. I felt talking to family members posed a threat to all of us.

I intuitively had a sense that Todd's life might be over. At night I lay in bed sensing Todd was now at peace, a thought that in some odd way brought me comfort. But in the daylight, it was back to worrying and waiting for a phone call. I lived in fear for our family that the people looking for him might come after us, too. I found myself often looking out a window of my house expecting to see a shadowy figure outside, or wondering if someone was following me in my car. I did receive a couple of phone calls, with a mysterious person on the other line saying, "I've been watching you." I was scared. I wondered why I could not live as normal families do.

• • •

Growing up in Marysville, Washington, Todd and I took care of ourselves during the week. My mother, a single parent, had a good-paying job and was career driven. She had to be. Our father had left when we were very young, and he was not providing financial support. While my mother's job in the lumber industry provided us with a beautiful, comfortable home, Todd and I were left to fend for ourselves. I remember the burden and sadness I felt at being left alone. Today, I realize my mother's amazing strength and courage raising us without the help of our dad.

During long summer days, Todd and I played until sundown, and even into the evening. The woods near our home became our playground. We were both independent kids, and although he was fourteen months older than me, I was the more responsible one. I often noticed Todd making poor, erratic decisions. He was also a prankster. But I loved him dearly and trusted him. I became like a mother to him. I would often have to correct him as a parent would. This mothering tendency developed into a pattern of putting others' needs before mine, a behavior I carried into adulthood like a cumbersome piece of luggage.

Our lives changed dramatically when my mother married Gary, a man she had been dating. She was trying to choose a man who would be a good provider and a fit for the family, but he also came with three of his own children. This would not be our version of *The Brady Bunch*. I remember feeling concerned that I would not matter anymore.

Todd's demeanor changed. Seething with anger, he began acting out to get attention. One day he rode his motorcycle through the house. I feared Mom would punish me for allowing it to happen. He started oil-rag fires in the driveway. At times he even directed his anger at me. He once chased me down the hallway with a knife in his hand. He was trying to scare me to elicit a reaction. He was lashing out. He needed his father. Boys growing up without a healthy relationship with a male father figure are susceptible to a life of struggle and self-sabotage. My brother was no exception.

In middle school, Todd began hanging around the stoners. Drugs became his escape from his inner turmoil. While on occasion we still rode horses and motorbikes through the woods, the time we spent together became less and less.

Years later, Todd started dating a young woman who encouraged him to attend the church where she was a member. Todd dove deep into religion. He affixed religious bumper stickers on his car. He had a good job and appeared happy and clean from drugs.

But then a devastating series of events occurred. Todd's girlfriend became pregnant but decided to have an abortion. The anger he had suppressed through religion eventually reappeared. All his life Todd had yearned to have a father. Now, here was his chance to be a father, but it was taken away, apparently without him having a say. Perhaps becoming a father would have helped heal some of his pain.

Around the same time, my mother and stepfather decided to divorce and sell our horse farm. It was too many losses for Todd. He left the church, ended all relations with his girlfriend, and reverted to his partying and drug-induced ways. Todd's life fell apart again.

Todd got reacquainted with a childhood friend. They discussed moving to California. His friend had connections there, and a way of making some fast, good money. Apparently, this friend had ties to the Mafia. Believing he had few choices, Todd left Washington State for Los Angeles in March 1986.

At that young age, I was in denial of the world outside me. I do not recall having fears of what could happen to Todd. I also knew his friend. He was a nice, good-looking, clean-cut guy. I did not suspect trouble ahead. I also felt Todd needed a change. That six-month period of his life remains a mystery to me. We spoke once on the phone that summer.

• • •

As months turned into years, I felt Todd's spirit did not want to be found. He had made it clear that he did not want me looking for him. His disappearance left a hole in my heart, but we all continued with living. My mother hired a private investigator; he came up with nothing. Later, we discovered the first missing person's report had been lost. Todd remained missing.

I worked hard to raise my son and daughter, as well as nurture and encourage my husband, Rick. All I wanted to have was a typical family that stayed together. We did, but there were enormous challenges. I developed cancer in my early forties. To pay mounting debts, we liquidated all of our assets. Eventually, we filed for bankruptcy. I lost everything in the material world, but I still had my family and inner drive to succeed and overcome. When you are at your lowest, the only way to go is up.

Interestingly, I began experiencing strong, intuitive feelings to move to Arizona. I thought it centered on our daughter continuing Junior Olympic gymnastics training in Phoenix. Or, I thought, maybe it was to escape all the failure and loss we had experienced in Washington. There was an inner pull to move to the desert. The feelings were real, but the motive was not clear. Over time, I listened to the still voice within me — my true self — and surrendered to intuition. I had no idea that our move to Phoenix in 2002 would eventually reunite me with Todd, and that he was only thirteen miles away from my home.

In 2012, the Everett, Washington, police department suggested our family submit DNA for testing against the more than 60,000 remains of people buried in unmarked graves and lying in boxes in medical examiner's offices across the country. At the time of Todd's disappearance, the technology that could link missing persons with found remains was nonexistent. By 2010, the National Missing and Unidentified Persons System had been created to help find the names and identities of missing loved ones.

Sometimes life-changing moments occur when you are doing the most mundane things.

That May, I was busy cleaning the house when the phone rang. My mother called to reveal that Washington authorities had found Todd's DNA matched that of a man killed in Phoenix in 1986. Through an informant, the picture of Todd's disappearance became clear. The tipster told Maricopa County detectives that the husband of a friend had killed a man in 1986. The informant said the dead man's name was Mike.

Police pieced together what happened after Todd's frantic phone call to me that day in September 1986. Todd drove east on Interstate 10 to Phoenix and paid for a room in a house on the west side of the city rented by Michael Root and his wife, Carol. My theory is Todd was using the name Mike to avoid detection. One evening not long after he moved in, police say Todd and Michael had an altercation in the living room. To this day I believe it was over Carol. There may have been something going on between her and Todd, and Michael sensed it. Carol had a young child. Perhaps Todd was drawn to her because this was another chance to be a father.

According to the police reports, while Carol was in the bedroom, Michael pulled a knife and began stabbing Todd repeatedly in the stomach. He fell to the floor in a large pool of blood. Later, police say the couple stuffed Todd's body into a sleeping bag, hauled it 50 miles to the west of Phoenix to a remote part of the desert near Tonopah, and lit the sleeping bag on fire. In February 1988, a hiker discovered a human jaw in the desert near the Palo Verde Generating Station and called the police. Investigators soon found the rest of the remains.

A year later detectives interviewed Michael, who by then had moved to Michigan. He refused to answer questions. Arizona prosecutors would never file charges. A court later convicted Michael in the killing of an elderly couple. He died in prison in 2008 while serving a life sentence. I tried to contact Carol a few times but had no success. My guess is she took a plea for immunity. To this day questions remain unanswered.

News of the DNA match was surreal. I could not believe it. Part of me was skeptical. I have faith in all that is spiritual and unseen, but when it comes to human beings, I can be suspicious of their motives and agendas. Were authorities just saying they had a DNA match to wrap a cold case with a nifty bow so they could move on? I was not convinced.

But then I met Dr. Laura Fulginiti, a forensic anthropologist at the Maricopa County Forensic Science Center in Phoenix. Fulginiti analyzes unknown skeletal remains and provides biological profiles. Bone examinations include looking for any trauma that occurs to a body. While bones don't have a voice, they still speak of a life lived and the damage done.

Fulginiti inherited case number 88356 when she started her career in 1991. At that time, skeletal remains were overlooked because forensic professionals felt there was nothing they could do with the information. While there were numerous boxes of remains at the Center, 88356 haunted Fulginiti.

Periodically, she pulled out the box of bones and spoke to them. "Who are you? Why can't we get you identified?" The remains became a teaching tool for her new students, who would reanalyze the remains to make sure no clue was missed.

Eventually, Phoenix police created a missing persons cold case unit in their homicide division. Fulginiti alerted detectives to case 88356. They told her the case was still open, the full story was not known, and that the missing person was called "Mike" in their department.

After twenty-two years, Fulginiti's relationship with "Mike" suddenly changed. Through advanced DNA testing, a match hit on a missing person in Washington State named Todd Mertes.

I felt close to Dr. Fulginiti, as if she were a family member. She had been caring for Todd for decades. She kept a small blue hand-knitted blanket positioned under his skull in a box in her office. She'd formed a close relationship with Todd's bones. She had spent as much time with him as I had. And her forensics office was just 15 miles from my home. For ten years I had been that close to Todd, but I did not know it.

When I met Fulginiti in person for the first time, we hugged and cried from relief for the ending of a long, emotional journey. As we shared our stories, I learned Fulginiti's brother had died when she was twenty and he was twenty-two. We had a similar bonding: losing an older brother.

As our family processed the confirmation of Todd's remains, my son, Tyler, called me one afternoon.

"Mom, do you think it's strange that I want to see Uncle Todd?"

"You want to see him? What do you mean? You want to see his skeletal remains?"

"Yes," he said.

Honestly, I found his request strange, but I reluctantly agreed to accompany him to the morgue at the Forensic Science Center where we would meet Dr. Fulginiti. I had no intention of viewing his bones. I couldn't do it — or so I thought.

As Tyler, Dr. Fulginiti, and I stepped slowly down a staircase into the morgue, she warned us about the distinctive odor we would encounter. I already felt nauseous. The lower we went, the more pungent the subtle scent grew. My heart was pounding.

We entered a large room. A gurney with a cloth draped over it sat in the middle. I noticed a bulkiness under the fabric and the shape of a head at one end of the gurney. I stopped, turned around, and headed for the door. Tyler walked toward the remains. I stayed near the door, ready to leave immediately.

"Come on, Mom, it's not that bad. Come and see him."

He walked over to me and lovingly and gently took my hand to usher me closer. After a few nervous steps, there was Todd after all these years. Dr. Fulginiti had laid out Todd's skeleton out, bone by bone. Surprisingly, a sense of calm came over me. I knew it was Todd. It was as if he was there meeting me again, too. Any reluctance over seeing his remains dissolved and was replaced by loving gratitude for my son who had urged me to have closure.

Dr. Fulginiti asked if I wanted a remembrance to take away. I decided to take a few of his back teeth. I still have them, and I'm glad I do.

On a beautiful Washington day, we buried Todd in a cemetery in the small town of Machias, Washington, near Lake Stevens. He lies next to our cousin, who died at about the same age as Todd. My mother visits the grave and keeps the grass trimmed around a headstone my husband handmade.

There is tragic irony in Todd's murder. Drug hitmen did not end his life. Instead, he made a fateful decision to rent a room from an acquaintance who was a psychopath. How can death be so random? Did Todd unconsciously attract his violent end? If thoughts are things, can negative thoughts be the creative force that shapes a negative reality?

I do not wish for my life to be defined by what happened to my brother. Nevertheless, I am who I am, to a varying degree, because of it. Todd died young, but I believe now that everything is for a purpose. His death taught us about forgiveness. Not just forgiveness of another, but, first and foremost, forgiveness of one's self. Sometimes we have to strip ourselves bare — down to the bone — to discover all that remains. When we pull back the ego, the experiences and messages of our childhood, when we forgive ourselves the choices we made as adults, when faced with death itself, we are altered forever. We realize that love is all that remains and all that matters.

My brother's life and death demonstrate how we all come full circle. We are born as love, and we spend the rest of our lives trying to return to love. Sometimes a body dies before we reach that point, but it may be that our death is designed to help others return to love before they die.

My brother's death helped me to return to the true essence of being, which is love.

Wendy Gless is a certified life and money coach, with a Bachelor of Business Administration in accounting and a minor in psychology. A master empowerment coach trained in the law of attraction, Wendy guides women in creating and manifesting more money, more love, and everyday miracles in their life and business. She's a dream-life designer and a passionate lover of life. Wendy lives in southern California, USA, with her husband. Visit wendygless.com.

Life Always Finds a Way

WENDY GLESS

•

*i*t was 6 p.m. on Mother's Day, and I was alone. My three teenagers were off hanging out with friends, pretending to be finishing up last-minute school assignments before summer vacation. I laughed knowing they were way too excited to get much accomplished, and honestly, I didn't even mind. The thought of all of us not having a tight, rigid schedule for a few months was pure bliss.

Bliss! When was the last time I said or felt this word ... if ever?

While mulling over the *bliss* word, I heard a tap on the door, some whispering, and feet running away. Oh, for heaven sakes, what are the kids up to now? I opened the door and saw a beautifully wrapped gift with a card that said *To Mom & Wendy*. Although I wasn't expecting a gift, I felt like a kid in a candy store. This Mother's Day was getting better by the second. I went inside, lit a few candles, sat down on our sofa with my surprise gift, and began to reflect on just how wonderfully the day had gone.

This Mother's Day I had tried something different. Rather than waiting for a gift that may not come or the typical, although valuable, you're-the-best-mom-in-the-world hug, I treated myself and my three teens to a nice lunch and a mini-shopping trip where we each received a gift to celebrate having each other. I thought of the delight on my daughter's face when she selected a small bottle of perfume she had been waiting so long for, and how my sons ripped off their old shoes and left them lying on the floor when the cashier handed them their new ones. I fiddled with the charm bracelet that I bought for myself, and I smiled. Megan was so excited for all of us to be together. It reminded me of what she was like as a little girl waiting patiently for her big brothers to come inside from playing for a family dinner.

You see, my kids are my life, but it wasn't always possible for me to spend money on them, frivolously. Today I could. I felt giddy with happiness by being able to treat them. I got to express my love to them, and it felt good.

Truth be told, Mother's Day had not always been so great. For many years, I felt alone and empty and not very appreciated. For some reason, Mother's Day was the most important day of the year for me, and I often found it hard to keep my chin up. I was a single mom trying to play the good guy/bad guy game, and I always seemed to be putting out fires instead of relaxing, surrounded by candles, and opening up a surprise gift like today. Life had been hard over the last few years. Scary and unpredictable. But I felt at peace today. After years and years of being alone, I felt perfectly okay.

I was perfectly okay.

As I sat back, opening up my beautifully wrapped gift and reflecting on our smiles and laughter of the afternoon, I said out loud, "Wow, *he* still sure knows how to make me happy, when he wants to." I thought about my ex-husband. "A cozy soft Barefoot Dreams blanket from the kids and a bottle of white wine, Cakebread Chardonnay, from him! My favorites."

Although the wine was not chilled enough, I was too impatient to wait. I uncorked the bottle and poured myself a small glass, wrapped up in my new cozy blanket, and thought back to the first night we shared a glass of this same wine.

Twenty years earlier, this wine was way out of our budget, but we'd splurged anyway. We had talked late into the night, sharing our dreams for the future. I was crazy about him. And he was crazy about me, too. We were beside ourselves when we were both presented with amazing job offers in California. I was not quite thirty, with three small children, and although we were leaving Texas, our families, and loved ones — the only support system we had ever known — this adventure was worth the risk and just way too good to pass up. So we packed up our stuff and set out to create the life we had always dreamed of: full of love and money and happiness!

Or so we thought.

Our picture-perfect life soon turned into one of fear and uncertainty. Yes, we had the big house, the cars, the clothes, travel, and money in the bank, but I was lost, hurting, and lonely. I missed my family in Texas. And my once-doting husband now felt untouchable and unreachable. He was so consumed with work that he didn't have time to focus on what was going on at home. Days would go by when only small talk was exchanged; we stopped asking how we really felt or if we were happy.

My days felt fast and furious, spinning on a treadmill. I was busy with the kids and busy with work, and yet, I craved a deep, meaningful relationship with my husband. I couldn't be the mother I wanted to be within this lonely chaos. I missed the man I married, but he was no longer my best friend.

I stood in my bathroom staring at myself in the mirror. My eyes were swollen and puffy, and my heart was broken. I didn't know where my husband was. He was constantly traveling around the world or working late. I felt as if I were engulfed in flames. Despite my stoic outside, I was smoldering ash on the inside. I had a decision to make. Was it time to step away from the man I had loved since I was sixteen years old? Leaving him meant leaving the dream of a picture-perfect marriage along with a $25-million+ bank account. But we were no longer each other's dream.

I filed for divorce.

Along with the divorce came guilt and shame. Every single day I woke up and went to bed feeling as if I had failed at being a great mom and wife. I clung to hope with borrowed strength, praying I would find a way to create peace in the midst of the chaos. It would take time to adjust to our new family dynamic. I didn't want to hurt him, and he didn't want to hurt me, and we both didn't want to hurt our kids, but our worlds were drifting further and further apart. As the last thread unraveled, I stood alone. We were no longer "Matt and Wendy." Our divorce had been finalized.

The shattering of my life seemed to happen in slow motion, and I felt pieces of myself change. I clung to the only serenity I could find: the strength of my faith and the love of my children. I felt like I was watching a scene of my life in a movie.

During the months that followed the divorce, I got clearer on what I wanted from life. Letting go of my marriage opened my mind to all the other things that no longer served me. One by one, I let go of old belief systems. I took charge of how I wanted to love and show up in this world. I learned how to set healthy boundaries of what and who was allowed into my life. I stopped blaming him, and I was secure and comfortable with being alone.

I feel as though the "gift of grace" carried me through the next few years, and even though there were times that I vacillated between gratitude and grief, struggling to stand on unsteady ground, I reminded myself daily that my life had been made up of many choices. Choices I had made. My new life as a single mom had not been done to me. I wasn't being punished. I surely wasn't a victim. Maybe my husband and I had grown apart, but I knew for many, many years we really had loved each other.

I was now able to recognize that we all go through different phases and stages in our lives, and at some point one area in life may take precedence over the other. I was able to let go of how we could be in such different places after wanting the same things for so long. I could see the value we'd both put on my ex-husband's career. I wanted the finest things in life, too. I wanted the big house and financial security, and he'd given it to me. But with every choice, there is a trade-off.

With this realization, I could breathe for the first time in years. I had freedom. In the face of all that had been lost, I could see the beauty in what had been found. Instead of staying angry at him for not being there enough, I found forgiveness — something I didn't believe was possible. I forgave myself, too. And yes, I had walked out of the nightmare that I had helped create. But now I had a new list of amazing dreams.

I began doing things that felt good and made me proud at the end of the day. For the first time in a very long time, I began to enjoy the simple things in life. I found myself feeling neutral toward my ex-husband — the emotional, angry charge was gone. And then our friendship began to flourish.

I am in awe of what can happen when we forgive despite unforgivable actions, when we walk despite weak knees and we love against all odds. The fear that once consumed me has been replaced with so much faith.

Fast-forward to the Mother's Day gift.

As I took a sip of that chardonnay, reminiscing, I felt the tingly butterflies over the thought of being close to my ex-husband. I knew I had a decision to make. My ex-husband still loved me. And as hard as it was for anyone around us to believe, I realized I still loved him, too. We still wanted each other. We still believed in each other.

A few weeks later, when we finally sat the kids down and told them we were getting back together, we were worried they'd be upset. Worried they'd feel angry for the emotional roller coaster we'd put them through. Their reaction couldn't have been more opposite. They were happier than we'd ever seen them.

My husband and I are back together, stronger than ever, and beyond grateful that our kids approve. We all have another shot at love. Now, years later, I realize this could only have happened because I became a soul mate to myself first and foremost. If I could give any woman advice regarding navigating a breakup, I would urge them to focus on themselves. Focus on mastering your own money, focus on your dreams, and focus on healing your heart. Knowing I was responsible for every aspect of my life was both terrifying and eye-opening. I realized the tremendous pressure my husband was under for years upon years to produce, provide, and take care of us the way I'd told him that I wanted to be taken care of.

Becoming a single mother forced me to learn how to take care of myself. I have a flourishing business of my own now, coaching women every day on how to master their money and life.

Is being in love and sharing the responsibilities with someone else easier? Hell, yeah! However, I didn't go back because I was angry, scared, or helpless. I didn't go back because I couldn't make it on my own. I went back because I chose to. Because I love him. I'm grateful that I held a "space" for us to heal and that I didn't think in black-and-white terms of *never* or *always*. It was this neutral space that paved the way for the future.

There is nothing in life without flaw. There are still moments that are difficult. But when we refuse to give up on ourselves, our joy, and our happiness, new life is found. There is a great line in the old blockbuster movie *Jurassic Park* that goes something like this:

> *Life will always find a way. You can try to bury, douse it, or destroy it, but life breaks free. Life expands to new territories. Painfully, perhaps even dangerously. But life finds a way.*

Love does, too. Love will always find a way. Trust in that.

Today, I am equal parts my past and future. I have been broken and mended. I am messy and beautiful. I am living the life I dreamed of and here is where I'm staying.

My choices
patterned out
played
on this wind
sailing   *then become*
straight through   *all I was meant*
these currents   *to be*
where mightier   *destiny was*
ships   *tricked then*
are lost in the   *perhaps*
night   *coming calling at*
on shoals and   *my door*
reefs   *when I wouldn't*
with mermaid   *believe or accept*
enchantments   *defeat*
to lull them   *or lessening*
to sleep   *of what I knew*
but I never slept   *inside*
only waited   *was a greater*
until this   *purpose*
sea began   *so I asked*
to part   *these gods for*
and I could   *help*
     and in helping myself
     our purpose
     became one.

—Sara (Navasi) Hartman

Resources

·

Millions of women worldwide have experienced tough times and traumatic experiences, yet have healed and found happiness. Regardless of circumstances, please know that you aren't alone. In this section, we've compiled a list of support services you may find helpful.

Al-Anon

Visit Al-Anon at **al-anon.org** to find your local helpline.

Alcoholics Anonymous

Visit Alcoholic Anonymous at **aa.org** to find your local helpline.

Assaulted Women's Hotlines

If you live in the USA, visit **thehotline.org** to find your local helpline.

If you live in Canada, visit **awhl.org** to find your local helpline.

If you live in the UK, visit **womensaid.org.uk** to find your local helpline.

Children and Teens Help Phone

If you live in the USA, visit **yourlifeyourvoice.org** to find your local helpline.

If you live in Canada, visit **kidshelpphone.ca** to find your local helpline.

If you live in the UK, visit **childline.org.uk** to find your local helpline.

Eating Disorder Support Services

If you live in the USA, visit **nationaleatingdisorders.org** to find your local helpline.

If you live in Canada, visit **nedic.ca** to find your local helpline.

If you live in the UK, visit **beateatingdisorders.org.uk** to find your local helpline.

Mental Health Support Services

If you live in the USA, visit **mentalhealthamerica.net** to find your local helpline.

If you live in the Canada, visit **mentalhealthhelpline.ca** to find your local helpline.

If you live in the UK, visit **mentalhealth-uk.org** to find your local helpline.

Mothers Against Drunk Driving

Visit **MADD.org** to find your local helpline.

Rape Crisis Helplines

If you live in the USA, visit **centers.rainn.org** to find your local helpline.

If you live in Canada, visit **wavaw.ca** to find your local helpline.

If you live in the UK, visit **rapecrisis.org.uk** to find your local helpline.

Suicide Prevention Helplines

Visit International Association for Suicide Prevention (IASP) at **iasp.info** to find your local suicide prevention helpline.

United Nations Women

To learn more about how you can help and get on board with the women's movement, visit United Nations Women at **unwomen.org/en**.

• • •

The S.W.A.T. Institute

Founded by Crystal Andrus Morissette in 2009, the S.W.A.T. Institute (Simply Woman Accredited Trainer) is an online global empowerment coach certification exclusively for women. The Institute offers both Personal and Master certifications in over thirty countries. Women from all over the world — including Iceland, Palestine, Ireland, Switzerland, France, Spain, Romania, Canada, Holland, Slovenia, New Zealand, Namibia, United States, Australia, England, and South Africa — have enrolled. Trainers call themselves the new "Special Weapons and Tactics," and we strongly believe they will help heal this world by empowering one woman at a time.

One of the most beautiful aspects of the S.W.A.T. Institute is its Empowerment Mentorship Coaching program. Any woman, living anywhere in the world, can sign up to be mentored — at no charge. It's easy to get started, and there are no upsells or hidden fees. Visit **SWATinstitute.com** to learn more.

12-Week Emotional Edge TeleCourse

The 12-Week Emotional Edge TeleCourse is Crystal Andrus Morissette's flagship course. It's been featured three times on *Oprah.com*, as well as in the *New York Post* and the *UK Daily Mail*. Take Crystal's Emotional Age Quiz at **oprah .com/inspiration/emotional-age-quiz** — discovering your "emotional age" and learning how to become your most empowered self is life-changing!

Simply Woman Magazine

Written for women by women, *Simply Woman Magazine* is a global coalition and celebration of women's rights, needs, wants, and dreams. This innovative and influential online magazine covers healthy living, spirituality, femininity, world issues, and more. It is a place where like-minded women come together to share what they've learned and how they apply that knowledge to their daily lives. If you would like more information or wish to become a writer for *Simply Woman*, visit **simplywoman.com**.

Simply Woman Accredited Yoga

Many people don't realize that classical hatha yoga was developed for men, by men (including most of the texts). Created by women for women, SWAYoga helps women regain the soft, feminine sway of our hips, the gentle rocking of our pelvic floor, the natural curve of our backs, and the beautiful sweet embodiment of woman. For more information on SWAYoga, visit **swaynetwork.tv**.

Acknowledgments

•

*P*utting a book like this together in the short time that we did took the full collaboration, trust, and effort of everyone involved. The process was, literally, the divine feminine in action — there was no ego, no arguing, no resistance. We each knew our capabilities and strengths, and we allowed the process to unfold. Each person was in what some people call the "flow"! I am so grateful to everyone who helped make this book happen.

Thank you, Jackie Brown, my frontline editor, for meeting one-on-one with all of our contributors, honing their stories, and ensuring we were able to reflect as many different perspectives as possible. Your chapter was compelling and honest, and I sincerely respect your work in the world. You're a Rock Star!

Thank you, Tracy Bordian and Kyle Gell, for your exquisite book production, editorial, and design services. I could not have done it without you. I'm grateful beyond measure. You took this dream and in a very short period transformed it into something beautiful.

Thank you, Lori Rennie and Marquis Book Printing, for your adept guidance every step of the way. You connected all the dots and made this process easy for me.

My eldest daughter, Madelaine Dantas, thank you for being you. Not only are you an incredible executive assistant, but you also have the gentlest, kindest, smartest brain and heart. I love you. Thank you for gracing the cover photo with us.

My youngest daughter, Julia Dantas, thank you for taking the beautiful cover photograph and providing my makeup. Thank you for your creative energy, your passion, and your incredible talent. I'm so blessed to have you as my child. I love you.

My husband, Aaron, thank you for believing in me and my work. You are often the unsung hero, but I know that I couldn't do what I do without you. I love you.

My biggest thank-you goes to all of the courageous women in this book who told their stories. You trusted me every time I told you "I got you," and I mean it. Thank you for believing in me and for believing in yourself. It is women

like you who are going to change this world. I applaud you.
I celebrate you. I love every one of you.

#TogetherWeRise

#TimesUp